Writing a First Novel

Writing a First Novel

Reflections on the Journey

Edited by

Karen Stevens

First published 2014 by
PALGRAVE MACMILLAN

Palgrave Macmillan in the UK is an imprint of Macmillan Publishers Limited,
registered in England, company number 785998, of Houndmills, Basingstoke,
Hampshire RG21 6XS.

Palgrave Macmillan in the US is a division of St Martin's Press LLC,
175 Fifth Avenue, New York, NY 10010.

Palgrave Macmillan is the global academic imprint of the above companies
and has companies and representatives throughout the world.

Palgrave® and Macmillan® are registered trademarks in the United States,
the United Kingdom, Europe and other countries.

ISBN 978-0-230-29082-2   ISBN 978-1-137-36840-9 (eBook)
DOI 10.1007/978-1-137-36840-9

This book is printed on paper suitable for recycling and made from fully
managed and sustained forest sources. Logging, pulping and manufacturing
processes are expected to conform to the environmental regulations of the
country of origin.

A catalogue record for this book is available from the British Library.

A catalog record for this book is available from the Library of Congress.

For Joe, Jamie and all my wonderful friends
Thank you

Contents

Acknowledgements   ix

List of Contributors   x

Introduction   1
Karen Stevens

Part I 'Inspiration' and the Novel

1 Something Given: Reflections on Writing   17
   Hanif Kureishi

2 Look Back in Angst   26
   Valerie Martin

3 Illuminating the Shadows: The Space between Fact
   and Fiction   36
   Johanna Skibsrud

4 Genesis   44
   David Vann

Part II Research and the Novel

5 Treasure, Trash and Planned Obsolescence   49
   Maile Chapman

6 Writing Home   58
   Edward Hogan

7 Walking the Tightrope   66
   Kishwar Desai

8 The Reluctant Aficionado   76
   Wena Poon

Part III Voice and the Novel

9 Hearing Voices   89
   Alison MacLeod

10 'This Won't Do': *Pig* and the Temptation of Silence 99
    Andrew Cowan

11 Knots and Narrative 108
    Jane Rusbridge

12 'Voice' and the Inescapable Complexity of Experience 119
    Isabel Ashdown

Part IV Form and the Novel

13 Giving Shape to One's Universe 129
    Helon Habila

14 Another Fine Mess 138
    David Swann

15 Man of Letters 148
    Soumya Bhattacharya

16 Belief 154
    Jane Feaver

Part V The Business of Publishing

17 An Agent's Perspective 167
    Hannah Westland

18 The Role of the Editor 172
    Helen Garnons-Williams

19 Baby, You've Got It Made 180
    Lionel Shriver

Index 189

Acknowledgements

My biggest thanks go to the writers who contributed to this anthology. I am sincerely grateful for their patience and astonishing generosity. I would like to thank the University of Chichester for supporting this project. My gratitude extends, in particular, to my creative writing colleagues Stephanie Norgate, Alison MacLeod, Stephen Mollett, David Swann and Hugh Dunkerley. Their support and encouragement has been invaluable. Thanks to Jacqueline Boyce for her excellent typing skills. Thanks also to the reviewers of the manuscript *Writing a First Novel*, whose comments were timely and helpful. Many thanks to Bethan Roberts for her support. Finally, I would like to thank Jenna Steventon, Kate Haines and Felicity Noble at Palgrave Macmillan, also Sumitha Nithyanandan at Integra Software Services in India. Their vision and support has been truly appreciated on this book's journey to publication.

List of Contributors

Isabel Ashdown is the author of three novels. After giving up a career in marketing, she studied English & Creative Writing at the University of Chichester, UK, where she was awarded The Hugo Donnelly Prize for Outstanding Academic Achievement and completed her MA with distinction. An extract from her debut novel *Glasshopper* won the Mail on Sunday Novel Competition, judged by Fay Weldon and the late Sir John Mortimer, going on to be named as one of the best books of 2009 in the *Observer* and *London Evening Standard*. Her second novel *Hurry Up and Wait* was released in 2011, followed by her latest, *Summer of '76* in 2013. Excerpts from *Glasshopper* are reproduced by permission of Myriad Editions (www.myriadeditions.com).

Soumya Bhattacharya's books about how cricket defines India – *You Must Like Cricket? and Why India Can Never Do Without Cricket* – were published to wide acclaim. His novel, *If I Could Tell You*, was longlisted for the Crossword Book Award, and he was a finalist for the *Hindu* newspaper's Best Fiction Award 2010. He is the author, most recently, of the fatherhood memoir, *Dad's the Word*. His work has appeared in the *New York Times, Granta, London Magazine*, the *Guardian*, the *Observer*, the *Independent*, the *New Statesman* and the *Sydney Morning Herald*.

Maile Chapman is the author of the novel *Your Presence Is Requested at Suvanto*, shortlisted for the Guardian First Book Award in 2010. Her stories have appeared in *Stand Magazine, Dublin Review, Boston Review* and *Best American Fantasy Writing*, among others. After completing her MFA in Fiction at Syracuse University, USA, she spent a Fulbright Grant year in Finland. She has recently been a fellow at the New York Public Library's Dorothy and Lewis B. Cullman Centre for Scholars and Writers, working on her second novel. She is currently Assistant Professor of English in the MFA programme at the University of Nevada, Las Vegas, and Fiction Editor of *Witness* magazine.

Andrew Cowan is the author of five novels and a Creative Writing guidebook, *The Art of Writing Fiction*. His first novel *Pig* was longlisted for the Booker Prize, shortlisted for five other literary awards and won a Betty Trask Award, the Authors' Club First Novel Award, the Ruth Hadden Memorial Prize, a Scottish Arts Council Book Award and the Sunday Times Young Writer of the Year Award. His other novels are *Common Ground, Crustaceans, What I Know*, which won an Arts Council Writer's Award, and *Worthless Men*. He is Professor of Creative Writing and Director of the Creative Writing programme at the University of East Anglia, UK.

Kishwar Desai is the author of the critically acclaimed biography, *Darlingji: The True Love Story of Nargis and Sunil Dutt*. She has also written three novels. Her debut novel *Witness the Night* won the 2010 Costa First Novel Award, was shortlisted for the Author's Club First Novel Award, longlisted for the Man Asian Literary Prize, the Waverton Good Read Award and the DSC Jaipur Literary Festival Prize. Her second novel in the Simran Singh series, *The Origins of Love* was published in 2012 and her third novel in the series, *The Sea of Innocence* was published in May 2013. She is now working on another book about Indian cinema. She has worked as a journalist, TV anchor and producer, as well as the head of an Indian TV channel. She is also a regular columnist for three Indian publications: *The Week, The Tribune* and *The Asian Age*. She lives between London, Delhi and Goa.

Jane Feaver's first novel, *According to Ruth*, was published in 2007 and was shortlisted for the Author's Club Best First Novel Award and the Dimplex Prize. *Love Me Tender* (2009), a collection of linked short stories, was shortlisted for the Edge Hill Short Story Prize. *An Inventory of Heaven* was published in 2012. Jane is a lecturer in Creative Writing at the University of Exeter, UK.

Helen Garnons-Williams is Editorial Director for Fiction at Bloomsbury, UK, where her authors include Jon McGregor, Jane Rusbridge, Anne Michaels and Stephen Kelman. She began her career in publishing as an editorial assistant at Hodder & Stoughton. She then became Editorial Director of Sceptre, Hodder & Stoughton's award-winning literary imprint. In June 2003, she moved to Weidenfeld & Nicolson, where her acquisitions included *Salmon Fishing in the Yemen* by Paul Torday, *The Rose of Sebastopol* by Katharine McMahon and *Belle de Jour* – the call girl confessional. She moved to Bloomsbury in 2007.

Helon Habila is the author of three novels. His debut novel *Waiting for an Angel* won the prestigious Caine Prize in 2001 and the

Commonwealth Literature Prize in 2003 for the best first novel by an African writer. His second novel, *Measuring Time*, won the 2008 Virginia Library Foundation Fiction Prize. His short story, 'The Hotel Malogo', was featured in the 2008 Best American Nonessential Reading anthology. He was a writing fellow at the University of East Anglia, UK, 2001–2003; in 2005–2006 he was the first Chinua Achebe Fellow at Bard College, New York. In 2006, he co-edited the British Council's anthology, *New Writing* 14. He teaches Creative Writing at George Mason University in Virginia.

Edward Hogan is the author of three novels. His first book, *Blackmoor*, was shortlisted for the Dylan Thomas Prize and the Sunday Times Young Writer of the Year Award and won the Desmond Elliot Prize. His other novels are *The Hunger Trace* and *Daylight Saving*, a young adult ghost thriller set in a sports holiday village. He was born in Derby in 1980 and now lives in Hove, working as a mental health mentor at the University of Sussex, UK.

Hanif Kureishi is the author of six novels, several story collections, plays and screenplays. Among his other publications are the collection of essays *Dreaming and Scheming, The Word and the Bomb* and his memoir *My Ear at His Heart*. His screenplay *My Beautiful Laundrette* won the New York Film Critics Best Screenplay Award and an Academy Award for best screenplay. His novel *The Buddha of Suburbia* won the Whitbread Award for best first novel. He has been awarded the Chevalier de l'Ordre des Arts et des Lettres, was appointed a CBE in 2008 for services to literature and drama and was awarded the PEN/Pinter Prize in 2010.

Alison MacLeod's debut novel, *The Changeling*, was awarded a Canada Council for the Arts Award, while her second novel, *The Wave Theory of Angels*, won an Arts Council England Award. In 2008, she won the UK's Society of Authors' Award for short fiction and, in 2009, her short story collection *Fifteen Modern Tales of Attraction* was named one of the 'Top Ten Books to Talk About', in association with World Book Day. She was shortlisted for the 2011 BBC National Short Story Award and is currently completing her next story collection. Her third novel, *Unexploded*, was published in 2013 and was longlisted for the Man Booker Prize. She is Professor of Contemporary Fiction at the University of Chichester, UK.

Valerie Martin is the author of nine novels, three collections of short fiction and a biography of St. Francis of Assisi. Her novel *Mary Reilly* won the Kafka Prize and was made into a film directed by Stephan Frears.

Her 2003 novel *Property* won the Orange Prize and was shortlisted for France's Prix Femina Étranger. She has been the recipient of a National Endowment for the Arts grant and was awarded a Guggenheim Fellowship in 2012. She is currently teaching at Mount Holyoke College in South Hadley, Massachusetts.

Wena Poon is the author of five books of fiction. Winner of the UK Willesden Herald Prize for best short fiction, she was nominated for France's *Prix Hemingway*, Ireland's Frank O'Connor Award, England's Bridport Prize for Poetry and the Singapore Literature Prize. Her first literary novel *Alex y Robert* was made into a BBC Radio 4 *Book at Bedtime* series; a story based on the book was performed in French at the Roman amphitheatre in Nîmes. Her short story *The Wood Orchid*, based on the Chinese heroine Hua Mulan, was staged in Westminster Abbey and the Bush Theatre. Born in Singapore and living in America, she is also a lawyer and a graduate of Harvard University and Harvard Law School, USA.

Jane Rusbridge is the author of two novels published by Bloomsbury. Her debut, *The Devil's Music*, was nominated for the 2011 International IMPAC Literary Award, while her second novel, *Rook*, was one of *Guardian* Readers' Books of the Year 2012. In 2005, Jane won the *Writersinc* 'Writer-of-the-Year', judged by Mario Petrucci and Tobias Hill. Her short stories have won or been placed in several national and international competitions including the Bridport Short Story Prize, the Bluechrome Experimental Fiction Award and the Fish International One Page Story Prize.

Lionel Shriver is the author of eleven novels. Her writing has appeared in the *Guardian*, the *New York Times*, the *Wall Street Journal* and many other publications. Her novel *We Need to Talk About Kevin* won the Orange Prize and has been adapted to a feature film starring Tilda Swinton. Her 2010 novel *So Much for That* was a finalist for the National Book Award in fiction. Her most recent novel is *Big Brother*.

Johanna Skibsrud is the author of the 2010 Scotiabank Giller Prize winning novel, *The Sentimentalists*, a collection of short fiction, *This Will Be Difficult to Explain and Other Stories*, shortlisted for the Danuta Gleed Award in 2012, and two collections of poetry, *Late Nights with Wild Cowboys* and *I Do Not Think That I Could Love a Human Being*. Originally from Nova Scotia, Canada, Johanna currently lives in Tucson, AZ, where she is working on a collection of critical essays and a second novel.

Karen Stevens is Senior lecturer in English and Creative Writing at the University of Chichester, UK. She teaches on both undergraduate and postgraduate programmes. She has a special interest in the novel and short fiction, publishing short stories. At present, she is undertaking a PhD in Creative Writing, in which she is writing a novel.

David Swann is the author of *The Privilege of Rain* (Waterloo Press, 2010), a collection of poetry and prose about his residency in a high-security jail, supported by the Arts Council of England. The book was shortlisted in 2011 for the inaugural Ted Hughes Award for New Work in Poetry. His stories and poems have appeared in small press publications and won many awards, including five successes at the Bridport Prize. A short story collection *The Last Days of Johnny North* was published by Elastic Press in 2006. Once a journalist, he is now a senior lecturer in English & Creative Writing at the University of Chichester, UK.

David Vann is an internationally bestselling author whose work has been translated into 19 languages. He is the winner of 14 prizes, including France's Prix Médicis Etranger, Spain's Premi Llibreter, the Grace Paley Prize, a California Book Award, the AWP Nonfiction Prize and France's Prix des Lecteurs de L'Express. His books (*Legend of a Suicide, Caribou Island, Dirt, A Mile Down* and *Last Day on Earth*) have appeared on 70 'Best Books of the Year' lists in a dozen countries. A former Guggenheim Fellow, Wallace Stegner Fellow, and National Endowment for the Arts Fellow, he is a professor at the University of Warwick in England. He has written for the *Atlantic, Esquire, Outside, Men's Journal, McSweeney's*, the *Sunday Times*, the *Observer*, the *Sunday Telegraph*, and many others, and he has appeared in documentaries for the BBC, NOVA, National Geographic and CNN.

Hannah Westland was a literary agent at the Rogers, Coleridge & White Agency, where she represented a range of fiction and non-fiction writers. In 2012 she left to become publisher at Serpent's Tail. Serpent's Tail publishes literary and crime fiction, and non-fiction. Publishing fiction from all over the world, they are best known for championing edgy, boundary-breaking books.

Introduction

Karen Stevens

As a teacher of creative writing I meet students who join our university expressing a strong desire to write a novel, both on our undergraduate and graduate programmes. Our annual publishing panel, literary events and book launches are also increasingly attended by the public. From discussion with colleagues at other universities it appears that this flourishing interest in the novel is happening across the UK, the US and beyond. Universities have been responding accordingly by offering courses aimed specifically at writing novels, as well as opening up literary events to the local community. Public readings by novelists, storytelling events and reading groups are as strongly attended as they ever were. Literary festivals, many of which are devoted to new fiction, are booming and evolving with the emergence of micro festivals which cater to their own surroundings and local literary interests. A new and imaginative breed of literary event is thriving on both sides of the Atlantic, drawing heavily on the relaxed interactive ethos of comedy nights. And writing programmes across the UK and US are buoyant, generating an extraordinary explosion of varied new fiction.

Consequently, I feel this book is timely. Indeed, the idea came to me after several weeks of hunting through books in search of wisdom. I was teaching an introductory session on writing the novel and wanted to encourage and inspire my students with insightful words from published authors. I believe there is no better way to understand the novelist's art and craft than by listening to professional writers reflecting on their process: 'this was the starting point, this was the block, this was the breakthrough moment, this was the method that kept me going'. As the weeks progressed I read much on writing fiction, but only a few lines and paragraphs on the specific task of writing a first novel. However, my searching, though yielding little, proved to be

1

worthwhile. It made me aware of the need for a book dedicated to this subject.

This collection is for those who write, want to write or simply love the novel and wish to share the experiences of professional writers. The writers included are a mix of award-winning, established and new writers, offering the reader an inspiring blend of seasoned reflection from experienced novelists and fresh discoveries from newer writers.

Writing a novel is the longest and loneliest journey a writer can embark upon, and one that is difficult to articulate to the uninitiated. For this reason, I would particularly like to thank all the writers in this collection for their great generosity; each one has given of their precious time in order to open up their process to us. The resulting chapters are written with conviction, authority and passion, identifying in a visceral and personal way that place where the literary rubber meets the road. This book's usefulness for developing writers does not rest with the single chapter but in the aggregate, as the balance of personal, inspirational and practical materials reveal what it really takes to be a novelist. As a result this book is illuminating of writers' own particular methods rather than prescriptive or didactic.

In an age when students seek definitive answers on the process of creation and 'how to' books simplify the process of writing a novel into a linear step-by-step form, it can appear to the aspiring novelist that the journey is a straight run from start to finish: a Roman road without hills, dips or detours. Please do not think that I am damning the 'how to' book. As these chapters attest, writing a novel is exhilarating but also frustrating and any help is welcome. Nigel Watts' *Writing a Novel*, for example, is an excellent 'how to' book which I often suggest to students. Rather, what I hope this book reveals is that good writing does not simply come from a 'how to' book, a check list or from being told what to do and when to do it. When a novel is 'boiling up', Margaret Forster has no clue as to where it is heading. It is simply a 'shadowy vision and odd lines'[1] in her head. Forster's trust in this elusive process suggests an openness to chance and unpredictability, which is something professional writers welcome, for these unquantifiable qualities allow for the mysterious gift of discovery. Alison MacLeod states that, 'All good writers have to rest easy with uncertainty, or with what Milan Kundera calls *"the wisdom of uncertainty."* ' And Hanif Kureishi asserts, 'There is a sense – there has to be a sense – in which most writers do not understand what they are doing.'

The writers in this collection talk of arduous, uncertain and chaotic journeys with unforeseen obstacles, dead ends and the occasional hair-pin bend which forced them off the road and into the unknown: the desert. One must be patient but also impatient as one listens to each word and each sentence, vigilantly listening for what comes next as one makes one's way – crawling, stumbling, finally sprinting euphorically – towards the welcome oasis.

Hilary Mantel, winner of the 2009 and 2012 Man Booker Prize, says, 'From the practitioner's point of view, there is a sense in which every novel is your first novel... If you're saying to yourself, "This is my tenth novel, it will be fine, I know how to do it," it's probably time you stopped.'[2] Like every child, every literary novel is an individual that demands a singular approach. Creation is not a blueprint. Time and again writers in this book talk of the magic of channelling some new discovery that goes beyond ego. Isabel Ashdown describes the excitement of the 'unexpected moments of synchronicity' in her writing. David Swann talks of surprise and disorientation as the plot of his novel came to him in the form of dictation, as if it already existed 'in some other dimension'. The elation of the inspirational self, or the 'not-self'[3] as George Eliot calls it, are rare moments in the dogged devotion of writing thousands of words 'in the best order'. Gustave Flaubert describes these moments as his 'great days of sunlight'.[4] So enchanting is it that fame and even happiness cannot compare. This is the nub of it; this is why writers write. It is also why readers read – for these inspirational moments are the heartbeats that pulse delightfully.

My own path towards reading the novel began when I saw the controversial adult drama series 'Bouquet of Barbed Wire' as a child in the 1970s. Watched secretly in my bedroom on a tiny black and white portable, I was captivated by the story of infidelity and incest and how it devastates a family. I loved the haunting music and picture of a young girl running in the opening credits. I was shocked by the scenes of domestic violence and intrigued by the jealousies and intensity between a father and newly married daughter. *So this is what it's like*, I thought with an electric thrill, for I had discovered emotions that belong in the world of adults and were outside of my own experience.

I recall this because I felt what can only be described as a sense of loss once the series had finished. In the playground I relived (in inappropriately graphic detail) the torrid fallout from the father's incestuous infatuation with his daughter, only to receive confused or blank looks from my playmates. Desperate to experience that sense of 'discovery' again, I soon turned to reading fiction. My starting point was to read through the familiar lists of literary 'classics', beginning with children's fiction then moving onto adult fiction. I felt the strangeness of Jane

Eyre's preternatural experience of hearing Rochester calling to her from across the moors. I stepped inside Anna Karenina's anguished head and experienced her suicidal state of mind, when everything and everyone seems so ugly to her at the train station. I nodded uneasy assent at Humbert Humbert's savage and hilarious attempt to gain his reader's sympathy for his sexual obsession with 12-year-old Lolita.

I mention these three novels in particular because they so completely captured (and still do) my imagination. But why? What was I discovering through fiction that made such an impression during my formative years? I now see that novels such as these were indispensable to me because they connected with my own quest to discover who I was. They fought – with dramatic intensity – my own muted struggle to find my place or to impose myself on the world. I was enthralled by Jane Eyre's force of will as she battles to find a middle ground between her passionate and conscience-driven sides. I questioned time and again whether Anna Karenina is victim or immoral woman as she abandons her privileged yet empty existence to embark on a passionate affair with Vronsky. And Humbert Humbert? Well, I knew that his obsession was deeply wrong, yet I was entranced by the skewed story of a man who describes himself as both 'courageous' and 'a maniac'.

What is right and what is wrong? I had little real experience of the world and fiction enabled me to see – with a more crystallized clarity – that existence is incongruous, illogical and contradictory. 'The novel comes into contact with the spontaneity of the inconclusive present'; Mikhail Bakhtin wrote, 'this is what keeps the genre from congealing. The novelist is drawn toward everything that is not yet completed.'[5] Social scientist and academic, Shirley Brice Heath[6] says that for most women life today is very different from the lives their mothers lived. Therefore, life has an unpredictable quality that past family experience cannot prepare them for, and this is the void that fiction fills. Heath's claim chimes with my own need as a reader. What I seek is not a world simple enough to be complete and therefore predictable; rather, I want company in my imperfect understanding of it. And over the years, as my reading widened to encompass contemporary literary fiction, I felt (and still feel) an increasingly moving series of recognitions that inconclusiveness is the novel's 'truth'.

In contrast, David Shields, American novel-essayist, declared in his book *Reality Hunger: A Manifesto* (2010) that the crafted novel – neat, coherent, fathomable – is too artificial with its completist attitude to reflect 'truth' in the speed of twenty-first century culture. '[F]iction has now become a museum-piece genre',[7] stated US critic, Lee Siegel, also in 2010. It is non-fiction, they argue (specifically the lyric essay for Shields), that now has the capacity to illuminate the complicated cultural moment in which we find ourselves. In 2003, US literary critic Harold Bloom[8] railed against the National Book Foundation for bestowing its annual award for 'distinguished contribution' to Stephen King, opening up the debate on the state and decline of fiction. In 2001, the BBC's Andrew Marr wrote an article in the *Observer* about contemporary British novelists' lack of ambition, announcing that 'the great work, the time of discovery, is over and done and cannot be reopened'.[9]

Such funeral pronouncements raise one's awareness of certain anxieties relating to the novel genre and twenty-first century culture. How can the novel, with its very scope and breadth, truthfully reflect our technology-led culture as it evolves at such an unprecedented pace? How can the novel offer a distinct vision of life when language and culture are becoming increasingly 'globalized'? How can the novel give us intellectual significance in the intellectual decline of our current historical circumstance? The idolatry of consumerism is directly at odds with the extended narrative of the novel. Consumerism is consumption without absorption. It encourages reductionism which, in turn, discourages deep thought that we associate with the 'serious' novel.

When approaching a first novel, the aspiring novelist must not only tackle writing on a scale never experienced before, but must also contend with a vision of what the novel is, what it has already achieved and what it needs to achieve in discovering 'the various dimensions of existence'.[10] Susan Sontag says, 'Setting out to write, if you have the idea of "literature" in your head, is formidable, intimidating – a plunge in an icy lake.'[11] For the new novelist this can raise issues of entitlement and insecurities relating to authenticity. Indeed, Andrew Cowan, Edward Hogan and Kishwar Desai discuss their feelings of inadequacy when embarking on their first novels. Jane Feaver offers good advice to the fledgling novelist, weighed down with the burden of self-consciousness and the insecurity that can come from daring to approach this supreme literary form. 'We must develop some counter-confidence that will temporarily overcome or pull the rug from whatever it is that tells you, you have no right to be there.' Cultivating a sense of entitlement, it seems, is a crucial step in writing a first novel. You have the right to be there. It is, after all, the new writer – the new voice and vision – who makes the future of literature. Craig Seligman, writer and editor, feels it is first novels, rather than later ones, which exude the spirit of their age because, '[f]irst novelists are seldom conscious of the zeitgeist they're inhaling, they're too busy just trying to get the words down on the page.'[12]

In response to Marr's declaration that the 'great work' is over, writer and academic Terry Eagleton asserts, 'Whenever people say "the novel is dead", it usually means it is transforming or metamorphosing into something else, a new kind of fiction, and that may be what is happening again now.'[13] Eagleton's words are reassuring. They remind us that the novel – 'so clumsy, verbose and undramatic, so rich, elastic and alive'[14] – is a living thing that dies only to be reborn; it is all part and parcel of the novel's continual evolution.

Indeed, announcing the genre to be an endangered species can only serve to ensure its survival. As one critic, theorist or novelist points to the decline of the novel, passionately declaring that he or she is bored by its traditional confines, another responds by passionately defending its riches. The result? The novel does still matter. One is reminded of what it can do and needs to do, yet one is also reminded that there is not necessarily a definitive answer as to the novel's 'purpose'.

As such, new writers need not be spooked or irked. While critics thrash out the state of the novel (sickly, buoyant, dull, vibrant) writers continue to go about their business and readers continue to read their books or Kindles (yes, the novel also adapts to and survives the innovations of the IT revolution), absorbed and marvelling at some new discovery that speaks to them alone. The choice of writers for this collection could be nothing but personal. They are writers whose work speaks to me and whom I admire. Their fiction seeks to go beyond the surface to capture contradictions, revealing not only the poetry in the everyday but also the world's strangeness.

Unexpected gifts mysteriously come to the imagination and it is the rational authorial mind which alters them to create meaning. The novelists' dilemma when asked to demystify their process lies in the difficulty of expressing what is largely inexplicable – for creation occurs in the dumbfounding tussle between the unconscious and conscious. The writers in this book also had the additional task of demystifying their process still further, focusing their discussions around particular elements of writing: *Inspiration, Research, Voice* and *Form*. These are key elements that a writer must consciously consider in order to proceed. Of 'form' Soumya Bhattacharya says, 'Without making a decision about the form . . . one is simply stuck with the material, unable to fashion it into a story.'

Of course, decisions made often change as a novel develops and the 'imagined ideal'[15] takes shape. Writers talk of crucial hours of research that were finally not crucial; of bringing in a new voice or changing viewpoint which led to many more hours of intensive labour, only, at times, to switch the whole thing back. Jane Rusbridge, concerned that her second-person narration might alienate readers, painstakingly switched it to third person, only to find that her character was truly alive in the second person.

This book, consequently, is divided into the four parts – *Inspiration, Research, Voice* and *Form* – to offer the aspiring novelist a specific focus that may shed helpful light on an aspect of their own process. Though chapters focus on these four separate elements, I hope readers see that these are necessarily interconnected. As pointed out by Helon Habila, 'any separation is really artificial', for when talking about one thing the writer cannot help but talk about the other things.

'Writing is so personal, so subjective, so deeply and intricately threaded through, in, under, over, around a writer's life'[16] that it seems fitting to begin this book with Part I on *Inspiration*. Of course, where else can this book begin – for without inspiration there cannot be a novel. Where does inspiration come from? How does a writer start? What makes people want to write? The chapters in this section by Hanif Kureishi, Valerie Martin, Johanna Skibsrud and David Vann are rich, diverse and highly personal as the writers reflect on these questions and the imagination's process in turning life into art. Kureishi explores the artist's subject matter and where one gathers one's material from for writing. Martin reveals the tremendous power of reading in the formation of her creative imagination. Kureishi and Martin offer fascinating insight into personal history and how it informed their remarkable debut novels, both directly and indirectly. Skibsrud and Vann pinpoint the genesis of their ambitious first novels in a moment's recognition when both (interestingly) look down into lakes. Vann talks about the 'certainty' of the moment, 'a certainty that it will not mislead', while Skibsrud analyses, with freshness and eloquence, the 'growth' of an abstract recognition into its final dramatic form.

Curiosity, undoubtedly, is the writer's primary preoccupation, but as Kureishi points out, 'There are certain ideas, like certain people, that the writer will be drawn to.' These chapters show how it is the singular perception or impression that begins a story. Write what you know is a controversial cliché, but perhaps it should not be quickly dismissed, for what one knows does not only come from experience, but from what is central to us: our interests, obsessions, cares and preoccupations. Lorrie Moore says, 'None – or at least very few – of the things that have happened to my characters have ever happened to me. But one's life is there constantly collecting and providing and it will creep into one's work regardless – in emotional ways.'[17]

Part II focuses on *Research*. Maile Chapman, Edward Hogan, Kishwar Desai and Wena Poon offer lively and revealing insights into how research is undertaken and how it dictates the shape of a story. 'Nothing is more irritating to the reader,' Janet Burroway says, 'than to be told a character is a doctor when it's clear he doesn't know a stethoscope from a stegosaur.'[18] These chapters highlight the writers' acute awareness of how one must immerse oneself in research in order to produce good writing that is authentic and rich with detail. Research is absorbing, moving and can open up new directions and possibilities, yet the writers here are also acutely aware of how research can delay, distract and devour you. Maile Chapman explores the process of collecting and letting go of information and how this time-consuming process contributed to the compelling and unsettling atmosphere of her first novel. Edward Hogan considers how research offered reassurance – indeed, the right – to write about a fictional mining town in his home county. In her impassioned account of Punjab gendercide, Kishwar Desai explores how research is employed in different ways in the writing of non-fiction and fiction. Wena Poon explores her alien experience of bullfighting and offers an enthralling discussion on how research can vanquish initial ignorance and even distaste. Interestingly, Chapman and Desai talk of the almost 'mystical' moments in researching, when an invented detail, speculation or feeling is confirmed by the outside world. At times, research is as mysterious as the imagination itself, it seems. Professional writers often talk of the surprising and magical connections that arise through the act of researching, and which offer a strange sense of rightness that feels somehow predetermined.

In Part III writers explore *Voice*. Alison MacLeod, Andrew Cowan, Jane Rusbridge and Isabel Ashdown discuss with honesty and integrity the essential and arduous goal of finding the right language, imagery and rhythms to give voice to their novels. MacLeod feels that 'voice' is a 'primitive and essential gift... Without it, a novel might be well developed and fluently composed, but the "spirit" of the story will not have entered it.' In writing we talk about voice in different ways: the unique voices of characters, the novel's 'voice' and the recognizable voice of the author. In her book *Imaginative Writing* (2007), Janet Burroway reminds us of the writer's skill and struggle, for writers have only the words – their choice and arrangement – with which to create voices as distinct as those we *hear* with their different accents, tones and rhythms. MacLeod examines how writers capture the 'inner signature' which is the voice of the novel, and explores the exciting and mysterious process in which her characters' voices and *the voice* of her novel came to her in the gaps of research. Cowan offers fascinating insight into the devotion and labour involved in giving voice to his poignant first novel. He explores the anxiety of writing the 'real thing', and the challenge of achieving a consistent and singular narrative voice. In her search for the right way to tell her story, Rusbridge illuminates the complex development of three narrative voices, offering rare insight into the trial and error involved in bringing characters to life through language and viewpoint. Ashdown discusses the advantages and disadvantages of choosing first-person narration for her teenage character in her impressive first novel. She examines her uncertainty over readership (adult or young adult) and how she resolved this through her gradual realization that another voice had been 'quietly but insistently' waiting to speak.

MacLeod and Rusbridge both express a creative preoccupation that stems from research, when voices are absent or lost in the documentation of 'fact'. Cowan and Ashdown give voice to marginalized characters: the disaffected working class, the drunk. While giving voice to the 'voiceless', writers are also working to establish their own voice. The desire to be heard is, after all, life's purpose. Margaret Atwood in *Negotiating with the Dead* – her excellent book about the purpose and the pleasures of writing – offers the final words of her book to the poet Ovid: 'But still, the fates will leave me my voice,/and by my voice I shall be known.'[19] These words are spoken through the Sibyl of Cumae, and Atwood suggests that the Sybil speaks not only for herself but also Ovid, 'and for the hopes and fates of all writers'.

In Part IV writers explore *Form*. Helon Habila, David Swann, Soumya Bhattacharya and Jane Feaver offer comprehensive and enthralling accounts of their own particular methods of giving shape to their first novels. 'What Fancy sends, the writer must order by Judgement',[20] says John Gardner. 'He must think out completely...what his fiction means, or is trying to mean. He must...get at the truth not just of his characters and action but also of his fiction's form.' Some writers structure their novels through careful attention to narrative sequence. E. M. Forster spoke of writing a novel as 'moving toward some imagined event that loomed as a distant mountain'.[21] Others write without paying attention to shape or structure, preferring to see what will emerge. Hilary Mantel's aim is to think first about the people in her books; such things as plot and structure can take care of themselves. 'There are bound to be as many different approaches to form as there are people, as there are books to be written', Feaver assures, for as Habila points out, '[i]n giving shape to a novel one is also giving shape to one's universe'. Habila explores how personal circumstance produced the fragmented structure of his powerful debut novel, and how presenting his material in reverse chronological order served to strengthen conflict in his story. Swann illuminates how content and form are intimately bound together through the arduous and thrilling process of structuring his tricky dual monologues. Bhattacharya examines how the epistolary form – intimate, discursive, non-linear and inconclusive – enabled him to shape his poignant narrative of a man's spectacular failure. Feaver offers tantalizing insights into 'the beauty of organization', and how the very act of writing dictated the shape and form of her remarkable novel. Here, we see the writer wrestling with the actual material of her making, and share her exciting discovery – both structural and material – that 'making it up' offers as much truth as the didactic narrative of memory.

As Feaver points out, writing is an intangible activity, and both Swann and Feaver found the act of visualization – drawing on pictorial images (two streams crossing and making an 'X' for Swann; a tent for Feaver) – offered dimension and patterns which helped them to shape their stories. This method allows for a degree of flexibility – rivers flowing and kinking, tent poles moving – within the decision-making process which, surely, can only benefit the novel in the long run. As Gardner warns, '[N]eatness can be carried too far, so that the work begins to seem fussy and overwrought, anal compulsive, unspontaneous . . . on the other hand, mess is no adequate alternative.'[22]

While there is no specific part of this book dedicated to revision and editing, such issues run throughout. Writers often refer to the drafting process – 'the shaping, honing, and cut, cut, cutting' (Feaver) – that is crucial in creating a living, breathing world which coheres and is consistent. Some of the writers find the drafting process enjoyable – especially line-by-line editing – as it satisfies the desire to polish and improve the writing. At other times, with weightier revision, it can be somewhat alarming for new writers. Skibsrud's novel was thinned down to almost half its original size, and she found the editing process to be 'violent or even cruel' at times before she came to see that the editing stage was essential to realizing her novel's initial intent.

Helen Garnons-Williams, Editorial Director for Fiction at Bloomsbury UK, talks of the organic and collaborative process of editing. Through being asked a pointed question, some writers are shocked to discover their characters still exist in their heads rather than on the page. Conversely, some writers have overly researched and there is too much on the page. In those cases, the editor's job is to help the author to sift the novel so that research shakes down and the characters and story rise up. As with the writing process, working with any editor – whether a relative, friend, tutor, mentor, thesis supervisor, editor at a publishing house – is something of a necessary leap of faith.

'Bravery', 'belief', 'confidence', 'faith' are fundamental words that run through the chapters like stitches. These are qualities that one must possess – or cultivate – if one is truly committed to writing and wishes to enter into the practical business of getting a novel published. Being courageous and having faith in oneself, however, does not guarantee publishing success, rather, it thickens the skin and gives the writer the necessary endurance to keep going.

The fifth and final part of this book considers the completed novel's journey to publication. Publisher and former literary agent Hannah Westland, editorial director Helen Garnons-Williams and writer Lionel Shriver give insights into a tough and subjective business from their own particular perspectives. Written with focus, clarity and passion, these chapters reveal that the business into which the new novelist strains to enter is 'built on taste' (Garnons-Williams), and taste is as unpredictable and personal as writing itself. Westland gives useful and practical advice to aspiring novelists seeking an agent. Garnons-Williams illuminates the fascinating process of publication and the sometimes crucial role of editors in drawing out the very best from a writer. Shriver's pointedly humorous reflections on her first publishing experience offer grounding and a sense of 'ownership' to would-be novelists as they surmount the various hurdles of getting a first novel published.

The publishing business is driven by gut instinct. There are no hard and fast rules, no precise and helpful answers to the problem of getting a first (or second or third) novel published in an overcrowded and unpredictable market. Even though publishing is going through a period of intense change, with the rise of digital technology, which is challenging the very nature of how agents and publishers work, debut novels *are* getting published. Publishers are *always* looking for new, original and distinct voices; it is what the industry depends on.

Several years ago, Annie Proulx was giving a writer's talk at a venue in Brighton and asked the packed audience who wanted to be a writer. Her eyes travelled over the field of raised hands swaying like corn. 'So,' she said with a wry smile, 'why aren't you at home writing?' She makes an obvious yet pertinent point: before a novel can be published it has to be written. This book is intended to help writers to write and to continue writing. It offers insights and advice for new writers, but also deep reflection that is useful to more experienced writers. Martin says, 'Writing novels didn't get any easier after I finished the first one; in fact because I have a much clearer idea of what I'm doing now than I did

then, the process has become more complex and therefore more difficult.' Yet Martin – writer of nine novels and winner of the esteemed
Orange Prize in 2003 – continues to write novels, as do all the writers
in this book. Once one has aspired or submitted to the inspirational self
and felt the 'great days of sunlight' perhaps one doesn't mind the rain so
much. As Susan Hill says: 'Heady stuff. Writing is. Gets more so. *That's*
why. That's all really.'[23]

And so here I'd like to finish with Lionel Shriver's wonderful words
to every aspiring novelist: 'you're a fiction writer. You like story. How
marvellous, that yours is just beginning.'

Indeed, how marvellous!

Notes

1. M. Forster (1993) 'Cooking the Books' in C. Boylan (ed.) *The Agony and the Ego* (London: Penguin), p. 162.
2. H. Mantel (June–September 2006) in C. Seligman article, 'The First Novel', *Bookforum* (volume 13, issue 2), p. 33.
3. G. Eliot (1965) in M. Allott (ed.) *Novelists on the Novel* (London and Henley: Routledge & Kegan Paul), p. 119.
4. G. Flaubert, Ibid., p. 149.
5. M. Bakhtin (1981) *The Dialogic Imagination* (Austin: University of Texas Press), p. 27.
6. S. Brice Heath, cited in 'Perchance to Dream: in the Age of Images a Reason to Write Novels' by Jonathan Franzen, *Harper's Magazine* (April 1996), pp. 48–49.
7. L. Siegel (22 June 2010) 'Where Have All the Mailers Gone?', *The New York Observer*, www.observer.com/2010/06/where-have-all-the-mailers-gone.
8. H. Bloom (24 September 2003) 'Dumbing Down American Readers', *The Boston Globe*, www.boston.com/news/globe/editorial_opinion/oped/articles/2003/09/24/dumbing_down_american_readers.
9. A. Marr (27 May 2001) 'Death of the Novel', *The* Observer, www.guardian.co.uk/books/2001/may/27/fiction.
10. M. Kundera (2005) *The Art of the Novel* (Chatham: Faber & Faber), p. 5.
11. S. Sontag (2001) 'Directions: Write, Read, Rewrite. Repeat Steps 2 and 3 as Needed', in *Writers [on Writing] Collected Essays from The New York Times* (New York: Times Books), p. 224.
12. C. Seligman (June–September 2006), article, 'The First Novel', *Bookforum* (volume 13, issue 2), p. 31.
13. T. Eagleton (2001), 'Fact or Fiction', *The Observer Comment*, www.observer.guardian.co.uk/comment/story/0,6903,497137,00.html.
14. V. Woolf (1965) in M. Allott (ed.) *Novelists on the Novel* (London and Henley: Routledge & Kegan Paul), p. 198.
15. C. Boylan (ed.) (1993) *The Agony and the Ego* (London: Penguin), p. xi.
16. M. Dooley (ed.) (2000) *How Novelists Work* (Wales: Seren), p. 7.

17. L. Moore (1993) 'Better and Sicker' in C. Boylan (ed.) *The Agony and the Ego* (London: Penguin), p. 204.

18. J. Burroway (2007) *Imaginative Writing*, 2nd edn (New York: Pearson Longman), p. 213.

19. M. Atwood (2002) *Negotiating with the Dead* (Cambridge: Cambridge University Press), p. 180.

20. J. Gardner (1983) *The Art of Fiction* (New York: Vintage Books), p. 7.

21. J. Burroway (2007) *Imaginative Writing*, 2nd edn (New York: Pearson Longman), p. 211.

22. J. Gardner (1983) *The Art of Fiction* (New York: Vintage Books), p. 7.

23. S. Hill (1993) 'Heady Stuff' in C. Boylan (ed.) *The Agony and the Ego* (London: Penguin), p. 122.

Part I
'Inspiration' and the Novel

1
Something Given: Reflections on Writing

Hanif Kureishi

Where do stories come from? What is there to write about? Where do you get material? How do you start? And, why are writers asked these questions so often?

It isn't as if you can go shopping for experience. Or is it? Such an idea suggests that experience is somehow outside yourself, and must be gathered. But in fact, it is a question of seeing what is there. Experience is what has already happened. Experience, like love and hate, starts at home: in the bedroom, in the kitchen. It happens the moment people are together, or apart, when they want one another and when they realize they don't like their lover's ears.

Stories are everywhere, and they can be made from the simplest things. Preferably from the simplest things, if they are the right, the precise, the correct things, and if the chosen material is profitable, useful and sufficiently malleable. I say chosen, but if the writer is attentive the stories she needs to shape her urgent concerns will occur unbidden. There are certain ideas, like certain people, that the writer will be drawn to. She only has to wait and look. She cannot expect to know why this idea has been preferred to that until the story has been written, if then.

There is a sense – there has to be a sense – in which most writers do not entirely understand what they are doing. You suspect there might be something you can use. But you don't know what it is. You have to find out by beginning. And what you discover probably will not be what you originally imagined or hoped for. Some surprises can be discomfiting. But this useful ignorance, or tension with the unknown, can be fruitful, if not a little unreliable at times.

The master Chekhov taught that it is in the ordinary, the everyday, the unremarkable – and in the usually unremarked – that the deepest, most extraordinary and affecting events occur. These observations of the ordinary are bound up with everyone else's experience – the universal – and with what it is to be a child, parent, husband, lover. Most of the significant moments of one's life are 'insignificant' to other people. It is showing how and why they are significant and also why they may seem absurd, that is art.

The aged Tolstoy thought he had to solve all the problems of life. Chekhov saw that these problems could only be put, not answered, at least by the part of yourself that was an artist. Perhaps as a man you could be effective in the world; and Chekhov was. As a writer, though, scepticism was preferable to a didacticism or advocacy that seemed to settle everything but which, in reality, closed everything off. Political or spiritual solutions rendered the world less interesting. Rather than reminding you of its baffling strangeness, they flattened it out.

In the end there is only one subject for an artist. What is the nature of human experience? What is it to be alive, suffer and feel? What is it to love or need another person? To what extent can we know anyone else? Or ourselves? In other words, what is it to be a human being. These are questions that can never be answered satisfactorily, but they have to be put again and again by each generation and by each person. The writer trades in dissatisfaction.

How then, can the novel, the subtlest and most flexible form of human expression, die? Literature is concerned with the self-conscious exploration of the lives of men, women and children in society. Even when it is comic, it sees life as something worth talking about. This is why airport fiction, or 'blockbusters', books which are all plot, can never be considered literature, and why, in the end, they are of little value. It is not only that the language in which they are written lacks bounce and poignancy, but that they don't return the reader to the multifariousness and complication of existence. This, too, is why journalism and literature are opposed to one another, rather than being allies. Most journalism is about erasing personality in favour of the facts, or the 'story'. The personality of the journalist is unimportant. In literature, personality is all, and the exploration of character – or portraiture, the human subject – is central to it.

Writers are often asked if their work is autobiographical. If it seems to me to be an odd, somewhat redundant question – where else could the work come from, except from the self? – I wonder whether it is because there remains something mysterious about the conversion of experience into representation. Yet this is something we do all the time. We work over our lives continuously; our minds generate and invent in night-dreaming, day-dreaming and in fantasy. In these modes we can see that the most fantastic and absurd ideas can contain human truth. Or perhaps we can see how it is that important truths require a strange shape in order to be made acceptable. Or perhaps it is simply true that the facts of life are just very strange.

Still, it is odd, the public's desire to see fiction as disguised, or treated, or embellished, autobiography. It is as if one requires a clear line between what has happened and what has been imagined later in the construction of a story. Perhaps there is something childish about the make-believe of fiction which is disconcerting, rather like taking dreams seriously. It is as if we live in too many disparate worlds at once – in the solid everyday world, and in the insubstantial, fantastic one at the same time. It is difficult to put them all together. But the imagination and one's wishes are real too. They are part of daily life, and the distinction between the softness of dreams and hard reality can never be made clear. You might as easily say, 'we live in dreams'.

Sometimes I wonder whether the question about autobiography is really not a question about why some people can do certain things and not others. If everyone has experience then everyone could write it down and make a book of it. Perhaps writers are, in the end, only the people who bother. It may be that everyone is creative – after all, children start that way, imagining what is not there. They are always 'telling stories' and 'showing off'. But not everyone is talented. It is significant that none of the many biographies of Chekhov – some have more of the 'facts' than others – can supply us with an answer to the question 'why him?' That a man of his temperament, background and interests should have become one of the supreme writers, not only of his time but of all time, is inexplicable. How is it that he lived the life he did and wrote the stories and plays he did? Any answer to this can only be sought in the work, and it can only ever remain a mystery. After all, everyone has some kind of life, but how that might be made of interest to others, or significant or entertaining, is another matter. A mountain of facts don't make a molehill of art.

Writing seems to be a problem of some kind. It isn't as if most people can just sit down and start to write brilliantly, get up from the desk, do something else all day, and then, next morning start again without any conflict or anxiety. To begin to write – to attempt anything creative, for that matter – is to ask many other questions, not only about the craft itself, but of oneself, and of life. The blank empty page is a representation of this helplessness. Who am I? it asks. How should I live? Who do I want to be?

For a long time I went to my desk as if my life depended on it. And it did; I had made it so. Therefore any dereliction seemed catastrophic. Of course, with any writer the desire to write will come and go. At times you will absolutely rebel against going to your desk. And if you are sensible, you will not go. There are more pressing needs.

There are many paradoxes here. Your work has to mean everything. But if it means too much, if it is not sufficiently careless, the imagination doesn't run. Young writers in particular will sometimes labour over the same piece of work for too long – they can't let it go, move on or start anything new. The particular piece of work carries too heavy a freight of hope, expectation and fear.

You fear finishing a piece of work because then, if you hand it over, judgement starts. There will be criticism and denigration. It will be like being young again, when you were subject to the criticism of others, and seemed unable to defend yourself, though most of the denigration people have to face has been internalized, and comes from within. Sometimes you feel like saying: Nobody dislikes my work quite as much as I do. Recently I was talking to a friend, a professional writer, who is conscious of not having done as well as she should have, and hasn't written anything for a while. She was complaining about her work. 'It isn't any good, that's the problem,' she kept saying. But as good as what? As good as Shakespeare?

You don't want to make mistakes because you don't want a failure that will undermine you even more. But if you don't make mistakes nothing is achieved. Sometimes you have to feel free to write badly, but it takes confidence to see that somehow the bad writing can sponsor the good writing, that volume can lead to quality. Sometimes, too, even at the end of a piece of writing, you have to leave the flaws in; they are part of it. Or they can't be eliminated without something important being lost, some flavour or necessary energy. You can't make everything perfect but you have to try to.

At one time I imagined that if I wrote like other people, if I imitated writers I liked, I would only have to expose myself through a disguise. I did this for a time, but my own self kept coming through. It took me a while to see that isn't a question of discovering your voice but of seeing that you have a voice already just as you have a personality, and that if you continue to write you have no choice but to speak, write, and live in it. What you have to do, in a sense, is take possession of yourself. The human being and the writer are the same.

Not long ago I was working with a director on a film. After I'd completed several drafts, he came to me with pages of notes. I went through them and some of his ideas and questions seemed legitimate. But still I balked, and wondered why. Was this only vanity? Surely it wasn't that I didn't want to improve my film? After thinking about it, I saw that the way I had originally written it was an expression of my voice, of my view of the world. If that was removed, not much remained apart from the obligatory but uninspiring technical accomplishment.

I started to write seriously around the age of 14 or 15. At school I felt that what I was expected to learn was irrelevant and tedious. The teachers didn't conceal their boredom. Like us, they couldn't wait to get out. I felt I was being stuffed with the unwanted by fools. I couldn't make the information part of myself; it had to be held at a distance, like unpleasant food. The alternative was compliance. Or there was rebellion.

Then there was writing, which was an active way of taking possession of the world. I could be omnipotent, rather than a victim. Writing became a way of possessing, ordering, what seemed like chaos. I soon learned that writing was the one place where I had dominion, where I was in charge. At a desk in my study, enwombed, warm, concentrated, self-contained, with everything I needed to hand – music, pens, paper, typewriter – I could make a world in which disharmonies could be contained, and perhaps drained of their poison. I wrote to make myself feel better, because often I didn't feel too good. I wrote to become a writer and get away from the suburbs. Stories were an excuse, a reason, a way of being interested in things. Looking for stories was a way of trying to see what was going on within and without. People write because it is crucial to them to put their side of the story without interruption. This is how they see it; this is how it was for them – their version. They need to get things clear in their own minds, and in everyone else's. To write is to be puzzled a second time by one's experience; it is also to savour it. In such reflection there is time to taste and engage with your own life in its complexity.

Experience keeps coming. If the self is partly formed from the blows, wounds and marks made by the world, then writing is a kind of self healing. But creativity initiates disturbance too. It is a kind of scepticism which attacks that which is petrified. Perhaps this is a source of the dispute between Rushdie and the mullahs. Art represents freedom of thought – not merely in a political or moral sense – but the freedom of the mind to go where it wishes; to express dangerous wishes. This freedom, of course, is a kind of instability. Wishes conflict with the forbidden, the concealed, with that which cannot or should not be thought, and certainly not said. The creative imagination is usefully aggressive; it undermines authority; it can seem uncontrollable; it is erotic and breaks up that which has become solid. I remember some of my father's friends complaining to him about my work, particularly *My Beautiful Laundrette*. For Asians in the West, or for anyone in exile, intellectual and emotional disarray can seem unbearable. The artist may be a conduit for the forbidden, for that which is too dangerous to say, but he isn't always going to be thanked for his trouble.

I wrote, too, because it was absorbing. I was fascinated by how one thing led to another. Once I'd started banging on my typewriter, I wanted to see what might be done, where such creative curiosity might lead me. You'd be in the middle of a story, in some unfamiliar imaginative place, but you'd only got there because you'd been brave enough to start off. I was impatient, which hindered me. As soon as I began something I wanted to get to the end of it. I want to succeed rather than search. I wanted to be the sort of person who had written books, rather than a person who was merely writing them. I am still impatient; it isn't much fun sitting at a desk with nothing happening. But at least I can see the necessity for impatience in writing – the desire to have something done, which must push against the necessity to wait, for the rumination that allows you to see how a piece of writing might develop or need to find its own way over time, without being hurried to a conclusion.

I conceived the idea of what became *The Buddha of Suburbia* on the balcony of a hotel room in Madras, my father's birthplace. Until then, as a professional writer, I had written plays and films, though I'd already published the first chapter of *The Buddha of Suburbia* as a short story. Ever since it had appeared in print the characters and situation remained with me. Normally you finish something with a sense of relief. It is over because you are bored with it and, for now – until the next time – you have said as much as you can. But I had hardly begun. I knew – my excitement told me – that I had material for a whole book: south London in the 1970s, growing up as a 'semi-Asian' kid; pop, fashion, drugs, sexuality. My task was to find a way to organize it.

Often, to begin writing all you need is an idea, a germ, a picture, a hint, a moment's recognition – an excuse for everything else you've been thinking to gather or organize around, so that everything falls into place. In the search for stories you look for something likely and malleable, which connects with the other things you are thinking at the time. I have to say that with *The Buddha of Suburbia* I was also excited by the idea of being occupied for two years, of having what was, for me, a big project.

Looking at the journal I kept at the time, I can see how much I knew of what I was doing; and, concurrently, how little. It had to be a discovery – of that which was already there. I am reminded of a phrase by Alfred de Musset: 'It is not work. It is merely listening. It is as if some unknown person were speaking in your ear.'

I spent ages trying to unblock myself, removing obstacles, and trying to create a clear channel between the past and my pen. Then, as now, I wrote pages and pages of rough notes; words, sentences, paragraphs, character biographies, all, at the time, disconnected. There was a lot of material but it was pretty chaotic. It needed order but too much order too soon was more dangerous than chaos. I didn't want to stifle my imagination just as it was exploding, even if it did make me feel unstable. An iron control stops anything interesting happening. Somehow you have to assemble all the pieces of your puzzle without knowing whether they will fit together. The pattern or total picture is something you have to discover later. You need to believe even when the only basis for belief is the vague intuition that a complete story will emerge.

The atmosphere I had already. But the characters and the detail – the world of the book – I had to create from scratch. Establishing the tone, the voice, the attitude, the way I wanted to see the material, and the way I wanted the central character, Karim, to express himself, was crucial. Once I found the tone, the work developed independent life; I could see what should be in or out. I could hear the wrong notes.

The Buddha of Suburbia was written close to myself, which can make the writing more difficult in some ways, if not easier in others. I knew the preparation – living – had already been done. But in writing so directly from the self there are more opportunities for shame and embarrassment. Also, these characters are so much part of oneself that you can almost forget to transfer them to the page, imagining that somehow they are already there.

There are other dangers. You might want the control that writing provides, but it can be a heady and disturbing sort of omnipotence. In the imaginative world you keep certain people alive and destroy or reduce others. People can be transformed into tragic, comic, or inconsequential figures. They are at the centre of their own lives, but you can make them extras. You can also make yourself a hero or fool, or both. Art can be revenge as well as reparation. This can be an immense source of energy. However, the desires and wishes conjured by the free imagination can make the writer both fearful and guilty. There are certain things you would rather not know that you think. At the same time you recognize that these thoughts are important, and that you can't move forward without having expressed them. Writing might, therefore, have the aspect of an infidelity or betrayal, as the pen reveals secrets it is dangerous to give away. The problem, then, with explorations, or experiments, is not that you will find nothing, but that you will find too much, and too much will change. In these circumstances it might be easier to write nothing, or to block yourself. If we are creatures that need and love to imagine, then the question to ask has to be how, why and when does this stop happening? Why is the imagination so terrifying that we have to censor it? What can we think that is, so to speak, unimaginable?

A block holds everything together; it keeps important things down, for a reason. A block might then work like depression, as a way of keeping the unacceptable at a distance, even as it continuously reminds you that it is there.

Once I'd embarked on *The Buddha of Suburbia* I found characters and situations I couldn't have planned for. Changez, in particular, was a character who sprang from an unknown source. I knew Jamila had to have a husband who'd never been to England before. In my journal of January 1988 I wrote 'Part of me wants him to read Conan Doyle. Another part wants him to be illiterate, from a village. Try both.' Originally I had imagined a cruel, tyrannical figure, who would clash violently with Jamila. But that kind of cruelty didn't fit with the tone of the novel. I found, as I experimented, that the naiveté I gave Changez soon presented me with opportunities for irony. If arranged marriages are an affront to the romantic idea that love isn't something that can be arranged, what would happen if Changez did fall in love with his wife? What if she became a lesbian?

Many of the ideas I tried in the book seemed eccentric even as I conceived them. I taught myself not to be too dismissive of the strange. There was often something in peculiar ideas that might surprise and startle the reader just as I had been jolted myself.

I like to work every day, in the morning. I miss it badly if I don't do it. It has become a habit but it is not only that. It gives the day a necessary weight. I'm never bored by what I do. I go to it now with more rather than less enthusiasm. There is less time, of course, while there is more to say about the process of time itself. There are more characters, more experience and numerous ways of approaching it. If writing were not difficult it wouldn't be enjoyable. If it is too easy you can feel you haven't quite grasped the story, that you have omitted something essential. But the difficulty is more likely to be internal to the work itself – where it should be – rather than in some personal crisis. I'm not sure you become more fluent as you get older, but you become less fearful of imagined consequences. There has been a lot to clear away; then the work starts.

Extract from *Dreaming and Scheming: Collected Prose: Reflections on Writing and Politics* (2002), Faber & Faber.

2
Look Back in Angst

Valerie Martin

I grew up in New Orleans, where I attended a public grammar school and a Roman Catholic high school. My father, a sea captain for Lykes Brother's Shipping Company, was a great reader, as was my mother. He had wanted to be a writer and had, in fact, a degree in journalism from a college in Missouri. I remember that he sent out a few stories to the men's adventure magazines of the period and that he received at least one response suggesting changes. Changes were beyond him and somehow, I gathered, beneath him. The letter was torn up in disgust.

I was very young, but this lesson lodged in my memory. Stories could be rejected.

My childhood was a miserable, largely friendless business, but I was blessed with a child's pantheistic passion for nature, and when I was up in my tree house in the vacant lot near our apartment, I was as happy as such a child can be. I believed in Martians and talked to dogs and trees, both of which, I knew, understood me.

At Mt. Carmel, the Catholic high school I attended, the nuns opened the lid of my imagination and stuffed it with visions of saints and of Jesus. Jesus was everywhere, no room was without his image, and the nuns had literally married him – they wore wedding rings and were the brides of Christ.

I quickly fell under the spell of this suffering, marrying Jesus, and I was entranced by the romance of the nuns in their graceful habits, their chanting voices drifting out from the chapel into the yard, their silences, their fingers working the rosary beads, their inalterable routines of teaching and prayer, and even their names, which were not their real names, but assigned names that connected them to dead women who had been brutally martyred in defence of their virtue or their faith. Though I was not raised a Roman Catholic, my mother had been, and most of my relatives were practicing Catholics. I found everything about the church, and particularly the nuns who were my teachers, fascinating. Obsessively, I read the lives of the saints, stories packed tight with pathology, visions, voices, fantastic acts of masochism, hysteria and, requisitely, miracles. What struck me was that many of the saints didn't get along well with their families until it was universally acknowledged that their bizarre, anti-social behaviour was 'saintly' at which point, as far as the families were concerned, the rebellious youth could do no wrong. I determined to become a saint.

I prayed a lot and paid attention to my teachers. I was a girl who wanted to please and the nuns were willing to be pleased, but they were also intelligent women, many with advanced degrees, and they were rigorous in both their thinking and their expectations. I learned to study. I wrote poems and stories and was encouraged by my teachers. I toyed with the idea of entering the convent, an option my father dismissed as 'throwing your life away'. In the end, I agreed with him and went to college.

It was the 1960s, about which it has been said that if you can remember them, you weren't there. Revolutionary ideas were afloat on the airwaves, but Louisiana State University in New Orleans, the students joked, was a 'hotbed of apathy'. I read a great many books and listened to some truly excellent lectures. My taste in literature was unformed, but my sensibility was that of a confirmed romantic. As I read the novels of Camus, Crane and Steinbeck another possibility presented itself, and unbeknownst to me a tiny fissure appeared deep down in the tectonic plate of my imagination, one that would widen, shifting soundlessly and relentlessly beneath the swamp of ordinary life for years to come. On one side was Romanticism, urging the superiority of passion over reason, the personification of nature, the taste for superstition, darkness, all things spooky and otherworldly. On the other side was Realism, with its 'scientific' method, interest in moral ambiguity, distrust of religion and emphasis on the meaninglessness of human endeavour. Both appealed, yet it seemed to me that one must triumph and rule out the other. The stories I was writing sometimes seemed to have come from two different heads. Then, in my third year at college, I read *Madame Bovary*, and a light bulb switched on in my brain. In the emotionally tumultuous opera scene, when Emma, a bourgeois wife whose romantic education (by nuns!) has ill fitted her for the world, looks upon the upstart Italian tenor pouring out his passion on the stage before her and finds in her heart nothing but scorn for him and everything he represents, scales, not tears, fell from my eyes. And when the narrator concludes (in the excellent Steegmuller translation), 'Now she well knew the true paltriness of the passions that art painted so large', I felt the stab of truth like a wound. I understood that Flaubert had closed the gap that so confounded me simply by choosing as his subject a woman despoiled by romanticism and following her with a clinician's eye to her inevitable ruin. Romanticism stalked and exposed as folly by Realism; no wonder the book was banned.

I resolved not to become Emma Bovary, and to worship forever at the altar of her creator, Gustave Flaubert. I still genuflect to his name.

In 1969, having graduated from college and equipped with a fresh and largely useless degree in English Literature, I began to look for work. After a brief stint as a temporary secretary (thanks to the pragmatism of the nuns at my Catholic high school, I was an excellent typist), I settled at the Louisiana Department of Public Welfare, Food Stamp Division. I had no particular calling for social work, but several friends from college were already there, the pay was barely adequate to support life, and the work was not difficult.

My job was simple: on Monday I received a stack of folders with the names and phone numbers of people who were applying for Food Stamps. I called each one and scheduled an interview during which I obtained the answers to a series of very specific questions provided on the 'intake' form. Following the equally specific guidelines about eligibility and allotment of food stamps, I made a recommendation and sent the record on to my supervisor. I neither liked nor disliked the work, nor was I particularly good or bad at it. I talked every day to people in varying degrees of degradation, and I had only a little power to make their lives much better or worse.

No knowledge of English Literature was required to do my job, but because so many of my fellow UNO graduates were now my fellow welfare workers, the conversations behind the scenes (the scenes took place in dreary particle board interview booths) were about literature. Many of us had ambitions to write, some were poets, a few worked on stories, one wrote plays. On weekends we gathered at one or another dingy apartment and read our work to each other. We drank a lot of very bad wine. My life divided neatly into daily conversations with two very different kinds of people – my clients, who were largely uneducated, desperate, and living on the sketchy margins of society, and my friends, who, though poor, could afford to buy novels, have ambitions, and care about art. Another disturbing divide.

I was to serve two two-year terms at the Department of Welfare, one just after college, and another on my return from Graduate School at the

University of Massachusetts, where I spent two years obtaining a slightly less useless MFA degree in Creative Writing. I was married between term one and two, and pregnant at the end of the second instalment – I left the job a month before my daughter was born. By that time I had begun my first novel.

This epic was entitled *Set in Motion* and, unsurprisingly, it is narrated by a young woman who is employed by the Louisiana Department of Public Welfare in New Orleans. I worked on the novel steadily for a year, often between interviews, and every page I wrote was an attempt to answer the serious literary question heretofore frequently and ponderously posed by me, but as yet unanswered: would I be able to finish a novel. I understood that an affirmative answer to this question was the equivalent of passing the bar exam for a lawyer. If the answer was no, the profession I longed to enter was closed to me. A phrase the nuns used to describe the religious vocation applied equally to my ambition to be a novelist – many are called, but few are chosen. I'd done the requisite story collection in graduate school, and it had been published by the requisite small press run by fellow students, so I was on the track, nosing around at the starting gate. Now the gate was open and I was off and running.

What did I think I was doing?

I was a neurotic, depressive young woman, eager to dramatize my artistic struggles, but I had a practical bent which has stood me well over the years, and it came to the fore when, after several stabs at an opening, I made up my mind to begin in earnest. I believed that the way to proceed was to simplify the objective. I was a great fan of Vladimir Nabokov, Henry James, Edith Wharton, Junichiro Tanizaki, and, above all, Gustave Flaubert, writers whose mastery of subtlety, indirection, and the compound–complex sentence made me shiver with delight, and of course I tried to imitate them in my limited way, but I instinctively knew that for my first novel I should choose as a model a writer whose chief virtue was the straightforwardness of his style. I was much too impatient to wait several days for the *mot juste* to present itself or to follow a Jamesian sentence into a thicket of permutations and innuendo.

The novelist I chose was Albert Camus, and the book was *The Stranger*. I'd read it twice in college, once in French, and then in the Stuart Gilbert English translation. Though it was clear to everyone, including me, that Meursault, the alienated murderer who narrates this tale of his own undoing, was not admirable, I adored him. I wanted to be like him. His inability to hold up his end of ordinary human discourse, to proffer the required responses to empty gestures of courtesy, to pretend to feelings he does not have, or to entertain ambition of any kind – all this struck me as a kind of nobility. This was doubtless because I always tried hard to please anyone with a modicum of authority over me, I was an apt practitioner of the empty gesture, and I was consumed with ambition. I believed myself to be an existentialist by temperament and conviction, walking that lonely road on which existence precedes essence and not the other way around. The notion that human life is essentially meaningless, and that we make ourselves up as we go along, had a strong appeal to me. Authenticity, whatever that was, was the goal, in life and in art.

It's difficult to re-enter the confused and unarticulated intentions of that young woman setting out on her first novel, but I do recall clearly that I didn't really have a plan. I had a narrator, a setting and a method. The narrator is Helene Thatcher (no reference to any Thatcher living or dead intended; it just struck me as a good name for a character who is trying to hold a fragmenting identity together), a disaffected young woman working in the office I worked in, single, without artistic pretensions, and perversely attracted to her girlfriends' boyfriends. The setting is New Orleans, humid, florid, torrid, and doomed, my beloved hometown. The method was Camus's, though, of course, not original to him; a first-person narrator who is always writing at least a day after the events he describes. The effect is like reading a diary; neither the narrator nor the reader can see what's coming, and, though the story moves continually forward in time, as readers we never experience the present. It is infinitely richer than the currently popular first-person present tense, which flattens time to a sequence of photographs and has no possibility of retrospect. One could say that this method is all retrospect; the narrator looks steadily backward as she is carried forward by forces beyond her control.

My choice of *The Stranger* as the inspirational text for *Set in Motion* was conscious, but I didn't then understand why I felt the need to have, as I worked, another novel in my head, a novel that was, in some way, ever before me. The books that followed were not always so deliberately attached to a model, but there is a sense in which every novel I write is a conversation I'm having with a novel I've read. *Mary Reilly* is the most overt example of this; the story takes place inside another novel – Robert Louis Stevenson's *The Strange Case of Dr. Jekyll and Mr. Hyde*. My novel *Trespass* is a response to E. M. Forster's *Howard's End*. *Property* certainly has some things to say about *Gone With the Wind*, but it was also provoked by my sense of having romanticized the institution of slavery in a few scenes of my novel *The Great Divorce* – so *Property* is actually me having a conversation with myself about another novel by me – which may be why it's so claustrophobic.

Set in Motion begins, as many stories do, with a strange encounter on a highway. This scene, which is my favourite in the novel, is more Bronte than Camus – windy, dark, damp, and menacing. Unconsciously, I committed myself to a trope that has charmed me all my writing life: the double. As Helene looks out across the spillway, a young black woman, who seems to come out of nowhere, approaches and asks her for a ride.

This mysterious young black woman does not, as future doubles in my novels would, constitute a foil or a complement to the protagonist; she disappears before the first scene is done and reappears late in the novel among the largely faceless clients whose applications for food stamps Helene processes. After the interview is concluded, Helene realizes that this client is indeed the woman she encountered that night on the elevated highway and she rushes out to the street to question her further. 'I wanted to know what happened to her that night', she admits. But once again the luckless double has disappeared. 'She had escaped me twice, I thought, we were strangers.'[1]

I probably should have stuck with that unknown woman, but I had other obsessions – sex, betrayal, insanity and drugs – and evidently a great need to air them in fictional guise. *Set in Motion* doesn't really have a plot, or if it does, it could be described simply as 'things get worse'. Helene, who has driven to Baton Rouge in search of her college mentor and friend Clarissa, winds up in bed with a stranger, who is later revealed to be Clarissa's fiancé, Michael. On her return to New Orleans, she visits her soul mate Reed, a drug addict who never fails to offer her moral support. She spends her days interviewing food stamp applicants, who remind her that violence and mayhem are, for some, a way of life. In one notable interview, a man produces his amputated toe as proof of his disability. In another an old woman who is trying to raise a difficult grandson, confounds Helene with her strength, faith, and goodness. A young man, wheel-chair bound, who speaks with difficulty and cannot control his compulsively twitching hands, insists on signing his own name to a form.

Maggie, Helene's closest friend at work, reveals that she fears her husband Richard is becoming increasingly irrational. Gradually Helene realizes that Richard is following her. Michael makes repeated appearances at her apartment to have sex, which Helene, in rapturous passages, describes as definitive. Helene reads an article about a man who is going about the city with a woman's head in a bag. He knocks on doors and when the unsuspecting resident answers, holds up the head and laughs hysterically. She becomes obsessed with the idea that this man will come to her door. Reed invites her to stay with him. Richard closes in on Helene, sending her strange messages and inviting her to meet him at midnight in the Cathedral, but after an uncomfortable interview in a confessional, Richard flees, leaving her confused.

Things get worse. Richard sets his apartment on fire and is committed to an asylum. Clarissa confronts Helene with the news that Michael has informed her of his affair with Helene. Reed nearly dies of an overdose and winds up in the hospital. Maggie insists that Helene read Richard's diary-of a-madman, which documents his obsession with her. After a visit to the asylum to see Richard, and a mini-breakdown on the street, Helene goes to Reed's apartment. He comforts her, and she asks him if he thinks he could stop trying to kill himself. He says, 'I guess I could try.'[2]

Some of the decisions I made in writing this novel embarrass me, others just make me sad; they seem so raw and clumsy. Helene narrates several sex scenes that I believe could well qualify for the infamous Bad Sex Award. Apart from the banality of the descriptions, there is the breathless summing up of the meaning of it all. Helene's devotion to passivity as a strategy, her occasional asides about the power of weakness, her wilful self-delusion – which, ultimately, may be what makes her interesting as a character – all seem pitiful to me now. I recall that when a former writing professor called me and offered to show the manuscript of the novel to his agent, he said, 'I think you've done an excellent job of creating a psychotic character.' Psychotic? I thought. She's just doing the best she can.

I assumed he meant Helene, but he may have been talking about the character of Richard, who is actually psychotic and winds up in the asylum, but not before Helene shows her empathy by trying to have standing up sex with him in front of his psychiatrist. She does this because she identifies strongly with his need to be crazy. Or that's what she tells herself.

The presence of Richard in this novel, and particularly the inclusion of the 20-page diary that his wife gives Helene to read, strikes the mature novelist as a big mistake. Twenty pages in a 200-page novel is a considerable chunk. I recall that some of it was culled directly from a notebook in which I jotted my most outré notions, for example: 'I can see my whole experience as a history of treachery, others against myself.' It was a black notebook for black thoughts, and I had a lot of those. For reasons I don't now understand, I imagined that I might become insane. I thought insanity was interesting, possibly even optional. I was prey to the romantic notion that madness is genius run amok, that there is something admirable about being so destructive that one has to be locked up. Helene views madness as a kind of courage, a willingness to give up the one thing she values, the freedom to leave. Richard's journal strikes me now as a histrionic young woman's fantasy about what it would be like to be insane. I don't think the novel is enhanced by the presence of this silly bit.

So, what's to like about this maiden voyage of the novelist who is now me?

I made one good and very conscious decision, inspired partly by Camus and partly by having sat through one too many graduate workshops in which my characters were berated for manifesting a level of alienation that was not explained by anything their parents had done to them. My decision was to have a narrator with no past. Helene appears, speaking, on page one, and is so preoccupied with her present struggles that she doesn't take the time to explain how she got where she is. I like that, and sometimes I still do that.

Also, to give the youthful me her due, I note a good eye for detail, and the agreeable echo here and there, providing a little tensile strength amid all the disruption. The dismemberment duo – the client who brings his severed toe to the interview and the news story of the man who knocks on doors and holds up a severed head – was entirely accidental, as only true things can be; that is, both these events actually occurred during the course of writing the novel, but I failed to see the obvious thematic connection between them. This kind of serendipity is the stock-in-trade of the novelist, and I've learned to recognize it over the years and to make use of it. As a psychiatrist in one of Luis Bunuel's films observes 'the unconscious never sleeps'.

The motif of flight, the egrets (stupidly called cranes by me) in the swamp, the pigeons in Helene's house, the constant motion of the narrator, driving, walking, moving through rooms, up and down stairs, encountering snakes, birds, roaches, lizards, all manner of restless nature which is also on the move; I think all these work well in the novel.

And finally, the thing I like best about my first novel is the sensuality and the vividness of the setting. New Orleans, with its cool patios and dark alleys, its murderous heat, its alarming variety of scents and colours, its lushness and cruelty, its bad politics and general air of decay, is very nearly a character in the novel. When I came to write this book, I'd spent two years away from the city, and on returning I looked upon my hometown with fresh eyes. I never mistook its oddity for ordinary

American life again. It is a singularly Un-American place, and I had come to both love and despise it for that.

Interestingly, when the novel was published, two years after it was completed, it went straight out and found a reader who understood this perhaps better than I did. At the time, the critic Anatole Broyard was very respected in New York circles and a frequent reviewer of new fiction, about which he always had insightful and trenchant things to say. My editor called me shortly after the publication date with the joyful news that Mr. Broyard had given *Set in Motion* a very favourable review in the *New York Times*.

Anatole Broyard. How my provincial heart leaped at the news. I pictured him in some Greenwich Village cafe, his balding pate protected from the cold by a jaunty beret, puffing at his Gauloise, sipping a good, dry claret, glowering over the pages of my first novel with all his refined critical senses on the alert. And he approved of what he read! Though I remember little else about it, I can still quote the last line of that review: 'She [Martin] writes as if she felt that, now that we know the worst about ourselves, we might as well sit back and enjoy it.'[3] I was, very briefly, in writer's heaven. Years later I learned that Anatole Broyard was a fellow New Orleanian who had escaped from our swampy backwater to the high ground of the New York literary scene.

What did I learn from the experience of writing and publishing a novel? First, that I could do it, no small lesson. I had passed the bar, though the paltry advance made it unlikely that I had entered a profession that would support my family. There wasn't really any sense of triumph or joy, confidence didn't surge in me, I didn't think being a writer made me different from others, or that my novel was worth a penny more than the advance. What I felt principally was relief.

I'm not proud of my first novel, but I see that it was the book I knew how to write at the time, and as such, is the warbling harbinger of the books that followed, so I feel kindly towards it. I began my second novel almost at once and with a sense of having the liberty to be, literally, crafty. I decided to write a reverse Gothic bodice ripper, in which a man is spirited away to a big house in the swamp where two women, one an Amazon, have their way with him. I wanted to have some fun.

Writing novels didn't get any easier after I finished the first one; in fact, because I have a much clearer idea of what I'm doing now than I did then, the process has become more complex and therefore more difficult. Every novel I write makes me ambitious to write a better one. The form is inexhaustible and endlessly challenging. In the midst of writing a novel, I am sometimes frustrated, but never bored. I am one of those fortunate beings who actually enjoy sitting at the desk with my pen and lined loose-leaf paper, working over a recalcitrant sentence one more time. The publishing part is my least favourite, especially the notion that I should personally persuade strangers to read my books. By the time a book is done, I'm ready to move on to the next one.

Set in Motion didn't sell many copies, but Broyard's review gave me an aura of respectability, and when I finished my second novel, *Alexandra*, my editor exercised his option to buy it.

It was only later that things got tough.

Notes

1. V. Martin (2005) *Set in Motion* (London: Pheonix), p. 130.
2. Ibid., 187.
3. A. Broyard (23 June 1978) A Review of *Set in Motion*, the *New York Times*, p. 23.

3
Illuminating the Shadows: The Space between Fact and Fiction

Johanna Skibsrud

I was 23 years old in the summer of 2003, and working as a canoe and backpacking instructor in Northern Maine, USA. Flagstaff Lake was one of many lakes that I paddled that summer; a man-made lake, it was created as a result of a hydroelectric dam that was introduced to the area in the mid-1950s. The houses of the small settlement had been – as with many other settlements in the region during that time – either destroyed or relocated to form a small community nearby. Traces of the original town, which now lie submerged below the lake, are still visible above the waterline. Long poles stick out of the water, marking the old foundations of the relocated homes; a road, beginning on one side of an island, disappears back into the water again on the other without apparently leading anywhere at all. Finally and most evocatively (though it had long since disappeared from view) an old church steeple was rumoured to have remained for many years partially visible above the waterline, as though floating on the waves. These traces caught and held my imagination that summer. I was fascinated by the way that the lake's *present* (that which was visible, and could be encountered, on the surface of the water) was literally marked by its *past* (that which lay beneath). As I dipped my paddle into the water, it seemed that I could actually *feel*, in the water's perfect combination of resistance and give, the history that the lake contained.

I think most of my writing – my best writing, certainly – begins from a single moment that, like a photograph, offers a sudden illumination and consequent shape to an experience that it otherwise may not have held. And just like a photograph that you know too well, it sometimes becomes difficult to tell what came first: the experience itself, or its figuration. Is there actually something essential within the moment

36

itself – something towards which, afterwards, you can't help wanting to return? Or do such moments of sudden illumination indicate that the figuration process has already begun? That, without realizing it, the image, idea, or experience has already become a story.

The following fall, recently enrolled in the MA programme in English and Creative Writing at Concordia University in Montreal, I began working on my debut novel, *The Sentimentalists*, in which my unnamed narrator experiences a very similar revelation to the one I had experienced the summer before. Floating one day over the remains of the imaginary submerged town of Casablanca – modelled, of course, after Flagstaff Lake – she contemplates the congruencies between water and time, both of which may manage to obscure, but never to completely absorb, obliterate or replace, the past:

> One afternoon, I took the boat out on my own, to the far end of the disappearing road, where Henry's old place would have been. I stopped there, letting the boat drift slightly. Then I lay back on a pile of life jackets so that my head rested on the deck of the bow. I imagined the house below me, still standing like the old dock of the film. And the dam, too, that the grandfather built: still holding some things in and some things out.

> It's funny to think about. The way the whole world is disappearing like that. That every moment we get closer, until – and inevitably – there comes that one instant, that impetus, whatever it will be, by which we are one day blown, finally, from our furthest extremity. Like leaves from a thin branch at the end of a tree. (. . .)

> So that, in coming to live as we do at such a far remove from ourselves, it becomes possible – no, unavoidable at times – to float over certain essential objects without noticing them at all. As just in that moment, for example, I in Henry's boat bobbed above Henry's old house – from which vantage point I might have seen, if unobstructed, all the way down to the ruins of the grandfather's dam below. Time, it seemed – at once material, at once not – existed there, in that in-between: in the way I might have, but could not, see down.[1]

The first character that I conceived was not my narrator, however, but Henry, an eccentric old man living in Casablanca, the new town built on the shores of the lake that now covers his original family home. What would it be like, I asked myself, to live alongside such a constant, physical reminder of what you had lost? I was in the very early stages of working out this idea when, in what seems to me now a poignant coincidence, my father began to tell me about his experiences as a US Marine in the Vietnam War. These were experiences he had not spoken of, to anyone, for over 30 years.

In the fall of 1967, my father had been involved in the still controversial 'incident at Quang Tri', where he had witnessed the murder of a civilian woman at the hands of his Commanding Officer. My father had been so unsettled by the experience that he later reported the murder to the company chaplain, his report sparking a criminal investigation at which he was asked to testify. He was separated from his unit during this time – due in part to threats that had been made on his life – and given the solitary job of sorting through the bags of those soldiers who had been killed in action, making sure that no unsavoury articles (drugs, pornography or military souvenirs) made their way back to the grieving families. At night, he slept with his gun.

He never spoke of this experience after the war, attempting to forget that he had ever been involved in the conflict at all. In the early 1970s he relocated to Canada with my mother, and when it was assumed – as it often was – that he was a draft dodger, he would let it go at that. Because of this, when my father first spoke to me of 'the incident at Quang Tri', he was able to remember very little. Most of the details – having been buried for so long and at such a remove – had long since disappeared. The emotional trauma of the experience and the guilt associated with it had, on the other hand, remained.

The intersection between my father's real-life stories and the themes already emerging in my novel – first inspired by Flagstaff Lake – were immediately apparent: buried history and memory, the always implicit presence of the past. But how was I to demonstrate this intersection? How was I to expose the differences, as well as the similarities, between Henry's fictional story and my father's true one? How was I – through that exposure – to express the inherent truth that I felt existed in between?

I began piecing together the answers to these questions from the perspective most familiar to me. For my main character I chose a young woman of roughly my own age who, at a turning point in her life, goes to live at the lake house I had already constructed in the imaginary town of Casablanca with Henry and her father, Napoleon. Henry became the father of Owen, a friend of Napoleon's, who had been killed in the Vietnam War. After the war, Napoleon finally succeeds in tracking Henry down, and he becomes an integral part of the family. Every summer of the narrator's childhood is subsequently spent at the lake house in Casablanca, a place which becomes, as the narrator recounts, what 'all of us, including my father, secretly thought of as home'.[2]

Though the first half of *The Sentimentalists* is told solely from her perspective, the narrator remains unnamed. We are introduced to the lake and the narrator's early memories of it, to her family and its dissolution. Napoleon is a restless, damaged character, who 'disappears' from his daughter's life during her adolescence, only to 'resurface' again, years later. The question of Napoleon's connection with Henry, and the details of his life over the course of his 'disappearance' have remained a mystery to the narrator, but the connection that she has with her father – as well as to the lake, and her nostalgic memories of it – have continued to sustain her. When she is forced to re-evaluate her own life after a traumatic break-up, she flees to Casablanca, hoping to regain something there that she feels has been lost.

Over the course of the summer that the narrator spends with Henry and Napoleon at the lake house, both men's stories emerge. The narrative switches from first-person to third-person and we are taken back in time to 1959 – the year that the introduction of a hydroelectric dam forced Henry to relocate from his original home – and to 1967, the year of 'the incident at Quang Tri'. In each successive draft of the novel, emphasis on the details of the narrator's personal life decreased significantly. Eventually, and due to the sudden and extreme dislocation from her ordinary life that the break-up and subsequent retreat to Casablanca allowed, she is stripped almost entirely of her private concerns, and becomes, instead, the conduit for her father's and Henry's stories – as well as the source of illumination for the intersections between them. Increasingly as I revised, the unreliability of both experience and memory – and, by implication, the constructed nature of history – emerged as the novel's dominant theme.

A crucial addition to the final draft of the novel was the introduction of an excerpt from my father's real-life testimony at the military investigation into the 'incident at Quang Tri', which I have included in the epilogue of the novel. The transcript was given to me by my father – who had himself received it from an historian investigating the affair – but in the novel, the transcript is only discovered by the narrator *after* her father's death. The introduction of the testimony at the end of the novel serves to disrupt any notion of having established the 'truth' about her father's – or Henry's, or by extension even her own – experiences, opening up a space that I like to think of as existing *between* fact and fiction; the space in which we actually live. The (real-life) document fails, of course, to account for the (fictional) elements of the story with which the narrator and the reader have become acquainted; most conspicuously omitted is any mention of Owen, the absent connective thread between Napoleon and Henry. Both narrator and reader are therefore left with many more questions than answers, but also, I hope, a sense of the power that stories have to shape, and continuously reshape, our lives. The power, that is, not only of those stories that are suddenly illuminated and take shape either in our lives or on the page, but also, conversely, of those that never will; that have been left in shadow, forgotten, or concealed.

In all, seven years passed between the first moment of inspiration and the fall of 2009 when *The Sentimentalists* was first published by a small press in Kentville, Nova Scotia. Each time I returned to the manuscript I had to re-ask myself the question of what the novel was *really* about, and each time I realized more surely that it was about that space *between* fact and fiction, as well as the simple revelation of the palimpsest of history I felt as I canoed over Flagstaff Lake. The task, of course, was to be able to *express* this in a story that could exist *outside* of that instant and the personal context from which it arose – something that, in being brought to the surface, would not actually be *reduced* to that surface.

Towards the end of my novel, the narrator is confronted by her own high-school era poem, which her father, Napoleon, stumbles across in a drawer. When Napoleon reads it out to her she is embarrassed by what she sees as its simplicity and superficiality – in other words, its 'surface' quality. When her father praises it, calling it a 'nice little poem', she bitingly replies, 'I don't want ... to have written a nice little poem.' Her father is untroubled by the bitterness of her tone. 'So', he says, 'write another. But don't be too sad. Be like Whitman. I like it when you're like Whitman. He always made the most of everything.'[3] This advice to focus on the *process* of writing, rather than the product, points, I hope, both to the perpetual inadequacy of language (how is it possible to truly communicate any experience?) as well as to its saving power. There is, perhaps, no more worthwhile endeavour than to try: to 'make the most' of the potential that we have to shape, communicate, and therefore learn from, our personal as well as our collective experience.

Similarly, the novel as a whole – with its layered stories and multiple perspectives and narrative styles (the shift from first-person to third-person in the sections that relate the experiences of Henry and Napoleon, for example) – points to the idea that no one 'truth' about an experience may ever be established or expressed, while at the same time refusing to undermine the attempt. 'And so', the narrator concludes in the novel's epilogue, acknowledging the limitations of both language and expression,

> in these pages, I have also tried to record what I know to be true; the truth, anyway, as it exists at this, my own personal intersection of it; at this singular and otherwise obscure point along its complicated and transitional course. As it pauses here, I mean, almost imperceptibly and for only so long, before continuing on, in its uncountable directions.'[4]

In many ways I see this exposition by the narrator as a comment on my own process of creating the novel itself. From a complicated network of stories that evolved from a single moment, the process very quickly became one of locating the 'pauses': the characters, scenes and conversations that were essential to conveying the story and the impulse at its root.

There is, perhaps, a perpetual imbalance between the 'inspiration' behind a work and what is eventually produced. Even the material that seems to arrive in a single instant – as though already written, almost whole – must often be disassembled before it can be pieced back together on the page in a way that might actually *convey* that initial sense of completeness. During the process of writing, when the work-in-progress often fails to convey *any* of its original intentions, the writer must sometimes be sustained by simple faith. A faith that, in the end, the *process* of writing will result in a natural balance between inspiration and finished form.

Part of the reason 'faith' is such a necessary part of the process is that writing, like time, is bound to the limitations of its own measure. Just as the present – limited always by the very point at which it is drawn – opens onto that further, far less substantial element, the future, so language opens at every moment onto the possibility of renewed interpretation, even as it remains bound to the limitations of its form. The challenge and the joy of writing, as I see it, is the same as the challenge and the joy of living consciously at any time in history: the simultaneous sense of being tied to an inevitable past and the impulsive longing to be free of it. Literary writing grapples with – indeed embodies – our double investment in history and innovation, resignation and challenge, situated as we always are at a cross-roads – a waterline – between the past and the future.

If writing is understood in this way, however – as an indefinite, ongoing process – it follows that the inspiration behind a particular work (the initial moment that made you, as it were, 'catch your breath') is never completely expelled. Perhaps, indeed, the real task of the writer is not to fully express herself, but rather to formalize a space within the completed text for that original inspiration, a sort of conceptual 'holding in of breath'.

My own process in the first months after conceiving the idea for *The Sentimentalists*, was, in contrast, a steady, uninterrupted exhale. I did not look back over what I had written, but day after day – picking up whatever thread I had left hanging the day before – I proceeded towards what seemed (at that stage) a happily realizable end. It was with surprise (as well as a fair bit of dismay) that, after six months of steady writing, I assessed the amount of work still left to do in order to shape the material I had produced into something that even resembled a novel – let alone one that matched my original vision.

Much to his credit, when I submitted the manuscript to my thesis supervisor, he was far less alarmed by its size and state of confusion than I was. A writer of sharp, sparse prose, with many more years of experience behind him, he was accustomed to the necessary rigours of editing. Though at times the process could feel violent or even cruel, as though I were in fact working *against* the inspiration and the time invested in the work-in-progress, I came very quickly to learn that the editing stage was in fact the most essential to realizing my novel's initial intent.

With guidance, I whittled my manuscript down to roughly half of its original size, and a few years later I reduced it to roughly half again. Only then did I prepare myself to answer the tougher questions about detail and structure, or to consider – finally – how to construct within the work a space that might retain my original motivation to write it at all. At the end of this process, when I asked myself the question of what my novel was really about, I felt I could say with some confidence that it was, indeed, about the shudder of realization I'd had during the summer of 2003 as I floated over Flagstaff Lake: a realization not only of the constitutive nature of the past in the present, but also – and consequently – of the tremendous depth and infinite richness of the world.

When, last summer, I began my second novel, I remember thinking that I would go about it very differently. This time, I thought, it would be less a process of trial and error and more of a concentrated, considered effort from beginning to end. Instead, I have found the experience so far to be remarkably similar, and at this stage in the writing process I need (once again) to sustain myself on simple faith. It may be that, like history itself, the history of a particular work of literature is governed by the twin impulses of an endless forward momentum and a retrograde revisionist desire. For me, the real challenge and opportunity that writing presents is that of moving between these two impulses, in search of that delicate balance between the exuberant momentum of the present, as it moves ever-hopefully towards the future, and the dedicated focus, hard work, and resignation with which we both submit to, and endlessly revise, the past.

Notes

1. J. Skibsrud (2011) *The Sentimentalists* (London: William Heinemann), pp. 101–3.
2. Ibid., 13.
3. Ibid., 161.
4. Ibid., 176.

4
Genesis

David Vann

Two years ago, in late January 2009, I was walking on Skilak Lake, from the shore towards Caribou Island. It was early afternoon but looked like evening, the sun low. I didn't know how thick the ice was, or how safe to walk upon. The snow in drifts, like dunes of sand. No other human, and no bird or other animal or even wind. Just silence. The air so clear it seemed I should be able to touch things that were far away, the mountains above the lake.

I kept walking, but I was very afraid of falling through. I had no experience here. I'd visited this lake only in summer, when it was windy and blue-green from glacial silt, sometimes almost milky. I knew that if I fell through, there'd be no one to help and I'd simply freeze. But I wanted to walk out to Caribou Island. It had held a fascination for me for years. I'd begun writing a novel 12 years earlier. It was set here, but I'd never been able to write past the first 50 pages. I couldn't see the longer arc. I didn't know whose story it was or where to focus. And I felt that walking out to the island I might find how to tell the story.

I saw a long crack in the ice, indicated by the snow that had fallen on it differently. I knelt and swept away the snow with my glove and saw black. I'd wanted to see how deep the ice was, how thick, but the lake beneath was so dark the clear ice became essentially opaque. I was peering into nothing. The ice could have been two inches thick or ten feet thick. And something about gazing at the lake up close and not being able to see it or know it suggested something. I could imagine Irene walking out on this lake and trying to find her marriage and peering down and seeing nothing. I understood that it was her story, that I had to focus on her in this landscape, and that the rest of the novel would come from there.

And so this walk on the frozen lake became Irene's winter vision late in my new novel, *Caribou Island*, and I wonder whether other books are like that, with one scene or moment which was the genesis. The most important quality about this moment is its certainty, a certainty that it will not mislead. As I wrote *Caribou Island*, working on it every morning, I kept returning to describing the place, and the characters and story came from the landscape and the transformations of the landscape. At one point, Irene is running in the forest on Caribou Island and feels the earth tilting beneath her and knows the entire island is rolling over, top-heavy, and this is Irene being written in place, this is discovery of Irene in the landscape, and this is why I write.

Originally published on Powells.com.

Part II
Research and the Novel

5

Treasure, Trash and Planned Obsolescence

Maile Chapman

As a fiction writer, I'm spoiled in the kind of research I undertake. While it is important work, it feels luxuriously aimless and self-indulgent, in part because I usually don't know what I'm looking for unless I find it. This *I'll-know-it-when-I-see-it* method allows for a lot of poking into random dark corners and rooting around in second-hand bookstores. Ideas for my debut novel, *Your Presence Is Requested at Suvanto*, first came from the stacks of old architecture books on my desk, picked up idly because I like black-and-white photos. Through them Finland began to appeal to me because, as I was discovering, Finnish architecture was so forward-thinking and so influential, especially during the first half of the twentieth century, the era I had in mind. Finnish design elements were linked to the landscape through natural materials and curving shapes that mimicked the coastline. This made me wonder how such buildings might affect the people living in them, which strikes me now as a novelist's preoccupation.

I began as many first-time novelists probably do, with a set of ideas that felt compelling to me, and a vague sense of how to string them together. I knew I wanted to write about Scandinavia, functional building design, women working in architecture, surgery and medicine: mostly because I was curious about all of these topics and wanted to justify spending a substantial amount of time reading about them. Ultimately, my novel is set in a women's surgical hospital in southwestern Finland and includes all of the above. I called my fictional institution Suvanto, and I set my story there in the first half of the twentieth century, at a time when innovations in surgery were changing the way medicine could be practiced even in rural areas. I included elements of superstition and mythology, as well as direct and obvious references to medicine and architecture, because I wanted to pit scientific reason against passion by tapping into the strong emotions of patients who wish to remain just as they are, without medical intervention. At a deep level, the plot is based on that of the Greek drama *The Bacchae* by Euripedes, in which women retreat into the forest to practice an ecstatic mystery religion that celebrates divine madness. In my novel, American women come to Suvanto seeking privacy, solitude and indulgence, with equally uncontrolled results.

The novel is solidly fixed in the landscape of the coastal pine forest that surrounds the claustrophobic hospital complex, and Finnish culture plays a large role in how the story unfolds as well as in the whole atmosphere of quiet isolation:

> In summer, Finnish families arrive and reopen summer cottages everywhere in the shifting green trees, on the rocky shores of the clear cold water, but the cottages are so discreetly situated on the islands, on the coast, on the shores of the lakes that even from a boat you might not see them, might miss them except for the docks and the small moored boats. And there are the meadows for picnics and for picking berries and mushrooms, the forests for walking, the inlets and the lakes for swimming, provided one can withstand the mosquitoes, of course. The lakes are lovely for strolling around and then for taking naps beside on wool summer blankets under the deep, sunny sky. The locals quietly appreciate a good hard winter – of course! – but they don't fully understand why others might come only for the winter, when the summer is as it is.[1]

While reading about landscapes, I realized that the Finnish forests have similarities to the area where I grew up, in the heavily timbered Pacific Northwest. I knew we had a strong streak of Scandinavian influence, but I hadn't considered that many Finns, in particular, had settled in Washington State because of the landscape of evergreen trees, a rocky coastline and not too much daylight. This coincidence got me thinking about possible professional and social exchanges between Finland and the United States. Finnish women, I discovered, had the right to vote before female suffrage was granted anywhere else in Europe, and American suffragettes travelled to Finland in the early twentieth century, so I knew that women could and did go back and forth between the two countries. Reading about Finnish experiments in industrial and residential planning prompted me to speculate that big companies might have employed architects and planners. I began considering all the potential jobs that my characters could have, and this led to the creation of one of my first characters, an American woman married to a timber executive who relocates to Finland for work.

Writing a novel is a bit like standing back in a laboratory and waiting to see which of many billions of genes will switch on to create your unique story. There is both randomness and order in those selections, and each necessarily closes off other options. When I consider all the ways my book could have evolved, but didn't, I see all of those 'unrealized possibilities' as inactive genes, dormant but filled with potential for what might have been – and providing mysterious support for what actually is. Whatever isn't explicit still contributes.

At one time or another I had considered setting the novel, or parts of it, in Sweden, Russia and/or Estonia. That research (not only from books but also trips that I made to Stockholm, St. Petersburg and Tallinn) was eventually rendered down in the novel to pretty much the following: a glass of Estonian stout; a longing to visit St. Petersburg; and a mention that an archipelago of rocky islands leads out and away, eventually, to Sweden. Yet everything I learned about those places contributed to the atmosphere, as well as to the development of my characters – much like that massive but unseen amount of DNA that you and I share with frogs and mice that presumably adds to our existence in discreet ways. Thanks to the material I didn't use, I felt confident about the material that I drew upon because I had done my homework, and this holds true for every aspect of the book.

This was the big lesson for me in writing a first novel: I needed to work from a vast hoard of much more information and imagery than I could possibly reference explicitly in my story. If I tried to be more organized and more targeted in my research, say by only looking at sources I believed would serve me, I would have missed the kinds of stray facts that make a fictional world feel real to me. One example was a day-long excursion through the snow to an old fire station in the city of Tampere, designed by a female architect in the 1940s; on the surface it was not similar to the setting I was creating, but elements of the staff stairwell and the dormitory-style quarters eventually went into my fictional hospital, and, though I hadn't planned to write about Tampere, it became the homebase for my timber executive and his wife. I frequently found that tangentially related findings became useful, and that information I expected to be helpful often pushed me away in some other direction. I could only know this, however, after I'd taken the time to find it.

At first I believed the book would be about an innovative Finnish woman architect. It began as a hunch, based on the idea that Finland was socially progressive, combined with their amazing architectural history, and I hoped it was true that some Finnish women would have had the opportunity to train as architects earlier than their counterparts in other countries. When I got to Finland I discovered that a whole cohort of women had been working in the field in the early twentieth century: women who had been trained at polytechnic schools, who had studied in Russia, or Sweden, who came from families in which their fathers, brothers, or husbands had been architects or master builders or masons. But because those women typically worked on purpose-built, practical buildings – schools and military buildings, for example, as opposed to showpieces like opera houses or embassies – their work wasn't really showing up in the kinds of books I had been reading. I was delirious with delight and the feeling of triumph that comes with having a hunch confirmed. There was a lot more fact to support my fiction than I had known. Perversely, maybe, this meant that my main Finnish female character didn't have to be an architect, because even though there were lots of them, there were also women working as draftsmen and designers and in other roles of which I gradually became aware. I made my Finnish character a draftsman (or draftswoman), because it seemed better for the novel for reasons I will explain in a moment.

I was figuring out how to write about women working in architecture, and also weighing up how to write about women working in medicine. Originally I considered writing about a female doctor, and when I looked into the historical feasibility of this I was drawn into old medical, surgical and nursing handbooks. To my surprise, it was the nursing material that really held my interest. Those books were written in a more immediate style, directed at female readers. I decided that my female medical professional would be a nurse rather than a doctor, and here's why.

In both cases what interested me most was that women doing certain kinds of highly skilled work (like post-surgical nursing or architectural drawing) would have been the norm, rather than the exception. A woman architect or surgeon could well have been historically accurate, but giving my characters those professions would have made it seem in my narrative that History Was Being Made, and I didn't want anything that momentous. I realized that what I wanted was the banality of routine, as a counterpoint to the submerged violence of the plot, and this was how I conceived of the American nurse who became my main character, and her friend, the Finnish draftswoman. Making these women into what might seem like pioneers in their careers would have distracted from that goal of quotidian normalcy that I felt the story called for. This was a decision made by the dictates of craft rather than of what my research may have borne out as historically possible, and this is an important point to keep in mind, if an obvious one: things have to fit together in the way that feels right for the novel at hand.

The logical way to bring together characters working in medicine and architecture was to create an interesting hospital complex, which eventually became Suvanto in my novel. Very early in the project I had come across a photo of the Finnish tuberculosis hospital in Paimio, designed by Alvar Aalto and completed in 1933. The moment I saw those images I knew that I was going to write a novel that would take place in a hospital like it. It was only later, through those two characters – the nurse and the draftswoman – that I could write about such a building in a way that wouldn't feel too forced, since, after all, the building was central to the work of both. The first flush of ideas may have been a lot more grandiose – an architect, a surgeon, and a paragon of modern medical architecture! – but I'm much happier with the more understated final incarnations of each that grew together organically.

Regarding plot: I had done a year of classics as an undergraduate and was familiar with the principles of Greek drama through studying playwriting, and I knew I wanted to borrow from that traditional structure. Through this, the violence I intended could take place 'offstage' and be reported later by a plural narrator, my version of a Greek chorus. That plural choral voice went naturally with the idea of patients stuck in a convalescent hospital, observing and remarking on events as they unfold in a closed setting. From a craft perspective, adopting that dramatic structure gave me a blueprint to defer to while I worked (even if it may be invisible to anyone who reads my novel).

The Bacchae of Euripides had been lingering in the back of my mind for many years – I'd never forgotten the image of women in violent religious ecstasy, worshipping the god Dionysus in rites that men were expressly forbidden to witness, and this too seemed to fit well with the communal life of the patients at my fictional hospital. Deferring to *The Bacchae* also convinced me to make the hospital a women's facility, whereas in earlier drafts, it had been co-ed. This made so much more sense, thematically, yet somehow I didn't admit that until I brought *The Bacchae* more explicitly on board. In the play, the rites of the Bacchantes are kept secret (and my characters became correspondingly secretive and insular), until the stepson of one of the women decides to find out whether the grotesque stories of intoxication, delirious violence, killing animals by hand, bloodlust and nudity are true. But anyone who violates the privacy of the women gets a swift and serious punishment. Nobody is safe when the women are in a state of religious transport, and thanks to this I knew from the first that at least one character in my novel would be doomed to run afoul of a group of deranged patients. To fit that role I needed a character who would be too deeply interested in the lives of those patients: an interloper whose authority would be a catalyst for violence, even if the intentions were good. Reflecting the events in *The Bacchae*, it had to be a male relative of one of the women, and because of the hospital setting, it had to be a doctor. With that, I created another central character, in the form of a visiting American surgeon related by marriage to one of the patients, caught in a slow but steady plot leading to his destruction:

> Now he is walking in the hall quite naturally, as if he will never leave it. He turns his head so solidly attached to his shoulders, and there is a nagging in Sunny's brain – perhaps a premonition of things to come – an observation of the contour where Dr. Peter's head would be most efficiently separated from his body. There is an invisible red line sketched below his chin, curving where his head would be most easily scooped away from his neck.[2]

Research had helped me establish my setting, my characters and my plot, but I knew I needed more details. I was able to go to Finland to collect them through the good fortune of a Fulbright Grant exchange year. I wanted to be near Paimio, and by coincidence I had already studied Swedish – an activity that had seemed monstrously impractical at the time, years earlier, when I quit my job to take an intensive summer course. That pursuit served me well in the long run, because Paimio just happened to be in the bilingual part of Finland. The hospital wasn't far from the only Swedish-speaking university in the country, and the grant allowed me to use the university facilities, including the library.

I arrived in Finland with the outlines of the novel in mind, and, as I had hoped, details kept falling into place. I had known intellectually that Paimio had been built before the use of antibiotics, and that patients could expect to remain there for long periods, and I had read that Aalto, along with his wife, Aino Marsio-Aalto, a designer, had planned the rooms around the comfort of the patient. Practical details like heating, lighting, plumbing and ventilation were all oriented around an occupant spending a lot of time horizontally, in bed. Windows were designed to avoid drafts and the sinks were meant to be silent and unobtrusive. The descriptions in the books had prompted me to consider that old question of how living in such a building would affect the inhabitants, but it was hard to visualize such things until I found myself standing in the actual place, in a room that had been preserved in its original state. At Paimio, I could see the view from the window, the colour scheme of the room, the way the light fell, the way the trees looked, and no book could have given me this.

When you put yourself in a position to do your work and prepare the way through research, the world will provide you with endless material and encouragement, offering moments that are sometimes akin to the feeling of déjà vu. These moments arrive most obviously when invented or speculated details are confirmed in the outside world, reassuring you that your intuitions are on the right track. As an example, I searched without success for descriptions of what a nurse at Paimio or a similar hospital might have worn in the time of my novel. I'm sure it exists somewhere, but I couldn't find that information in any book. I checked museums and libraries in Turku and Helsinki, and had seen examples of other nursing uniforms as well as the metal emblems that indicated areas of special training, but nothing specifically about Paimio. I was comfortable making an informed guess, but still I was curious. Years later, when I went back to Finland to finish the book, it was to reconsider this kind of small detail. On my last visit to Paimio, this and other small final pieces clicked into place.

I went to see the local historian, as I had before, and she took me to meet the Head Nurse, who very kindly let me see a photo album that had belonged to Paimio's first Head Nurse. Her photo collection began even before the landscaping of the hospital grounds had grown out of the bare dirt of the construction site. I had known nothing personal about the staff before this, apart from seeing the formal portraits of the former administrators and matrons on display in the main corridor. I couldn't have known that the first Head Nurse's nickname was Tyyni, which means 'Peaceful' in Finnish, when I gave the name Sunny to my fictional Head Nurse: a name that is sort of orthographically similar and that also implies, like Tyyni, that the bearer has a pleasant personality. I had already named my fictional hospital Suvanto, which means 'a place of slow-moving or still water'. Later, when I looked up online the name Tyyni in baby name databases, I found that it meant 'calm, in reference to water'. And so I felt good about those names.

In that photo album I also finally got to see that nurses at Paimio wore dark cotton dresses, white aprons and a white cap that was tied on with ribbons, low and to one side at the back of the head. I hadn't seen exactly that cap before, and I later adjusted the caps in my novel to match. Tyyni's photos were in black and white, but the Head Nurse and the local historian both thought the uniform dresses had been blue, which was pleasing because in my book the nurses already wore blue dresses. I had also invented a character called Sister Tutor, after reading that in England nurses were addressed as 'Sister'. This name seemed to me both benevolent and stern, and I liked it a lot, but I was troubled that it might mislead American readers into thinking that Sister Tutor was a nun. It would be a natural assumption, but not quite correct to encourage, because Finland was a very Protestant country, especially then. Still, I was very attached to that name and I asked the historian whether there would have been any nuns around the hospital in the 1930s. She confirmed that it wasn't likely. We kept looking at the photos, paging through the years, sitting there on the sofa in the Head Nurse's office, and I was thinking about how quickly the years pass, watching those first nurses growing older. Suddenly in one of the passing photos I saw a diminutive nun, dressed from head to foot in a black habit. 'Wait', I said, 'go back: who is that?' The historian and the nurse conferred, and decided the nun was probably a visitor to Paimio, and that perhaps she was Eastern Orthodox – Finland being so close to Russia. Again I had that feeling of triumph. I could leave Sister Tutor alone, and whether she was a teaching nurse, or a nun, or a combination of both, it wouldn't matter all that much.

After that meeting I went back into town and passed a junk shop I had frequented when I lived in Turku during my Fulbright year. The place was packed to the rafters with shelves and tables full of all kinds of objects, from treasure to trash, but in the midst of the chaos something propped against the back wall leapt out at me: I could only see part of it, but enough to know I was looking at a portrait of a woman wearing one of the nursing caps I had just seen for the first time in Tyyni's album. The shop owner helped dig it out for me, and I saw that the woman was also wearing a white apron over a blue uniform dress. The signature in the corner said 'Vaino' or maybe 'Laino' or, more likely, a stylized signature of 'Aino', followed by the year, '33. At this, I felt yet another surge of triumph: here was a portrait of a local nurse, painted in the time period of Tyyni's photo album, the same time frame as my novel, which I might not have recognized if I hadn't just seen that very type of cap in the photos that afternoon. I could comfortably assume that the local nurses had worn blue dresses. And furthermore, the name of the painter, Aino, was a coincidence that made me happy, because Aino Marsio-Aalto had worked on many details inside the building, from furniture to glassware.

Those incidents feel like part of the writing process. They are part of the secret content of the narrative that exists outside the purview of the actual novel, along with so many other images I couldn't incorporate into the final version for one reason or another. There were scores of unusable but evocative details – I can't help but mention a few: an important nursing handbook of the time was called The Red Book (how wonderfully creepy; I could even have used that as my own title); a metal hospital bed frame could be sanitized by dousing it with flammable liquid and lighting it on fire (how elegant and how primitive, to start a sterilizing fire in the heart of the forest); poultices or enemas of common food items (bread, oatmeal, mustard) could be used in the wards to treat ailments between meals (routine and repetition doubling back on itself).

It was hard to let go of these details, but I find an apt metaphor in the old nursing handbooks, in the illustrated instructions for techniques and treatments that were once ultra-modern. The handbooks describe, with necessarily minute attention and accuracy, scores of procedures that have long since been abandoned due to improvements in medicine. Many seem almost frighteningly crude now, but each of those antiquated manoeuvres was vitally important in its time, in the very particular circumstance for which it was needed. Each did the important work of the moment. I see something very moving in this, and I think it also describes the process of turning research into a novel – all that work of collecting information, of refining and perfecting drafts, is vitally important, but only until some new and better development or discovery renders all of that critical work obsolete. For that reason it is important to make peace with the probability that only a small percentage of the material uncovered in your research will make it into the final form. Let it be the best percentage.

Notes

1. Chapman, M. (2010) *Your Presence Is Requested at Suvanto* (London: Jonathan Cape), p. 67.
2. Ibid., 153.

6
Writing Home

Edward Hogan

One afternoon, I took a call from my hometown newspaper back in Derby. I was feeling pretty excited. My first novel, *Blackmoor*, had been shortlisted for the Desmond Elliott Prize, the winner of which was due to be announced later that week. I'd had a few nice little reviews in the national papers, but I was hungry for recognition in the mother-land. My family would be proud, and it would be one in the eye for the doubters. I was the local boy done good, right? This interview was going to be a pleasure.

I live in Brighton now, and it's always good to hear a Derbyshire accent on the phone. The journalist briefly congratulated me on making the shortlist.

'I've just finished reading your book,' she said.

'Oh great!' I said. 'What did you think?'

There was a pause. 'I thought there were some good *descriptions*.'

'Thank you. That's great to hear!' I said, already sensing disaster.

'So what made you write about a mining town in Derbyshire?'

Good, I thought. I've got my sound-bite ready for this question. I started with my pretentious and well-rehearsed answer: 'Derbyshire will always be home for me. The landscape is spooky and beautiful. I love the collision of the prehistoric outcrop and the McDonald's drive-thru. I mean, Derbyshire is just so central to my imagination, and –'

'So why did you move away, then?'

Wallop. I knew how it was going to go from then on. The spiky questions came quickly: how come I wrote about a mining village when I had never lived in one? Didn't I go to quite a decent state school? Why did the favourable reviews in 'London newspapers' compare me to 'North-ern' writers? Don't they know Derby is in the Midlands? Why am I so down on Derbyshire?

I stammered my way through the interview, and later that week, on the evening before the awards ceremony, the article ran with a headline that didn't quite match up to the one I had dreamed of: *Author Paints Bleak Picture of County*.[1]

After grudgingly mentioning the good reviews, the journalist opened a paragraph with 'Praise indeed – but is it deserved?' thus teeing herself up for an account of my treacherous ways. There was talk of an 'unrelenting passion for Northern stereotypes', and after quoting a passage describing a night out in Derby, the journalist commented that it was 'not a picture which will get the county's tourism bosses clapping their hands with glee'.

I was a bit wounded at the time. The one paper I wanted a good review from! The one place I expected support! But reviewers aren't cheerleaders, and they don't owe you anything, regardless of your nativity. They have a job to do, and they must do it with absolute freedom, for all our sakes. That's why I'm now quite embarrassed about the snooty letter I wrote afterwards.

Looking back, the article was quite even-handed, but it brought attention to a few issues that had been central to my writing the novel in the first place. Issues that come from the anxiety and sense of responsibility borne by a first novelist writing about his home county. Issues that very much relate to research. All the way through that interview, and all the way through the review, I could feel the journalist silently asking the question that I had so often asked myself, even though I was writing a novel about a place I'd lived in for 20 years. *What gives you the right?*

I was 21 when I started writing *Blackmoor*. Write about what you know? I didn't know anything. I'd spent a lot of time in former mining villages, mainly through sport. In my late teens I was raking in sometimes as much as £40 per match at the base of the football pyramid, and I'd played for and against Miners Welfare teams. I wasn't much liked in these places. I was a slight boy, and not particularly committed to physical confrontation. I was seen as effeminate and – by their logic – gay. I didn't mind, and I restrained myself from pointing out that the cover-boys on the front of *Attitude* magazine usually had bulky, muscular torsos.

One rainy afternoon shortly before I quit, I gave some verbal to an old-timer I was playing against. 'You poof', he responded. 'Look at you, you spotty fuggin skellington. What's up with you? Have you got the AIDS?'

It was the aggression, rather than the content of the taunt, that did for me. I was wearing huge red shorts and a top with the shirt sponsor

MORCON. On my jersey, the 'C' had rubbed off. I was dejected; I'd had enough.

What's wrong with this place? What's wrong with these people? Why are they being like this? I thought to myself, as I dumped my boots in the garage. I kept thinking it, until the questions stopped being rhetorical and became a point of genuine interest. In the former mining villages I could see antagonism towards outsiders and a close and often wonderful community spirit. I witnessed – in some individuals, not all – a bit of racism and a lot of resentment, along with a certain attitude towards women.

I wanted to understand the atmosphere, and it didn't take long to see sources of potential bitterness. The industry which had nourished those communities had been brutally wrecked in the 1980s and 1990s by a government that failed to supply any provision for what came next. It was no real wonder that notions of gender identity had become contentious in a place where – for many generations – families had been set-up purely to fuel male labour, and it was no wonder that such notions of masculinity took another odd turn when, all of a sudden, the wives were bringing in the only income. I wasn't about to excuse or ignore misogyny or prejudice (hence my occasionally 'bleak picture'), but I also wanted to write about how this swathe of towns and villages had had their hearts ripped out, and then been left to bleed to death. I wanted to write about the political injustice and private ambiguity of these situations, without generalizing.

Close communities can be so supportive, but they can be oppressive, too, if you don't happen to fit the mould. I suddenly became aware of how close I was to these issues. I was four years old during the Miners' Strike. The village we lived in for the first three years of my life was, in fact, a former pit village. There were coalminers in my family only a few generations back. The violent history of the demise of mining wasn't so long ago, and it wasn't so far away. This was the history of my birthplace and it was massively important, but really, I didn't know enough about it.

I began my research hesitantly. I found an old story about a village called Arkwright that had been evacuated in the early 1990s due to noxious and flammable gases rising from the defunct pit works. The image was impressive. The past literally wafting up through the floorboards! Even as the metaphor gripped me, I felt my unworthiness. *Coming up here, with your metaphors.* What right did I have?

A few things happened, and quite slowly. Firstly, the idea took hold of me with such force that I couldn't let it go. Secondly, a group of characters arrived, a family called the Cartwrights. There was Beth, the pale mother, distinctive and terribly misunderstood by the other villagers. There was George, a cocky father who spouts about his desire to leave the village for the greatness he believes his talents will secure. And there was Vincent, their boy. Once I had these characters, along with the story of the smouldering village, I knew I would spend as long as it took in the library to do them justice.

It's interesting, and perhaps under-appreciated, how much the very act of research can dictate the shape and content of a story. I wonder how many first novels involve a young character who investigates the events of his past, or the lives of his parents. First novels often include an attempt to locate oneself, and mine was no different. I soon found that I was writing in two time frames. In the first, I was relating the life and death of Beth Cartwright, and the dissolution of Blackmoor, my fictional mining village. In the second, Vincent was a young teenager living in quite a comfortable village on the outskirts of Derby, slowly uncovering the truth about what happened to his mother, along with the history of his county. Of course, there are some obvious parallels between Vincent's quest and mine. One of the notable things about the research I was doing was that I had to do it at *all*. So I wrote about Vincent going through the same process.

My family doesn't resemble the Cartwrights, but there are similarities between Vincent and I, in terms of our perspective. My grandparents were proud, hardworking and clever people, who didn't expect the opportunity to go to university. By the time I finished school, I sort of did. Vincent, who feels similarly comfortable in his peaceful world of semi-rural birdwatching, is oblivious to the difficult circumstances in which his family lived just a few decades before.

During a school project on Blackmoor, Vincent starts to uncover the truth about his family and the old village. He finds out about his mother's illness and discovers why his father has always refused to talk about her death. He unearths the guilt they share. He's a local historian, just like I was for the duration of the novel.

In terms of the research itself, I accidentally did something that worked in my favour: I became obsessed with an idea that was actually quite obscure. Not many people know about the pit gas escaping from the disused mine in Arkwright Town. Arkwright's story is full of the upsetting ironies of the way mining villages were treated. British Coal demolished Arkwright when the gases were discovered and then built a new village across the A-road. The old village site subsequently became an open-cast coal mine, worth millions of pounds, only a few years after most of the men in the village were made redundant due to an apparent lack of coal to be mined. Although a few national newspapers covered the story in the 1990s, I didn't have much trouble fending off competitors for the idea. As a novelist with limited historical abilities, I don't want to be researching something too mainstream. The easier it is to find information on a subject, the less excited I become about that subject as a prospective novel.

At the start of the process, I didn't know what I was doing and spent most of my research hours in local studies libraries in Derbyshire trawling through piles of stuff that would never have made it into a university library or a bookshop. But in the end that worked out quite well. Local studies libraries are amazing because the information they contain is often hopelessly obscure, or – to put it another way – fantastically rare. At that time, all of the references were still listed on index cards in little wooden drawers. The articles they referred to were from local papers, or else they were diaries published by small presses and historical societies. I even remember reading an anthropological PhD thesis about how Arkwright residents had responded to the spatial design of their new village. I thought it unlikely that more established and able novelists would be pulling such index cards from the drawer.

The most important sources, I soon realized, were first-hand accounts. As much as I needed to wade through texts explaining the historical and political nuances of the Miners' Strike and its aftermath, they didn't provide me with the physical details of living in that time. There's a fascinating documentary produced by Jan Rogers of BBC Radio Derby about Arkwright Town – the demolition of the old village and the move to the new one. It's brilliant because it consists entirely of villagers speaking about the experience. You hear their voices – the intonation and sentiment, but you also gain access to their sensory world. They talk about how they moved around their homes. What they saw and touched.

First-hand accounts were also vital to my research on post-partum psychosis (PPP), the condition which Beth Cartwright suffers from in the book. I can't remember when I decided that Beth was suffering from the condition. The first image I got for the novel was baby Vincent, lying in a flower basin, looking up at the open second-floor window of the Cartwright family home, waiting for his mother to appear. And I had an idea of an older Vincent, living with his father, sharing a guilty secret. I suppose Beth's illness rose into the gaps created by those two images.

Most of my research on PPP took place in university libraries (you don't have to be a student at a university to use its library resources).

My early reading took the form of medical text books about bipolar disorder, which has a lot in common with the experience of PPP. The problem with that – and a common issue when writing about medical conditions – is that you risk reducing your character to a list of symptoms. It's true that PPP and bipolar disorder share common traits, but of course there are specific emotions relating to childbirth with the former. Slim pamphlets about PPP and post-natal depression, which contained first-hand accounts of the actual experiences of sufferers, ended up being far more valuable to the construction of Beth's character. In those publications, I could read about the day-to-day lives of the women, the actions they took and their thoughts.

Reading *Blackmoor* again, I'm conscious of how young I was when I came to write Beth. I'm also conscious of how much I wanted to protect her, along with the women who had contributed their life stories to the literature on PPP. In some of the pamphlets I read, there are lists of the sorts of delusions that many women suffered during psychotic episodes. Taken all together, and taken out of context, they seem lurid and horrifying and extreme. There were stories of mothers who were convinced – at the height of their illness – that their children were Jesus or the devil, or who felt that their babies were the wrong shape. Beth actually reads such a pamphlet in the novel, when she returns from hospital, and it scares her deeply. I steered away from the more outlandish delusions and towards the obsessive behaviours as I felt unsure of my ability to represent the delusions fictionally, without being exploitative. I was conscious of the fine balance I needed to strike: wanting to avoid presenting Beth as an interesting exhibit of madness, while also trying to communicate that, yes, this is a truly frightening experience for her, and many like her.

I think it's important to consider the limits of research, because it's here that writing fiction really begins. When I write, I try – in quite an old-fashioned way – to create characters with a true consciousness. I like to write about the private, intimate spaces of the home and the mind. Even the diaries I read, written by women during the Miners' Strike, or by those suffering with post-partum psychosis, were prepared as public-facing documents, and therefore came with in-built defence mechanisms. I feel that one of my jobs as a novelist is to strip away those self-conscious, protective reflexes. To do that, I have to make things up. I have to take a leap into the mind of my character, and into their home. And to do *that*, I first have to take a step back from my research. I spent a long time steeping myself in the details of the world I was seeking to portray. Eventually, those details became part of my imagination. I no longer had to look up – or even think consciously – about the type of fireplace in Beth Cartwright's house. I simply saw her moving towards it. I didn't have to pull out notes and quotes on what it was like for sufferers of post-partum psychosis to return to domestic life with their babies, because I no longer felt that Beth was just a composite of first-hand accounts and medical texts. I know the postmodernists will take issue, but I felt that in Beth I had created someone particular, with an idiosyncratic way of thinking. I knew how she would react to finding the good green wine glasses, which she had smashed during her manic phase. I knew how she would react to her husband, who is now unconsciously frightened to touch her, because her manic behaviour was triggered by pregnancy. That took time. Time for research, and time to move away from that research, to allow the information to become visual and sensory.

There was only one occasion on which I wrote a passage immediately after doing the research. About halfway through writing the book, I visited the National Coalmining Museum for England, in Wakefield. Much of *Blackmoor* takes place in the early 1990s, after the pit has closed, but many of the characters have worked down the mine. The museum is excellent. You're taken down in a cage and can wander around the pit, which is set up to show you what work would have been like through the ages. The experience of descending in the cage made a huge impression on me. I came home and wrote chapter nine – a sort of history of George's father, Harry, a miner responsible for drilling and dynamiting. I felt that I needed to write it while the physical sense of the pit was still fresh, and it took only about an hour from start to finish.

I approached the subject of *Blackmoor* with very definite views on mining villages and community and masculinity. Through my research, all of those views were made more complicated, not less so. I never really came to any conclusions, and perhaps that's the way it should be. I ended up having more sympathy for George than I had envisaged and tried to provide a redemptive note to the ending of the book when he finally talks to Vincent about his mother's life.

Writing – and reading – about one's hometown is complicated, and I understand the journalist's ambivalence because it springs from the same place as my anxieties. The fact is, there aren't a lot of contemporary novels about Derbyshire. Such novels are therefore judged – quite wrongly – as the writer's attempt to provide a definitive guide to the area. Or, God forbid, a tourist brochure. When a writer sets a novel in London or New York, reviewers often give just a passing mention of the location. Not so when you write about a Derbyshire village. I totally understand how unsettling it can be to read or watch a fictional account of your home, because it's never quite *your* experience, or *your* viewpoint.

I remember the first time I saw *Dead Man's Shoes*, the Shane Meadows film set in Matlock, a few miles from where I was brought up. It was exhilarating. My brother and I sat watching the opening minutes, and when Paddy Considine spoke the first line of dialogue ('Don't mess around with that fire, Anthony') we looked at each other with amazement. The accent! The Derbyshire accent! On our television! And it's not the local news, it's a bloody *feature film*. I think Meadows completely nails the particular Derbyshire experience about which he writes, but I understand that it is only one part of Derbyshire. His standpoint is unique. So is mine, so is everybody's.

My research methods are much more organized these days. I have great lists of required sources, and a more thorough note-taking method. With a few books behind me, I'm also more confident about just calling an expert and interviewing them. With my first novel, *Blackmoor*, the anxieties that came along with writing about my home county were undoubtedly a huge motivating factor in my research. But even as I begin to write my fifth novel, I still hear that voice, asking, *What gives you the right?* In many ways, research gives me the right, but I hope the nagging voice never goes away.

Note

1. J. Gallone (4 April 2009) 'Author Paints Bleak Picture of County', *Derby Evening Telegraph*.

7
Walking the Tightrope

Kishwar Desai

Part of my problem when I start working on a book is that I simply can't stop researching for it. I worry endlessly about not knowing the subject thoroughly, about making mistakes, about not having the required skills to communicate a difficult story authentically. I worry about the library not visited, the book not read, the person not interviewed, the house not tracked down.

Simply put, I worry that I will be 'found out' – that actually I wrote the whole book sitting on a sofa, with a glass of wine by my side. Of course, it is entirely possible that luckier authors than I can actually do this. But since I am driven by these demons of insecurity, I tend to over-research. Sometimes I work for so long on the research, the book never gets written because I am so very intent on finding that little nugget of information which will make the book a triumphant success. And the irony is that a book is not about the information, but is actually about the *way* it is presented. But more about that later.

This dependency on never-ending research may have been due to my years as a journalist and later, a documentary film-maker. I still remember the hours spent by my protesting team as we hunted for that 'perfect' shot and that 'appropriate' sound bite. Of course, it may not have made any difference to the viewer if the film did not have that particular scene, but in my mind I was always relieved that I had pushed and gone that extra mile. I was a shy child lacking in confidence, and perhaps I could blame my childhood (if we must indulge in some psychobabble) for my tendency to overcompensate: *Look, even if you think I am bereft of all talent, perhaps you might appreciate my hard work!*

Anyone who indulges in the crime of over-researching knows that it is hugely addictive. No matter how many times you tell yourself, 'Now, this is absolutely the last article I am going to read on this', a few days later you will spot something and kick yourself for not having spent a little more time browsing the Internet or interviewing an expert. This is where deadlines help. Nothing concentrates the mind more, and this is why I now give myself self-imposed deadlines for book completion.

In fact, my experience with research for my non-fictional book and my novel were very different, in the manner in which they were finally used. This made me understand, somewhat ruefully, that research can sometimes limit your imagination, and the transformation of that research into literature does not always give an elegant result.

For my first book, *Darlingji: The True Love Story of Nargis and Sunil Dutt*, the biography of two very successful Indian film stars, I collected over 50 hours of interviews with their families and friends, and at least four boxes of newspaper clippings, books, letters, photographs, diaries. The research and interviews took nearly a year of hard slog mostly in Mumbai, Pune and Delhi. Yet, surprisingly, the book worked out well, despite the research – not because of it. The problem with non-fiction is that you can end up with far too much detail. One way of dealing with this, I found, was to spend a few days just reading through the material before I tackled a particular chapter. It was not necessary to remember everything verbatim, but just one attentive read-through was usually enough to give a structure to the chapter. And as I began writing, focusing on the 'big picture' or the broad strokes, I could subsequently dip into little details and reproduce them wherever required.

What I discovered from this process was that the author is like a sponge, absorbing the information almost at a subliminal level until she (hopefully) gains an almost visceral understanding of the subject. It might just be a conceit, but it seems to me that even without recollecting every tiny date or event, the research brings you ever closer and closer to the subjects until they become an extension of your own persona. You begin to eat, dream, even sleep, with them (metaphorically, of course!) by your side. Even if it sounds fantastical, it did appear to me that the book wrote itself, more or less. The characters became real and the strange serendipity that I developed with them (even though the two actors were no longer alive) gave me, I felt, a unique insight. I would write a line about them, and then, while going through their letters, find that they themselves had expressed very similar sentiments. I am sure other writers have this reassuring experience of identifying with and understanding their characters (both in non-fiction and fiction), almost at a mystical level. It was a quite magical and interesting experience: I realized that, as an author, *if I understood the main elements, I could construct the story.*

But while it was a relief that I had such a fascinating amount of detail, the arrangement of it was almost a forensic exercise. Further, since I was writing about two iconic and well-known figures, I had to be immensely careful about *what* I said. Sometimes, as I tried to interpret their behaviour, two very disparate sets of information could be drawn together in a single chapter because they best explained an event or experience. Often, even if an event took place much later in their lives, I found it was already foreshadowed in an earlier letter. Links developed in front of my eyes from unrelated elements – for instance, an interview in a magazine or an unguarded photograph. Even books which were written about similar subjects helped me find a resonance between the lives of the two actors and the environment in which they worked and lived. Thus the story explored their 'reel' lives and also their lives off screen, and the tensions which they experienced because one was a Muslim (Nargis) and the other a Hindu (Sunil). Fortunately for me, their story covered nearly one hundred years of Indian cinema and politics. So their lives were impacted by major events such as the Partition of India, the political upheaval during Emergency – even the Mumbai riots and the bomb blasts in that city, in which their son was arrested as an alleged terrorist.

Dividing the book into a chronological order, I found that each decade in their life was dominated by a particular event (usually a tragic one, alas) which forced a powerful change in their lives. Thus the book naturally flowed into chapters and it had an intrinsic strong narrative full of dramatic turns that made it very real – both for me and for others who read it as a book and were moved by the story of two people whom they may have never met.

So, I thought I had learnt a lot from *Darlingji*. Especially that research is often just a tool in the hands of the writer. It can be used to overtly impart information or it can be used subtly in context, embedded within the body of the main text, so as not to overwhelm the reader.

Lessons learnt are still not easy to repeat, however. If I somehow had succeeded in establishing the right tone for the first book, through a combination of direct and embedded research, I found I could not do so quite so easily in the next – especially when the second book I decided to write was a novel. My debut novel, *Witness the Night*, was again a research-based book, but this time exposing the horrific problem of female foeticide and infanticide in tradition-bound India. These are murders which routinely go unpunished and are discussed in the media with an unsentimental monotony. Most people have stopped listening to both the reports of gendercide and the steps which have been taking place to create awareness or eradicate the ghastly practice. A fictional account of this very real issue would affect readers more, I thought, as they would engage and empathize with the characters and their appalling situations. Also, fiction would enable me to draw on a more poetic and imagistic language that, I hoped, would express the reality of gendercide on a deeper, more emotive level than straightforward facts and figures:

> The headlines on television announced that saplings were being planted in memory of all the 'disappeared daughters'. Punjab is known for murdering its daughters. The sex ratio here is the lowest in the country – less than 850 girls per 1000 men – and despite all sorts of dire warnings from social scientists and demographers, girls are still considered inauspicious. In Chandigarh, the uber-urban capital that Punjab shares with Haryana, it is now 777 per thousand males. In some villages of Haryana it is a miserable 370. Delhi is also fast reaching those dismal figures. I thought of trees being planted all over the concrete mass of the city – and all the cities of the country. The bright life affirming green against the dead grey of the cityscape. Trees pushing out of windows, bedrooms, school rooms, offices, toy shops, bridal parlours, empty cradles … green leaves left like tiny footprints everywhere the girls would have been, had they lived.[1]

Some of the research for *Witness the Night* was done through informal personal interactions and through monitoring the news on this issue over the last decade. I read academic texts, googled and spoke to experts as well, but the main source of information was collected when I was a journalist and, later, the head of a TV channel based in India. During this time, I interviewed men and women who had been affected by the problem. I came across some very painful stories which stuck in my mind and which bothered me, much like a wound which refuses to heal.

Almost unconsciously, I drew upon a news item I had read many years ago about a young girl in Kolkata who had been accused of poisoning her whole family. To me it seemed that *Witness the Night* was her story. That is, I knew that this was the story of a girl who had been pushed to the limits of her endurance, who simply could not tolerate (what she thought was) the extreme punishment of having been born a woman. I hasten to add that I deliberately did not research the story of the real-life Bengali girl – but I took it as my starting point. So when I sat down to actually write the novel, I decided that the main protagonist, Durga, would be a teenager accused of a horrendous crime.

The novel is set in a small town, Jullundur in Punjab, where thirteen members of a family have been poisoned and their house set on fire. The only survivor is Durga, the family's teenage daughter who has been raped, beaten and bound. Ironically Durga becomes the chief suspect and is remanded, by the police, into judicial custody. An intrepid social worker, Simran Singh undertakes to prove Durga's innocence, and in the course of her investigation she discovers a world of deceit and betrayal, where women are treated with contempt from birth.

This was thus going to be a complex novel. On the surface it was a story about a horrific crime, but at another level I had to reveal the senseless prejudice and extreme bias which still exists in modern India, and which has led to the killing and 'disappearance' of over 35 million women.

Drawing on my experience of writing *Darlingji*, I dealt with the research in two different ways. Some stories I came across formed part of the information that the main protagonist, the social worker, Simran Singh shares with the reader:

> Not so long ago, the midwives used to take away newborn girls from their mothers, seal them in earthen pots and roll the pot around till the baby stopped crying. Or they would simply suffocate them. Or give them opium and then bury them.[2]

Other stories were woven into the personal narratives of the three female protagonists: Durga, Simran Singh and Binny. Durga recollects her own family history and writes of how she discovered that her family had been killing newborn baby girls and burying them in the field behind the house, sometimes in earthen pots. Durga and her sister would have met the same fate, had they somehow not beaten destiny and survived:

> Carefully, Sharda took out a paper envelope from which she drew out a tiny white skeletal hand. She made me hold it. I want you to know what they do in this house, Durga, she said. This hand was buried deep inside the vegetable plot. There was also a tiny skull and other limbs but they have all been crushed by the tractor. This is the only thing I managed to dig out. I would have been there too, if Jitu had not found me. You, too, because like me you refused to die.[3]

This particular scene was very important to me because I had met, during my research, a middle-aged woman from Punjab who had actually been given an overdose of opium when she was born in order to kill her. She lived to tell the story and I was haunted by the thought that she had grown up in a home where she knew that her parents were meant to be her assassins.

Thus, I kept poking at the agonizing wound, restless and angry. My anger made me long for a narrative which was shocking *and counter-intuitive* to my research. The protagonists had to be empowered women, capable of creating mayhem and challenging the notion that women can be easily ill-treated by a patriarchal society and tradition. They had to be caring and driven enough to want to stop the killing of baby girls, and yet calculating enough to expose those involved.

In short, the protagonists had to be everything my research did not reflect enough: rebellious, outspoken women, independent from men and marriage. While I could use my research factually to explore the practice of gendercide, the characters and plot would have to be mainly fictional, allowing for an independence of will that is in opposition to the reality of a culture based largely on inequality.

Though Durga is a teenager in the book and is incarcerated and vulnerable, I did not want her simply to be a submissive victim. Since her character is almost always silent, I could only convey her anger at the injustice of being born a girl and her subsequent victimization through her letters. From birth, she has been brutally treated, cheating death twice. She is a survivor who, I hoped, would pique the reader's conscience into truly recognizing the terrible injustices that are taking place in modern India. Though she doesn't speak directly (a reality for many women in India) the letters do give her a strong and subversive voice within the confines of her situation. I wanted my character Durga to be like her namesake, the many armed goddess (an avatar of Kali), who wants to destroy the demons of ignorance and evil from the world.

While Durga is quietly subversive, I needed a strong character who was quite the opposite; a woman who was loud and openly aggressive, who could fight social injustice on her own terms. This was crucial as I did not want the reader to have the impression that all Indian women are not liberated or modern. Simran Singh had to be an unconventional character – someone who has rebelled against the traditional path and is unmarried. Simran is in her mid-forties, smokes, drinks and is unafraid to challenge those who have brought her in on the case. I also wanted to introduce some humour through her relationship with her mother, who is extremely anxious that Simran finds a man and settles down. Because

Durga is still, in many ways, a child and her 'voice' in the book is some-what subdued, I wanted Simran to use a more colourful and confident language when expressing herself:

> I reach for a cigarette. The pleasures of not sharing a room are many. You can fart in bed, and you can smoke without asking, 'May I?' I look across the chintz printed bed sheets and imagine The Last Boyfriend sprawled there. Hairy, fat, rich. Better than bald, thin and poor. But unbearably attached to his 'Mummyji'. (...)
>
> I can still hear Mummyji's shocked voice, the solitaires shaking in opprobrium: 'Simran, you are a sardarni, a Sikhni, and you smoke!'[4]

The character of Simran is again based on many women I know, but is unlike most female heroines in Indian literature. She is neither attrac-tive nor particularly young. She has had a string of relationships and allows herself to become entangled with unsuitable men, much to her mother's anguish. And having just completed the second book in the Simran Singh series, *Origins of Love*, let me assure you that this is not a habit she is likely to give up any time soon. She is independent minded, and the important thing is she does not define herself through being a daughter, wife or mother – thus she is truly free and quite different from anyone who would have inhabited Durga's world.

Binny, who is the third female protagonist, is represented only through her emails, and because she is based in London, I was able to give her a completely different 'voice' and perspective. Yet her story is also based on research: the all-too-familiar tale of a young British Asian woman brought back to India to be 'persuaded' or 'forced' into an arranged marriage with the scion of a very traditional Punjabi family, regardless of her own desires and wishes.

I mused over many questions that became the driving force for my story. The primary question was why would a young girl want to kill her family? Women are usually the victims, not the perpetrators of vio-lence. As I began to ponder this, all the information I had collected – the myriads of stories of female oppression – began to parade in front of my eyes. The story of my fictional Durga unfolded during that epiphany, when the research synthesized into a single narrative. Along with this, were my own real-life experiences. As my father was in the police, and we, as a family, had been posted with him to various small towns and cities (including Jullundur where my novel is set), I could imagine, very well, what it would be like for a young girl to be brought up in a small town and then kept in judicial custody. While my own father was incorruptible, I had known plenty of other officers who were not.

Again, to my own observations from my childhood, I added the grist from current affairs in India – where the breakdown of law and order and the inability to provide gender justice has become a national shame. By reading accounts of women in jail, of women who were being trafficked, of women who had been raped or put into mental hospitals, I was able to construct sequences in the book which I hoped would seem authentic. I carefully cross-checked certain possibilities and events, but was equally careful not to copy any particular incident, episode or person. While I wrote about a school, a jail, a mental asylum, I did not want to describe journalistically an existing space. This was important for me because I wanted the debate to be focused on the larger issue of gendercide and not be dissipated by a discussion on whether my novel replicated any particular case or place.

And this is one of the most important differences I found between my first and second books. Though both are based on research, in the first the only freedom I had was in the planning of the book and in its style of writing and, of course, in the forensic connections I explored. There was, overall, a rigid structure in which the research had to be placed, as it was a biography and thus dictated by real incidents of which I was merely a narrator. But in my novel there was far more creative freedom in dealing with the research. I could use the research as a starting point for the story, or as a part of a conversation, or as the musings of the social worker, Simran Singh, or even as the culmination of a crime. There was no need for footnotes or acknowledgements because in fiction the research is largely embedded or camouflaged within the story.

Of course, I may not have been entirely successful in this endeavour. And I am conscious of the fact that in the first draft of my book, which I wrote over a frenzied few months during the wonderful monsoons at our home in Goa, there was a definite information overload. Since the book is written in the first person, and therefore knowledge is limited through the eyes of the three main female protagonists, I felt I had to push the material regarding the oppression of women and gendercide in every way I could, and sometimes (in my first draft) Simran Singh's thoughts became a runaway rant of facts and figures.

But fortunately, after it had been read (both by my publisher as well as family members) I was persuaded to cut down on dense portions of research which were thought to detract from the main story. At first I had staunchly resisted, assuming the main purpose of my book would be lost. What if people got carried away by the 'crime fiction' aspect of the book, and their focus was on who committed the crime, rather than the issue of gendercide?

Authors sometimes live in a delusional world where only they can communicate, and that too only in a certain fashion! Perhaps some first-time novelists, such as I, simply cannot (at first) see the fine distinction between a polemic and a tale. Also – and this may be a new writer's anxiety – a reader simply won't understand what you're saying unless it's clearly stated. If something is left unsaid will the reader be able to fill in the spaces and interpret those things implied through a character's action or gesture? Having been a journalist, perhaps writers like me are far too conscious of the requirement to transform society and the inequities which exist within, and so one tries to put too many ideas, thoughts and problems on the plate.

Fortunately, the gentle pressure exerted by my well-wishers (especially my daughter, my husband and my editor) ensured that some of the diatribe was removed. Reluctantly, I have to admit that its deletion actually helped the book. Prior to this edit, I had been told that, while most of *Witness the Night* was a 'gripping page turner', the pace was slowed by Simran's angry thoughts about the prejudice against baby girls in India. And so, having listened to my family and very efficient editors, I removed those stumbling blocks from the final version of the book.

Let me also add, that like many other first-time novelists (nervous about whether the book will be published at all) I mourned any extraction from the book. When the cuts were first suggested, I thought, quite irrelevantly, of the hours spent in data collection, or the days spent in writing those (crucial!) pages which were being ruthlessly edited out. Indeed, I now know that it is not necessary to say everything in words, because in fiction, much of the research becomes the subtext. The moment it is made obvious or apparent, the writer is really showing off his or her own knowledge. The story is then snatched away from the characters – to whom the novel rightfully belongs – and becomes an editorial.

So while the research was very obviously celebrated and enjoyed quite openly in my first non-fictional book, in my novel I had to disguise it within the dialogue, filter it into scenes, or just carefully weave it into description. The moment it popped up, like a previously underwater shark, it ate into the body of my novel, creating disturbing and distracting waves for the reader. Obviously, by basing my novel in reality I had to make it authentic, but then I had to sufficiently disguise the research so that the reader would not realize the tight rope I was walking between two very different genres of fiction and non-fiction.

While these are all wise words in hindsight, please do not think I will not tumble off the tight rope into a deep chasm of research in my next novel. I can only say that I will *try* not to!

Notes

1. K. Desai (2010) *Witness the Night* (Chatham: Beautiful Books Limited), p. 63.
2. Ibid., 63.
3. Ibid., 162.
4. Ibid., 4.

8

The Reluctant Aficionado

Wena Poon

Alex y Robert is a story of two friends, inspired by two real-life friends. Bea and I grew up together in Singapore. Bea always wanted to be an actress; I always wanted to write. We were precocious children and were prolific artists by age 14. I went to see all her plays and she read all of my novels. Fast forward 20 years: Bea is an actress; I am a novelist. We live in different countries and haven't seen each other for many years. One day, Bea stumbled upon a bullfight in Madrid. She was traumatized by what she saw, but also haunted by its tremendous theatrical potential. She contacted me out of the blue. 'You have to write a bullfighting story. Any story, as long as it's set in Spain, with bulls. Please. I can't write, I never could, but oh! The *drama*. The *colors*. You are the only person who can do it.'

This was the way we used to talk to each other as children. Nothing, apparently, had changed.

I sat on this assignment for a whole year because little about bullfighting appealed to me as an artist. I associated Spain and bullfighting with certain passé images and attitudes: deep-breasted women wearing frilly flamenco dresses and clicking castanets; muscled matadors with oiled hair and clefts in their chins taunting poor, bleeding bulls. And, of course, there is Ernest Hemingway. He visited Spain in the 1920s and was so fascinated by what he saw that he wrote *Death in the Afternoon*, his famous treatise on bullfighting, as well as short stories and novels on the subject. Hemingway believed bullfighting was of great tragic interest, 'being literally of life and death',[1] and early Hemingway critics lauded his world of masculine pursuits. How could a young Chinese woman novelist from Singapore possibly write about bullfighting in Hemingway's overbearing shadow?

I met up with Bea again. 'Can't do it. It's too alien, too impenetrable.'
'Find your point of entry,' she said solemnly. 'Everyone has a point of entry.'

It was an impossible commission. I had never been to Spain and didn't know a single Spanish-speaking person. I'd never read a book about bullfighting or seen a bullfight, nor had I ever wanted to. What could possibly be my point of entry?

My first instinct was to Wiki everything: Spain, the Spanish Civil War, Spanish bullfighting. Inspiration did not strike, yet I dutifully wrote a ten-page treatment for Bea. It was a typical nineteenth-century story about a famous macho matador. It was all I could think of: clichés, stereotypes. I was lazy. She took the story to a theatre producer. The feedback: 'This reads like *Les Misérables* in Spanish costumes. This is 2009. We need something contemporary.'

I thought of polite ways to reject the commission. But because we were childhood friends, I made a last ditch effort and bought an air ticket to Spain. I covered Valencia, Madrid and Barcelona in eight days: it was all the time and money I could afford. But I was lucky. My short visit coincided with some lower-ranking bullfights. Tickets were cheap and easy to obtain. For five Euros I had a front-row seat.

Women – I realized – do not go to watch bullfights alone, and there were few Asian tourists. People stared at me. I was intimidated by the gruff old men that filled the stands, and felt horribly lonely and displaced. The first bullfight seemed cruel and repetitive; I was depressed, disgusted and bored. But in the second fight, something unbelievable happened. The bull hit the matador and flung him into the air like a doll. Everyone in the stands screamed. My God, it was a horrible thing to see. Ashen with blood loss, the matador picked himself up and persisted in completing the bullfight. I couldn't speak Spanish with the people around me, so I couldn't even share my horror. It was a curious experience, to witness tragedy, alone and mute, in a sea of people.

The injured matador stayed on his feet and finished the bullfight, despite his injury. He was awarded a trophy: the ear sawn off the dead bull, which was cut off right there, in front of my eyes. It was rubbed against the sand to staunch any excess blood and handed to the matador, who walked a victory lap around the ring, still bleeding from his wounds, flourishing the detached ear and sobbing with happiness. I was appalled, but also very curious. Why would any teenager in this day and age be interested in this profession, when he could be a Web developer, a teacher, an analyst, a lawyer, a banker – you name it. Of the myriad of twenty-first century professions to aspire to, why bullfighter?

I realized I had been quite wrong about the Spanish macho male bull-fighter. None of the matadors I saw in person were particularly macho – they looked more like narrow-waisted girls, if anything. I looked them up on YouTube and reviewed innumerable interview clips. Most were shy and softly spoken. Some went to the States to learn English and came back with a degree; others were country boys who were more comfortable on farms than in cities. Without doubt, all were twenty-first century men. They had iPods and played videogames. When they were not in traditional costume, they wore cycling shorts and brand name T-shirts and went to dance clubs, just like everyone else. And yes, they were on social networking sites.

'Modern matadors', wrote a knowledgeable friend in an e-mail, 'are more interesting than any historical bullfighter you can make up.'

I could Google, Wiki, YouTube my subject to death, but nothing was comparable to the real experience of seeing these modern matadors and sitting in a cramped bullring, smelling the sweat of an expectant crowd fanning themselves feverishly in the evening heat. If I hadn't taken a chance on going to Spain, I wouldn't have seen the white haze of cigarette smoke above the ring that turned the evening into an ugly, ashen grey. Or the unexpected interruptions during a bullfight, such as the ominous staccato of a police helicopter, or a cloud of balloons emblazoned with SpongeBob, Hello Kitty and Dora, floating merrily across the sky above the open bullring while life-and-death was in progress. All these details went into the book.

I was interested in incongruity, in how the modern world – with all its unedited interruptions – constantly encroached into the ancient world of bullfighting. The story that began taking shape in my mind was a modern, cosmopolitan tale, one that would explore the tradition of bullfighting from the perspective of the Facebook generation.

In the 1950s, the story goes, two famous Spanish matadors who were best friends died in the bullring. In the twenty-first century their grand-children, Alex and Roberto, meet for the first time. Alex, an American college student, has inherited her grandfather's affinity with the bulls. She has trained as a matador on her American ranch since age ten, and knows that the chances of women – especially foreign women – making it in the world of the Spanish bullring are virtually nil. She dutifully goes to college and promises her family she will obtain an MBA thereafter.

One summer, Alex pretends to enrol in a language course in Spain, but never shows up for class because she is there to track down Roberto, the son of their old family friend. Roberto is her age but already a famous bullfighter and worshipped by fans. He is envious of young urban Spaniards who study overseas and return to found dot-com companies, and feels inferior to Alex. To him, the young American woman represents the sophistication that he aspires towards. They will trade places, I decided. Alex will fight bulls in Spain and Roberto will study for a degree in America. It was the perfect platform for cultural commentary: a story of the New World finding the Old World; a story about how Europeans and Americans view each other.

Once I decided on this plot, the hard work began. How would I convert my eight days in Spain into a credible bullfighting story?

Many Spanish diehard aficionados believe that you have to have Spanish blood in your veins in order to have *afición* (the love of the bulls) and the appreciation of *toreo* (the art of bullfighting). The fact that I just had to use two Spanish words tells you how untranslatable bullfighting concepts are in English. The bullfighting world continues to be a closed, mostly male circle, and there is even a special Spanish word for it: *mundillo*. Since I could not speak their language, few Spanish experts would – or could – talk to me. And English-speaking aficionados, most of them older generation, snubbed me for daring to barge into their fraternity.

I went back to Spain again, this time for 15 days. I met every Spaniard who could speak English and who wanted to talk about bullfighting: a very narrow slice of Spanish society. But being an international lawyer – my day job – helped. Many Spaniards who mastered English and other languages went – naturally – into international law. The idea of helping a lawyer colleague write a bullfighting novel was a delicious one: they rallied round. They volunteered as interpreters and helped me solve plot problems. For instance, I wanted the novel to build towards the point where Alex and Roberto appear in the same bullfight. However, I discovered this was impossible under bullfighting regulations. They did not have the same qualifications and would not have been allowed to compete together.

I complained to a female Spanish lawyer, who was busy introducing me to my first glass of dry sherry. 'Sí, es posible!' she reassured me, pouring the *manzanilla*. 'In a charity bullfight, bullfighters of different levels are permitted to perform together.' I'd never heard of charity bullfights and researched them further. A charity bullfight went on to play a big role in the book.

I was also delighted by my discovery that matadors, dressed up in sequined suits, Tweet on their phones as they wait to go into the ring. What a great comment on the old world and the new! What could they be saying to their fans? This led me to convey an entire scene in

Tweets written by people milling about the ring before the charity fight begins:

> My mother and I are standing in line at the hotel hoping to catch a glimpse of the toreros.
> Does anybody speak English?
> They're not starting on time.
> Soubeyran's out. No Soubeyran. Spread the word.
> *DOWN WITH BULLFIGHTING I HOPE YOU ALL DIE BLOODTHIRSTY ASSHOLES!!!*[2]

I love technology and sought every opportunity to introduce it into the novel. The language of social networking was a vibrant way of bringing together the many disparate opinions that I encountered while working on the book. With the discovery that modern matadors were, after all, young people who worshipped the same technology as I did, Spain became more familiar and identifiable to me. The distance between 'my' world and 'their' world began to narrow.

At the back of *Alex y Robert*, I quoted the famous words of Japanese poet Basho:

> Go to the pine if you want to learn about the pine, or to the bamboo if you want to learn about the bamboo... Your poetry issues of its own accord when you and the object have become one – when you have plunged deep enough into the object to see something like a hidden glimmering there.[3]

If you go to the pine, the book practically writes itself. The key is total immersion and total experience: there are no short-cuts. Every artist instinctively understands this. It did not come as a surprise to me later to discover that Hemingway emphasized the value of research when telling a story. It makes your work far easier as a novelist, and besides, readers can detect false notes:

> The dignity of movement of an ice-berg is due to only one-eighth of it being above water. A writer who omits things because he does not know them only makes hollow places in his writing.[4]

To give my story authenticity and dignity I had to feel the story, simply because it was so alien to me. But as Hemingway suggests, one doesn't have to use everything that one uncovers. I knew I would gather more information than I ever needed to show in the book, but it would all be helpful. I visited ranches where bulls were bred. I talked to the ranchers and student matadors and watched them at work. I inspected their ranches and looked into bins of animal feed. I met their pigs and chickens, and touched the branding irons and the armour of the picador's horse. I went into the bull's pen and felt the deep scars along the wood left by his horns. I photographed the patterns of dried blood and fecal matter on the walls. I imagined the bull's apprehension at being trapped in a dark box like that. It was very moving.

I sneaked into the bullring's abattoir to see how they cut up the carcass after the bullfight, before I was waved away by a security guard. The bulls killed at the bullfight – I discovered – are put in refrigerated trucks and sold to restaurants. I ate beef steak and beef stew made with these fighting bulls just to see what the meat tasted like (awful).

Aside from my two trips to Spain, I also raided the municipal library back in Austin, Texas, where I lived. Since this was Texas, there were quite a lot of books about farms, cattle and bulls. After all, the symbol of Texas was the long-horn cow – which, incidentally, is a direct descendent of the Spanish *toro bravo*, shipped over here by the original Spanish conquistadors. Many forget that Texas was originally known as *Nueva España*, New Spain, and belonged to the Spanish crown. I was walking among ghosts, and once I was on the trail of the bull, he was everywhere.

Sooner or later, I had to confront Hemingway. I flicked desultorily through his novel, *The Sun Also Rises*, and gave up halfway. I did finish his treatise, *Death in the Afternoon*. It was a good read, but it was published in 1932. Reading this book in order to understand bullfighting now, which is what a lot of people still do, is like packing a 1932 guidebook for a modern-day trip to China.

There is much that I admire in Hemingway's writing – such as his spare, lean prose for which he is famous – but I have always felt a little asphyxiated by his masculine tone. For me, his is a universe that is barren of feminine sensibility. As a woman reading *Death in the Afternoon*, it was like climbing a rock face that had no footholds I could grab onto or use. For example, he says:

> To see bulls fight is a beautiful sight. They use their horns as a fencer does his weapon. They strike, parry, feint, block and have an exactitude of aim that is amazing. When they both know how to use the horn the combat usually ends as does a fight between two really

skillful boxers, with all dangerous blows stopped, without bloodshed and with mutual respect.[5]

Hemingway's descriptions often irritate me. He assumes the reader has similar life experiences to his own and will know how fencers and boxers behave in their sport. Although I happen to have dabbled in both fencing and boxing in college, I no longer remember what is a 'parry' and what is a 'feint'. I could see how modern readers think that bullfighting, put in such terms, glorifies combat and violence. I wanted to have a twenty-first century response to what I was seeing. Something younger, more relatable to ordinary life, even mischievous. I wanted to remark upon the absurdity of bullfighting that I sometimes felt as a modern, young, female viewer:

> Alex shivered. There was something pathetic about watching a bloodied man face death without his hat or his shoes. She suddenly realized how provincial and polite the matador costume was, down to the fake, black necktie that cinched the white ruffles at the neck and the cheery little Christmas tree ornaments that dangled from the shoulders.[6]

This portrayal ruffled a few feathers. 'Do you really believe that the matador's suit is like *a Christmas tree*?' wrote an enraged aficionado. In contrast, a friend, a rather jaded political reporter, read a draft and wrote, 'Don't be afraid to be yourself, trust your intuitions, and make such observations.'

I read many other English-language bullfighting books for research. The most remarkable bullfighting book wasn't by a novelist or an aficionado. It was actually a 1988 scientific study, *Bullfight*, by a professor of social anthropology, Garry Marvin. I came across this book by accident during a web search. In his chapter on the fighting bull, Marvin contrasted the city and the countryside in Spanish bullfighting. The bull was raised for years in tranquil surroundings in the countryside then trucked into the city to finish his last hours in the bullring. Marvin writes of the tender, secret life of the bull on the ranch, how the animal is given a name and is recognized and respected by the foreman throughout its life. When it is time for the bull to be sent to the bullring, however, its individuality diminishes. It is simply reduced to a number and bundled into a truck like ordinary cattle. Marvin's observation inspired me to create a very brief but critical scene in the novel featuring a ranch foreman. Jeremy Osborne, the producer of the BBC

Radio Four *Book at Bedtime* version of *Alex y Robert*, had to abridge the novel for the radio series. Most side characters were cut, but he told me he wanted to keep the foreman, who only had one scene. In this scene, he is riding a horse alone at the bull ranch. Alex drives up and asks what he's doing. He tells her he is saying goodbye to six of his babies:

'They're being trucked to Bilbao tomorrow morning, long journey. I wished them luck.'
'Are you going with them?'
'No. Do you know that I have *never* watched a bullfight in a city bullring in my life? I can't stand it. To me their beauty is all here. It is here that they are full of vitality. I don't need to see anything else. The city has nothing for me.'[7]

I didn't have much luck with other bullfighting books. Most were simply too prosaic and corny, swinging wildly between technicality and sentimentality. They were filled with Spanish/English glossaries, bullfighting jargon, and schoolboy crushes on famous matadors. I found them alienating rather than inspiring. After putting myself through the thirtieth raving fan book, I couldn't bear it any longer. I vowed never to lose the reader in the way those authors had lost me, in the dense thicket of their specialized knowledge, in the Technicolor sunsets of their gushing adoration.

I wanted bullfighting to be identifiable to the lay reader. I kept paring back the language. Instead of saying *capote* and *muleta*, I wrote, with deliberate simplicity, 'pink cape' and 'red cape' – these immediately conjure up for the lay reader the appropriate image. Research authenticates and enriches a piece of writing and can offer new directions to explore, but sometimes it can also impede the imaginative process that fuels the writing. An expert pointed out that it was technically inaccurate for me to call a *muleta* a cape, but do you care? I don't. Instead of saying the matador executed a *veronica*, I said a *veronica* pass. The *veronica* was already a 'pass'; there was no need to say '*veronica* pass', but it helped you remember what the foreign word meant. No need for glossaries. My objective was to invite the reader in. The story was important, not the jargon.

To illustrate, I'll take you through the only extended description of a bullfight in the novel:

The first two acts – the act of the spears, and the act of the darts, went according to plan. Determined to get a trophy this time, Roberto dared several dangerous *veronica* passes with the pink cape. The gigantic animal bumped into him several times, smearing him with blood. He did not seem to notice, just as you would politely disregard an impatient child pushing you on a crowded bus.[8]

At this point in the bullfight, a typical bullfighting book might tell you that you are watching the *suerte de varas,* and that the matador is performing a *quite* and in fact, doing a *capotazo,* or a *lance,* which is in the form of a *chicuelina,* but I would not be so cruel. So I wrote:

Come, said the glittering figure of the matador mutely, flaring the cape. *Come, please.* The bull whirled in bewilderment, then came galloping back. The man bowed his head and folded the cape around his body humbly, eyes downcast.[9]

I had come a long way from my first despairing meeting with Bea. I was no longer flailing about blindly. Slowly, in the random scatter of stars in the night sky, patterns began to form. I did not create them: they were there all along, waiting to be discovered. For the first time I saw constellations. Before, I had merely watched bullfights, but now I actually *saw* what was happening. There was a reason why there were two concentric circles in the sand, why the matador moved in an arc around the bull before placing the darts, why the bull had to orbit around him in ever-decreasing circles towards the centre. A gorgeous geometry was at work. I began to appreciate the frenetic vocabulary of the bull's movements, the mute sacrifice of the picador's horse, and the practical line of the picador's spear. The bulls, which at first seemed to me like brutish cattle, began to look beautiful. Time and again, I photographed the famous line of its muscled hump of back as it lowered its head to charge. It reminded me of John Ruskin's line about the Rialto: 'that strange curve, so delicate, so adamantine, strong as a mountain cavern, graceful as a bow just bent'.[10]

I was a writer, and a writer's first duty is to observe. As a guest in somebody else's country, I could not import my own customs. Instead, I listened humbly to an older world order. Even the rapid-fire of Spanish conversation began to make sense. 'She can't speak', said a Spanish friend proudly to his mates. 'But she understands. Don't say anything bad about her.'

In 2011, after the publication of *Alex y Robert,* I began writing *Novillera,* the sequel, and enrolled in a brief bullfighting class in Sevilla. The chance came for me to learn from an expert and to go before three small bulls (actually, females of the same fighting breed). I caped the first two cows gingerly and was completely useless with the third. There is a rather spectacular photograph of me catapulting through the air when she hit me. It has made the rounds on Facebook. This experience helped me to see that in *Alex y Robert* I was merely portraying the bullfight from the stands. Now I could bring the reader inside the bullring.

Bullfighting class taught me many useful things. The cows are thrillingly beautiful up close. They roar like dinosaurs. You never notice your wounds until you get home and take off your clothes. It takes twenty-four hours to feel the full impact of your bruises, and twelve days to heal from a horn scratch, which leaves a distinctive, scimitar-like scar. You will have no memory of being tossed, and if someone caught it on video, you will watch it afterwards and express surprise that so many people rushed to your rescue, for you did not notice them.

For days after, you brood over your mistakes. You imagine doing it again, of making it work properly; you think, *my left leg was in the wrong place, I should have directed the animal more to the right. My fear was irrational. I forgot everything I learned.* You begin to realize why matadors always say, whenever they are not in the ring, *I fight bulls in my head.* For the bull is not a piano or a bucket of golf balls, waiting there for you to practice whenever you want to. It is a live animal, it is expensive to purchase, and you only have a few precious moments to get it right in front of a large crowd of people. You have inherited the unique, collective anxiety that is shared by all bullfighters from time immemorial, whether they are beginner or professional. You have begun to dream of the bulls.

There is much in bullfighting that is introverted, psychological and muted. Your dealings with cattle are now mediated by a heavy sense of responsibility, of sobriety. You learn how to – absurd as it may seem – address the bull. During our lessons with the small cows, the rancher told us not to shout as fiercely as we had seen matadors do during bullfights. 'Remember, she is still a baby', he said, with a smile. 'So call her nicely, softly. Your cape is a lure, like a treat. Make her come towards you.' He demonstrated for us. With the cow, he was as gentle as a father to his child. He was very proud of his livestock. Whenever the cow knocked one of us to the ground, he would hurry in like an anxious parent trying to break up a fistfight. For all his kindness, I knew that at the end of the afternoon, if the young cow did not meet his requirements to breed fighting bulls, she would be sent to the slaughterhouse. After all, this was a working ranch, not an animal sanctuary. Every animal was kept for a commercial purpose. Each had a name, but none were pets. It was a world of moral ambiguity, of heartbreak and pity.

Twenty-four months ago, I packed for Spain grudgingly, convinced that I had nothing in common with a nation of square-jawed, macho men who enjoy killing bulls just to prove they are brave. Where I had expected cruelty, I found kindness; where I had dreaded rigidity, I discovered softness. I have shed, one by one, my prejudices. My feminine, Buddhist, Asian sensibility merged with one of the great tests of Western maleness, enabling me to create an entirely new kind of narrative. I am a scientist who has discovered a new element – every day I have to fend off sceptics and protect its right to existence. It has been a strange and wondrous journey.

Notes

1. C. Baker (1972) *Hemingway: The Writer as Artist*, 4th edn (Princeton: Princeton University Press), pp. 144–5.
2. W. Poon (2010) *Alex y Robert* (London: Salt), p. 286.
3. Y. Nobuyuki (1966) *Matsuo Basho: The Narrow Road to the Deep North and Other Travel Sketches* (London: Penguin Classics), p. 33.
4. E. Hemingway (1960) *Death in the Afternoon* (New York: Charles Scribner & Sons), p. 192.
5. Ibid., 127.
6. W. Poon (2010) *Alex y Robert* (London: Salt), p. 93.
7. Ibid., 235.
8. Ibid., 86.
9. Ibid., 87.
10. J. Ruskin (1891) *The Stones of Venice* (New York: Charles E. Merrill and Company), p. 60.

Part III
Voice and the Novel

9
Hearing Voices

Alison MacLeod

It's a strange thing to open the cover and turn the pages of my first novel *The Changeling*, a book I began writing 20 years ago. It's a big read that was written in a tiny room – just five feet by four – with one small window and a rickety blind. When I wasn't under the green, flickering spell of my Amstrad screen, I was staring at the bare wall. I favour the bare wall over the sublime view. I'm more easily transported, I suppose, and 'transport' is, for me, as vital as the dogged labour of novel-writing.

As I glance now at *The Changeling*'s lines, paragraphs and chapters, my feelings are a funny assortment of discomfort, relief and pride. I'm aware that the Alison MacLeod who wrote that novel is a different person than the Alison MacLeod who writes this essay, and who is in the final laps of her fourth book. As I re-read her novel, a part of myself thinks, gosh, I wonder how she did all this. Against every expectation, I'm impressed. But she is a sort of revenant now. I'm a different person, a different writer. My understanding of the form and my handling of it is more deft, more nuanced than hers, but equally, there are things that she could do that I cannot. She could write faster. She had a powerful dream life that she could readily tap. Imaginatively, her mind was almost without borders, although in life, she was more hemmed in than I am today. There is arguably greater bravura – greater *display* – in her novel than in the novel I am writing now, but hers is also hit-and-miss, as most first novels necessarily are. Today, I give my characters more opportunity to go deeper; I create more space for them, and I am no longer afraid – at least not most of the time – of the demands they, as characters, make of me as a writer.

Yet, one of the gifts the 26-year-old Alison MacLeod bequeathed me was an ability to trust, above all, in the voice of a novel and in the voices, or animate lives, of my characters. I don't think I've ever lost that trust.

'Voice', or the writer's dousing line to that semi-mysterious thing we call 'voice', is for me a primitive and essential gift. It is the unknown quantity every novel needs. Without it, a novel might be well developed and fluently composed, but the 'spirit' of the story will not have entered it. The story will never *surprise* us with the truth in the way that all living things do. And a novel, a good one, *is* a living thing. Its story is charged with the emotional, psychical and intellectual energies with which its maker has shaped it. As writers, those energies are ultimately all we have. The words might be our medium – our paint, clay or stone – but they're merely marks on the page until those life-giving energies breathe them into being. We might offer an impressively described view, or we might bring together a credible and interesting cast of characters. The story might be well drawn, in other words, but it won't *move*. Nor, without those energies, without that palpable sense of breath and voice, will it be able to *move us* – to tears, wonder, compassion or laughter. In this essay, I'd like to give you a greater sense of what it might mean when writers speak of 'voice', and 'the voice of the novel', in particular.

The Changeling, as a title, was inspired by the image of the 'strange child' or the changeling babe from Celtic folklore. The changeling is of course the fairy infant who is substituted for the beloved human baby, a baby whom the fairies, in all their cleverness, have spirited away to raise as their own. My novel is partly based on the story of a real-life figure who, like the 'strange babe', was both wayward and 'in-between'. Anne Bonny was born illegitimate in 1699, on the hinge of the eighteenth century, in a village outside Kinsale, Ireland. Her father was a small-time solicitor in Kinsale. Her mother was a housemaid. To protect all concerned from the scandal of her birth, she was raised as a boy, as her father's nephew, according to some accounts, or as his young clerk, according to others. When, however, her father decided his fate lay not in Ireland, but in the New World, Anne too was transplanted to South Carolina. In her teens, she was 'converted back' to female-ness and was presented to 'Society' as a young lady, but the conversion didn't take. In time, she was frequenting the Charleston harbour front, dressed once more as a boy, and soon, the dandy pirate Captain Jack Rackham would take a liking to her/him. Anne Bonny, history tells us, ran away to sea, joined his crew and became his lover – and perhaps the lover, too, of Mary Read, another cross-dressing woman sailor who would later join his crew. But who knows the truth of it all? In the shape of her life, one feels the full charge of the word 'story' lying in wait within the word 'history', like a lit stick of dynamite in a trusty perimeter wall. A few years later, in 1720, she would be sentenced to hang for piracy on the high seas, but would vanish from both the authorities and history before the sentence could be carried out. From that time on, she would slip between the pages of legend and history, ever elusive, and she would become, it seemed to me as I followed her, many things: heroine, female grotesque, debutante, bloodthirsty wench, 'sea-maid', lesbian threat, siren, spinster, pregnant woman and libertarian. I was tantalized.

My research, over three years or more, was intensive and wide ranging: Irish rural lore and old wives' tales; domestic arrangements for the Anglo-Irish middle classes and for the indigenous poor; early eighteenth-century British naval history and weaponry; slave-trade practices and slave rebellions; Irish, American and Caribbean period landscapes; pirate sub-culture and dialect; the invention of bedsprings. I am often entranced by the kaleidoscope-like process of research; by the details and historical contexts that offer, in turn, oblique, unexpected views on our own contemporary concerns. I love the gifts of facts I never could have invented. Finally, one distils the research down. The facts must be digested to sit naturally within the wider story. The story is the thing. And sometimes the story is something other than your plans or ambitions for it. It has its own wisdom.

All good writers have to rest easy with uncertainty, or with what Milan Kundera calls *'the wisdom of uncertainty'*.[1] Keats famously wrote of the significance of the state of 'Negative Capability',[2] while William James, the psychologist, philosopher and brother to Henry, called for the reinstatement of 'the vague', the ability to attend to and accommodate ideas that are only half formed.[3]

Research and 'the vague' collide, to dynamic effect, in the spaces or *gaps* between the recorded facts of any history. The gaps are the writer's lunar landing-strips; the places where he or she can plant the flag of the imagination; the lunatic point where the gravity of 'the known' gives way to invention. I had dreams at the time, dreams that seemed to 'fill in' for me the great chasms in my own experience or sympathies that almost stopped me daring to write Anne Bonny's story. They were dreams, very practical in their aid, that helped me to overcome my worries about elements of her biography in which I felt out of my depth. What was it like to carry within oneself such a history of violence? What was it like to be attracted to another woman? What did it feel like to be sentenced to death? One, two, three dreams. Brief but powerful, each. They gave me a vivid, if vicarious, sense of experience. I still worried, of course, that I might hit false notes, but at least I could now move forward and try to write her story.

It's in these gaps – gaps of research, gaps of experience – that the voices and *the voice* of one's novel can enter.

Let's talk about the 'voices' first, by which I mean the voices of our characters.

After a loved one dies, it's said that his or her voice is the hardest part of the person to summon in memory, and sadly, I think that's true. Similarly, in a historical or known factual account, the voices of its personages – their words, unique rhythms, phrases and verbal tics – are, it seems to me, the most absent. They are often the most profound 'gaps' in the official record. At a purely human level, I felt this absence keenly when I discovered, in the Public Record Office in London, the records of Anne Bonny and Mary Read's 1720 trial. Once it was revealed that two of Jack Rackham's crew were in fact women dressed as men, a separate trial was ordered for them, and it seems they were tried both for piracy *and* for their 'unnatural' assumption of male personae and a 'male' sense of agency.

I found the absence of both women's voices from their court record deeply moving. I could 'hear' their trial unfolding, the voices of witnesses and the judge, but neither Anne Bonny nor Mary Read had a voice in it. That lack or gap or silence would become another powerful source of inspiration for my creation of Anne – although, if I'm honest, I never absolutely felt that I 'got' her. She has great 'presence' as a character; she is also, by virtue of her history, stubbornly evasive. I wonder if, to remain true to her nature, a part of her had to exceed her author's grasp as well. Or perhaps I was too new a novelist to handle her vital contradictions. I'm not sure.

Instead, the narrative voice of the novel 'took over' from me, its author, and *revealed to me* Anne Bonny, my character, much as it now reveals Anne Bonny to my reader. Although the novel features, in a Russian-doll-like form, stories within stories and 'narrators within narratives', *the* true narrative voice of the novel is that of an Irish peasant woman called Annie Fulworth, a woman who is left with no choice but to adopt into her care the newborn, motherless Anne. To this day I cannot explain where Annie's steady but urgent voice came from. Not from any history. She arrived on the page, in between the gaps of history, with an invented life and a voice entirely her own as she began to find the words for Anne Bonny:

I pulled him from a sea of blood. I grabbed his small, straining shoulders and willed him into my hands...I weighed him in my arms:

healthy for eight months. I tried to begin again. I tried to forget the weight of Sally's legs, slack on my shoulders...I counted toes: ten. Fingers: ten, clenched and angry. As he wailed, I babbled above him, all the while searching for a mark on the face, for down on the spine, for a nub of a tail where only a tailbone should be. I found nothing – except a fold of soft flesh between two thrashing legs.

She was not the boy I had promised Sally...She had flouted all the signs. She had come true despite me.[4]

Annie's voice grows in power with the novel. Years later, in Charleston, after she herself has ended up on board the rotting vessel of Anne's getaway, she again describes for us the almost indescribable Anne:

[D]ay by day, week by week, Anne was changing too. Even as I faded, she was growing – ruder, heartier, comelier, longer, broader, more brazen; growing fleet of foot and flint-eyed, single-minded and hot-headed; growing larger than life itself. One moment, she'd be airborne in the rigging of the mizzen mast, and the next, she'd be tying knots like sleights of hand...Look again, and you'd find her on her back, dreaming new constellations into the night sky: the Four-Breasted Woman, Satan's Horns...the Pair of Crossed Eyes. The crew too would be flat out and face up on the unscrubbed salty deck, while Captain Cain altered his charts like a lost man.

We had put to sea and our bearings were gone.[5]

Annie's is a voice that announced itself to me and became mine. Or perhaps my voice became hers. Whatever the case, her words arrived with their own rich rhythm, a literary variation on my own perhaps, which I'm told has echoes of the Irish and Scottish cadences of recent generations of my family. (In my native Nova Scotia, my grandfather's grandmother, for example, only spoke Gaelic.) Interestingly, after publication, an elderly Irish woman reader living in England remarked to me that she was thrilled to discover phrases in *The Changeling* that she hadn't heard since her childhood in Ireland. She wondered how I'd come by them, while I hadn't known their provenance until then. Oral rhythms and idioms are a natural part of our literary DNA, and that's another gift for any writer.

But Annie Fulworth herself? Where did she come from? Where did the assurance of her voice come from? I have no idea. I was 26. She was a mature 'peasant' woman in her late thirties or early forties, and she knew infinitely more than I did. As Hilary Mantel has said: 'When you stand on the verge of a new narrative, when you have picked your character, you stretch out your hand in the dark and you don't know who or what will take it.'[6] Virginia Woolf wrote 'I think writing, my writing, is a species of mediumship. I become the person.'[7] Toni Morrison tells us that, for her, 'imagination is not merely looking, or looking at; nor is it taking oneself intact into the other. It is, for the purposes of the work, becoming'.[8]

I had been planning, I think, to write the novel mostly in the third-person voice, but Annie Fulworth's voice appeared on the page instead. Its strength, substance and knowing took me by surprise. Indeed it is arguable that Annie Fulworth upstages the main character of Anne in *The Changeling*. Anne is better spectacle, but Annie Fulworth has greater depth and perspective, and is a more reliable voice, even though she is uneducated in any formal sense.

The power of the storytelling voice and, also, the loss of one's voice are creative preoccupations of mine, and they direct both plot and structure in *The Changeling* at various points. In the course of it, I became a 'medium', to draw on Woolf's image, for many voices, all distinct from my own. As writers sometimes say, in what is perhaps a confounding declaration, I *hear* voices. *The Independent*'s reviewer noted the multi-voiced quality of *The Changeling*, and I liked her unconventional choice of verb: 'In true 18th-century style, [*The Changeling*] readily admits of other voices. Rumours, reports and old wives' tales jostle the narrator for space.'[9] *Admits*. Yes. One opens a door.

Oddly enough, I am perhaps most proud of the voice of a minor character, Virginia Lazarus, a character who came to me, seemingly, unbidden through that door. I am most proud, I think, because her life lies at the greatest distance from my own. There is every reason why I shouldn't have let myself 'write' this character. She is a very old woman and a former slave in Jamaica. As soon as she appeared, I was aware of issues of authenticity and cultural appropriation. Still, she wouldn't go. I let her pull up a chair. I did the research I needed to 'focus' her; I took care of her with every skill I had. I investigated the rhythms of her voice and the phonetics of her words. But ultimately, I trusted in the story that had brought her to life. To a very ill Annie Fulworth she says:

Staystay. I come ta de girl-boy. Dey get you on a donkey, don ask me how, an bring you here. She vex datJack for yu, and a good ting too. Everyone know wit shore folk it's each man for herself, which is why I live in de wood. Salt water creep into dey lungs at night like obeah and mek dem crazy. Lok, dere it is even now, splashin down yu whitey cheeks. Yu has a whole sea inside you, by now, womun. What yu see, eh, troo yu tears? A ol-ol woman wit a face black an fuzzy as a coco-nut shell. Yes, so old, she should be long-gone dead.[10]

But beyond *The Changeling*'s many 'speaking' voices is that mystery still: the voice *of the novel*. Is there such a thing? If so, what on earth is it? And what do writers mean by the phrase?

On Facebook recently, novelist Gerard Woodward posted this status: 'got the feeling that on the eighth draft of my novel I'm just beginning to find the right voice for it – but maybe not, still early days'.[11] Just beginning? On his eighth draft? You might well despair. It's a common story. Later he writes: 'novel getting so long and complicated every time I sit down to write it feels as though something is punching me in the face'.[12] On a good day, voices might arrive unexpectedly, but mostly, the discovery of the voice or life of one's novel demands resilience. I dig and excavate, write and re-write – I put a wrecking ball through the first 70 or 100 pages several times over – until I think, finally, that's it, that's it, I can hear it now, *my novel*.

The voice of one's novel is something like its tone, I suppose, but that word, for me, seems too inert, flat or one-note. What we're talking about here is the life of the book, enfolded in the *body* of its sounds, pauses and rhythms. That's how we feel its urgency (no matter how restrained the narrative style). That's how we feel its need to be told.

For *The Changeling*, THE voice, I eventually realized, needed both lilt and ballast; musicality and weight; the spell of the sensuous and the sharpness of grit. Although I couldn't explain it early in the writing process, that particular combination of aural qualities would suggest to the reader, through Annie Fulworth's voice, a deep wellspring of a story-telling tradition, one of yarns, legends and superstitions. It's also from this welter of tales and reports that Anne Bonny is all but literally born: half-human and half-invention; half-girl and half-chimera. The reader, I think, comes to believe in her birth 'from story', not only because of the events that unfold at the level of plot, but also because of the particular 'chemistry' *of sounds* in the prose itself.

In *Why I Write*, George Orwell notes his 'Pleasure in the impact of one sound on the other.'[13] Yet it can't be forced. One, it seems, can only wait, 'dig', re-write and listen out for it with a good ear. Sebastian Barry wrote the opening four paragraphs to *The Secret Scripture* in 2003. They sat alone until 2005 when he managed a little more of the opening chapter. Yet, it would be nearly the close of 2006 before he would 'see and hear the book, and so write it'.[14] The key, as he describes it, was the sound of those first paragraphs, which he knew was the 'herald' of the novel itself (or what Ben Okri has called the 'inner signature'[15] of a piece). Barry writes: 'But those paragraphs were at least a herald, a coin in the bank, and I suppose contained something of the whistle-tune, the bird-song of the book.'[16]

Of course it might not always be the best idea to wait three years until one hears the 'tune' or voice or signature-sound of one's novel, even though that sound is ultimately the body or the vessel for everything else within the novel. When I'm conscious that I can't hit the notes or find the novel's sound in a given chapter, I try not to stop writing. I tell myself that it will come; that I simply need to attend to the story for a time, forget about the question of voice, and wait until a truer version of it comes of its own accord into the given chapter. I tell myself simply to write the story journalistically – describing who, what, where, when, how – and to trust in that form of writing for a time until the 'voice' returns. You forget the pressure, but you remain willing to be surprised. You attend. You keep an ear out. You have to be receptive to the briefest of notes or to a fleeting bar. When you hear it, you write your way towards the sound as quickly and precisely as you can.

The power of an assured voice in our ear is an intangible force. It's seductive. It's an incantation. It's immediate and direct. It holds us like nothing else can. 'The ear does it', says Robert Frost. 'The ear is the only true writer and the only true reader.'[17] Unlike many novelists, I have to write my chapters in the order in which they will eventually appear, not out of any dedication to chronology or plot-logic as such, but because only in this way can I *hear* the rise and fall of the novel's voice/music. In some way, the final notes of one chapter's concluding lines prompt the sound – and with it the voice and the words – of the next chapter's opening lines. I don't know how I'd get there if I wrote in discontinuous sections, although I envy novelists who can work in this way. I need that thread of the voice, breath, music, beat and sound to guide me, just as I rely on the almost physical pressure of one chapter's events to yield the next.

For me, Paul Auster comes as close as any writer can to describing the seemingly airy force that is the voice of a novel:

> Writing is physical for me. I always have the sense that the words are coming out of my body, not just my mind...So much of the effort that goes into writing prose is about making the sentences that

capture the music that I'm writing in my head. It takes a lot of work, writing, writing, writing, and rewriting to get the music exactly the way you want it to be. That music is a physical force. Not only do you write books physically, but you read books physically as well. There's something about the rhythms of language that correspond to the rhythms of our own bodies. An attentive reader is finding meanings in the book that can't be articulated, finding them in his or her body. I think this is what so many people don't understand about fiction.[18]

It's mysterious, yes, but the voice-and-music of one's own novel, when it comes, when we hear it, is as familiar as our own heartbeat. It's as vital. As sure. After the labour of so much writing and digging, it moves, like a current of sound waves, ions and breath, from your heart and lungs, down your arm, and through your fingertips. It makes everything else possible.

Notes

1. M. Kundera (1986) *The Art of the Novel*, 2nd edn (New York: Harper Collins), p. 7.
2. 'I mean *Negative Capability*, that is, when a man is capable of being in uncertainties, mysteries, doubts, without any irritable reaching after fact and reason'; J. Keats (1899) *Letter to George and Thomas Keats: Dec. 22, 1817; The Complete Poetical Works and Letters of John Keats*, Cambridge edn (Boston and New York: Houghton Mifflin Company), p. 277.
3. W. J. Gavin (1992) *William James and the Reinstatement of the Vague* (Philadelphia: Temple University Press).
4. A. MacLeod (1996) *The Changeling* (London: Macmillan), pp. 3–4.
5. Ibid., 133.
6. H. Mantel (28 July 2007) 'Ghost Writing', *The Guardian*, www.guardian.co.uk/books/2007/jul/28/edinburghfestival2007.poetry
7. A. Olivier Bell and A. McNeillie (eds) (1985) *The Diary of Virginia Woolf, Vol. 5, 1936–1941* (London: Penguin), p. 101.
8. T. Morrison (1992) *Playing in the Dark: Whiteness and the Literary Imagination* (Cambridge, MA: Harvard University Press), p. 4.
9. M. Denes (6 April 1996) 'A swagger, a wink and a tomcat's daughter', *The Independent*.
10. A. MacLeod (1996) *The Changeling* (London: Macmillan), pp. 175–6.
11. G. Woodward (20 July 2011), status update, Facebook profile.
12. Ibid. (14 September 2011).
13. G. Orwell (1946) *Why I Write* (London: Penguin), p. 5.
14. S. Barry (11 October 2008) 'Barry on Barry' in 'As our ancestors hide in our DNA, so do their stories', *The Guardian*:www.guardian.co.uk/books/2008/oct/11/sebastian-barrybooker-prize

15. B. Okri (September 2010) The International Small Wonder Short Story Festival.
16. S. Barry (11 October 2008) 'Barry on Barry' in 'As our ancestors hide in our DNA, so do their stories', *The Guardian*:www.guardian.co.uk/books/2008/oct/11/sebastian-barrybooker-prize.
17. R. Frost (1991) cited in 'Frost's Dramatic Principle of "Oversound" ' by Tom Vander Ven, in E. Harrison Cady and L. J. Budd (eds) *On Frost* (Durham, NC: Duke University Press), p. 88.
18. P. Auster (2005) 'Jonathan Lethem Talks with Paul Auster' in V. Vida (ed.) *Believer Book of Writers Talking to Writers* (San Francisco: Believer Books), p. 27.

10
'This Won't Do': *Pig* and the Temptation of Silence

Andrew Cowan

I've published five novels now, most recently *Worthless Men*, and it strikes me that each of these novels is a renewed attempt to solve the problem of how to write a novel. The fifth has been no less difficult to write than the first. And in fact, were the process to become any less difficult I think I might begin to suspect myself of complacency and the work of being formulaic, inauthentic, 'unearned'. Which isn't such an unusual scruple. In the words of W. G. Sebald, 'The process of writing is a constant battle against the temptation of saying, "This will do and I will hurry on to the next scene because this one will do." Nothing ever does do.'[1]

Clearly this is to describe – and perhaps even slyly to advocate – an aesthetics of the impossible. And there is good and bad in this. Such an exacting degree of writerly vigilance can offer some guarantee of a work's quality: the more we doubt it, the more we will attend to it, and the better we may be able to make it. But such scrupulousness can equally lead to a kind of stasis or inertia. The work may become stagnant, all the life – all the oxygen – squeezed out of it.

In my own case, the battle is not so much against the temptation of hurrying on, but against the temptation of staying still. It's a battle against saying, 'This won't do and I refuse to move on to the next scene until I get it just right, because this one won't do.' Yet as Sebald observes, 'Nothing ever does do', and so the attempt to give voice to my novels becomes, at its worst, a struggle to resist the self-sabotaging impulse to silence myself.

This impulse is born out of fear, of course, and the simplest way to characterize that is to say it's a fear of failure. More complicatedly, I would say it's a fear of the language, and a fear of the anxiety that grips me whenever I presume to place myself in a position of authority over the language. Ultimately it's a fear of my reader, which is to say, a fear of being found wanting or of being found out – that is, exposed as an imposter, as someone who writes plausible facsimiles of novels, but isn't able to achieve the 'real thing'. And my customary defence against this fear is perfectionism, which is self-defeating because perfectionism can't allow for the contingent, the accidental or serendipitous, for the possibility of self-surprise; it can't allow for any of those qualities that make art alive. In other words, perfectionism is anti-creative and leads to the very thing I most fear: the novel that merely resembles a novel, that isn't the real thing, that isn't after all 'perfect'.

I've described something of the slowness of the writing that results from this double bind in a non-fiction book, *The Art of Writing Fiction*:

> Ever since school, and whatever the form – whether poem, short story or essay – my habitual method has been to begin with minimal preparation (rough notes seeming altogether too rough, too messy) and to proceed strictly from the beginning, painstakingly building one slow sentence upon another, until finally, eventually, I arrive at the last sentence and can declare my job done, no further revision required, no overhaul possible.

> The assumption underlying this approach is 'first thought, worst thought', and the consequence is that I will feel compelled to rewrite each line I put down, and to continue rewriting that line until I feel certain – in [Julia] Cameron's words – that it is 'final, perfect, set in stone'.[2] Only then will I be able to move on to my next line. Except that the rhythm or sense of the next line will inevitably require me to go back and re-revise the previous line, and the one before that. And though I will, eventually, achieve a paragraph in this manner, every subsequent paragraph will require me to comb back through the previous paragraphs, just as every additional page will require me to refine every previous page. More agonising still, just as this method requires me to make judgements based on the rhythm and sense of everything that has preceded the current sentence, it also requires me to anticipate the sense and rhythm of everything that is still to come, which I would rather hold in my head than commit to the page, however sketchily, however provisionally.[3]

In the case of my first novel *Pig* – much of which was written on a typewriter – the laboriousness of this approach was exacerbated by a possibly lunatic refusal to tolerate any mess or marks on the page. Should I mistype a word, or wish to insert a missing comma, or decide to rephrase a sentence, I would rip out that page and type it again. And while I found this time-consuming task of re-typing in some ways soothing – it was a mechanical, largely thoughtless activity that at least *resembled* writing – I found the act of composition to be quite the opposite: arduous, draining, frequently defeating. I abandoned my first novel repeatedly – on one occasion for nine months – and no matter how far advanced it became, no matter how many pages I had accumulated, each time I returned to it I would feel obliged to re-type every word from the start.

There is arguably some method in this madness, for if the biggest challenge in writing a first novel – or *any* novel – is to achieve a consistent and singular narrative voice, this process of perpetual revision and repetition helped maintain in my mind a sense of the shape and flow of my sentences as well as my story. It allowed me to arrive at a certain regularity of style and cadence and – because I was scrutinizing the pages so closely – a clarity of expression that might not have been possible had I been inclined to write more freely. Although the process was fraught, the end product appeared to be its vindication.

Unsurprisingly, *Pig* took a long time to write: six years for fewer than 60,000 words, which included almost a year of anxious prevarication before I wrote the first sentence, as I know from some diaries I kept in my mid-twenties. Here is an entry from August 1986:

> Got up with good intentions. Had no money anyway, but still ended up smoking yesterday's butts. Later bought a pack of 20 with our food money. Meanwhile, reading *A Room With a View*, which Forster started when he was 21 and published at 29. Depressing. I keep worrying over the pig novel, how I'll ever find the time, if I could ever write it anyway, what tone it should take, and could realism sustain the pig at its centre?

I finally began writing in May 1987, by the end of which year I had made 13 unsuccessful attempts to stop smoking and completed precisely 12 pages of my novel. Four years later I was still smoking, and had amassed 124 pages. Three factors then helped me to accelerate: I became a father, which required me to be far less wasteful of what little writing time was available to me; I acquired my first computer, which eliminated the need for re-typing, and gave my prose the irreproachable appearance on screen of a published work; and I realized that I'd produced one half of a plausible novel, which persuaded me I might plausibly produce the other half.

The exact circumstances will vary, but this has remained the pattern with each of my books: achieving the first page may take weeks, even months; the final page can be written in a matter of hours. Yet however halting my progress, the problem is rarely to do with the story. Even as I was forlornly comparing myself to E. M. Forster, for instance, I still had a clear sense of what would happen in *Pig* – from beginning to end – and my preliminary research amounted to just two sides of A4 (some notes on keeping pigs and a calendar of the gardener's year). I was after all writing about what I knew: the places, the people, and what the critic Raymond Williams has termed their 'structures of feeling'.[4] The choice of a first-person narrator – a choice I wasn't conscious of making; it seemed so natural – was the inevitable outcome of this. The narrator Danny was never a 'he', separate from me. He could only ever be an 'I'.

But while I remained sure of my narrator, and of my story, this close- ness to the material was also in some ways a hindrance. Throughout the writing of *Pig* my insecurities centred on the language – on the day-to-day technicalities of how to construct sentences and maintain a consistency of tone – but these insecurities were compounded by feel- ings of ambivalence, for in order to write about the place I came from – the town, the social class – I first needed to be educated out of it, and so the act of writing about it would always entail the possibility of betrayal, of adopting a voice that was not mine (and therefore not Danny's), a voice that was merely an imitation of what I thought a novel ought to sound like. The issue, in part, was one of authenticity. But it was equally one of self-belief, for in some deep-seated way I did not feel entitled to assume the authority of authorship. People like me did not write books. The language, like the literary canon, was already owned: it was somebody else's property and to write was to trespass.

Another short passage from *The Art of Writing Fiction* may help to explain this:

> I should say that my background is not at all bookish. Not only did I not come across anyone in my childhood who wrote books, I knew hardly anyone who bought or borrowed or read books either. And although I did well in the English classroom, and often lost myself in the novels I was required to study, it was rare that I recognised much in those books that chimed with my own experience, or encouraged me to believe that the world I knew might be depicted in a book,

much less a book that people like me might be required to study (much less a book that I might myself write).[5]

Of course, I did have antecedents; I realize that now. Numerous other novelists had trespassed before me, principal among them being the English provincial realists of the late 1950s and early 1960s, in particular John Braine, Alan Sillitoe, Stan Barstow, David Storey, Sid Chaplin and (from a slightly later period) Barry Hines.

Interestingly – even crucially – each of their first novels depicts the textures and fixtures of working-class culture as seen from the inside (albeit from a highly gender-conditioned perspective). The communities the books describe are confidently assumed to be 'knowable', though not quite in the way that the whole world was assumed to be 'knowable' by the realists of the nineteenth century. Typically (though not always) they insist on a first-person narrator – on a narrator as a participant in the events described – because, I suspect, they haven't the confidence to sustain a view of a whole society. They can't represent an entire world in a way that is cohesive and all-encompassing; they can't assume the authority of omniscience. And this is *because* their books are written from inside the cultures they describe. Their strength is also their great limitation; their limitation is also their great strength.

Such an assessment might fairly be made of *Pig*, too, which likewise strives to give voice to a sensibility and range of experience not often represented in literary fiction. But whereas these earlier novelists (Hines perhaps excepted) are writing at a time of increasing affluence and social mobility – and derive great vernacular energy from their depiction of a society becoming more prosperous and permissive – the first-person voice of *Pig* is more cautious and more pessimistic. It's conditioned by two decades of economic and industrial decline, and while the novel does contain a confident vernacular voice, this voice belongs to the past and is expressed through the reminiscences of the narrator's grandfather. It's contained in quote marks. The dominant tone is both more subdued and more lyrical; the dominant mood is one coloured by the experience of absence and loss.

The autobiographical aspect of *Pig* is undeniable, though complex, and while it's mostly true to say that 'any resemblance to real persons, living or dead, is purely coincidental' (the exceptions are the important ones, including the grandfather), the town in which it takes place is straightforwardly modelled on Corby, where I was born and grew up. A Glaswegian colony in the heart of England, Corby was created in the 1930s by a half-Scottish company called Stewarts & Lloyds, which discovered iron ore and built not only a steelworks but the housing in which the workforce would live, most of them immigrants from Glasgow, brought south by the company.

There were other immigrants, too. Briefly in fact Corby was one of the most multicultural towns in Britain: 27 nationalities were represented in the population, though in practice this actually meant a couple here from Slovenia, a few there from Poland, a small number of Yugoslavs, Hungarians, Ukranians.... Many of these were Jews, 'Displaced Persons' from the war. But in essence Corby was white and working class and Glaswegian. It was *mono*cultural, a company town that became a New Town, whose hinterland wasn't rural Northamptonshire, not quite, but the tenemented streets of the Gorbals and Govan, Parkhead and Ibrox. Corby's river, to many who lived there, wasn't the Nene or the Welland, but still the industrial Clyde.

One unfortunate inheritance from Glasgow was the simmering sectarian division between Catholic and Protestant, but it remained a relatively stable, cohesive community in which almost everyone lived in a council house and nearly every child attended a state comprehensive, almost everyone's father belonged to a union and nearly everyone's parents voted Labour. And then came Thatcherism, and monetarism, and denationalization, and the reform of trades union law, and the sale of council housing, and the fetishization of 'market forces', and – in Corby – the closure of the town's major employer. The result was a situation in which thousands were idle, yet living in a house that was unarguably theirs, though unsellable in a town that had no industry and little prospect of secure employment and in which the public spaces and remaining public housing were becoming run-down, visibly neglected, sometimes abandoned.

Corby steelworks was dismantled and the derelict site earmarked for the construction of a theme park called Wonderworld, which was intended to include a miniaturized mock-up of a steelworks, employing former steelworkers as actors, and for a number of years – on several approach roads into the town – visitors would be greeted by advertising hoardings erected on patches of wasteland announcing 'Welcome to WonderWorld!'

In this last detail, if nothing else, the story of Corby clearly offers itself to the possibilities of satire, or the absurdist ironies of a dystopian, even fantastical post-modernism. And in fact it was just these possibilities that I was considering when I asked myself in my diary 'what tone it should take, and could realism sustain the pig at its centre?' My university education had in some ways persuaded me that the conventions of realism were anachronistic and inadequate in a post-colonial, post-industrial, post-imperial, post-modern, post-structuralist age. And yet the most obvious thing to say about *Pig* is that it is not linguistically inventive or experimental; it is not formally playful or 'ludic'. Its commitment is to a style in which every sentence is constructed to the measure of every other. The rhythm and symbolic frame of the whole takes precedence over the individual sentence. And this is indicative, I think, of an attachment to an undemonstrative ideal of plain speaking that derives from my upbringing. It is also a recognition that the only authentic voice for *Pig* is one that registers something of the exhaustion of the world it describes; a more exuberant voice would be inappropriate or untruthful, lacking in what Virginia Woolf might call 'integrity'.[6]

And so the novel depicts, in often quotidian detail, a town of run-down council estates surrounded by a post-industrial landscape, where the only hope of regeneration comes in the form of a theme park called Leisureland and where the cohesiveness of the community – the white working-class community – has broken down. There is a retreat into family that is entirely defensive, and embattled, and belligerent. And it's in the guise of family loyalty that the narrator's parents and brother object to the idea of Asians living next door to them.

The narrator Danny is still in school, aged 15. But whereas the reforms of the 1960s had held out the promise of social advancement through education – a common theme in the realist novels of that period – Danny is already disillusioned and unmotivated and beginning to look backwards, beyond the failures of his parents' generation to the lessons to be learnt from his grandparents. In them he identifies all the nostalgically remembered virtues of a mutually supportive, self-dependent community, which includes the idea of stable marriage premised on fixed gender roles, which is something he half-heartedly attempts to recreate with his secret Indian girlfriend, Surinder.

This imagining of a harmonious past finds its key symbol in the keeping of pigs, which would be fed on scraps from the neighbours' tables and on the homegrown produce of the land, then slaughtered according to natural cycles, the meat being shared out among the neighbours. And if Surinder is somewhat sceptical about all of this, that's because she is a more diligent student of history than Danny. Her fascination with the poverty of the Victorian and Edwardian eras enables her to piece together an identity that is in some ways superior to the past. In amassing her knowledge of what's gone before, she is equipping herself to go beyond it, and her great advantage may be that she has no roots in this community. For Danny's family, busily forgetting their roots, this would be an impoverishment; for Surinder it might actually be an opportunity. A lack of historical ties means that she is free, whereas Danny's emotional attachment to his grandparents' cottage, and to what it represents, is perhaps what will doom him.

Among my many anxieties while writing *Pig* was that my own attachment to the virtues of literary realism might be what doomed my novel. The question of 'what tone it should take' was persistent, and even as I resisted the temptation to experiment with a more satirical, ironical or metafictional voice, my uncertainties about realism found a ready response in my insecurities about the idea of myself as a writer.

If the dominant mood in *Pig* is, as I've suggested, one coloured by the experience of absence and loss there are in fact three absences it attempts to address, three losses it wants to commemorate. The first concerns Corby, and my wish both to honour the place it used to be while registering something of my regret at what it had become. Entangled with this was a desire to examine the emergence in England of a racism that seemed symptomatic of a fracturing society, while also acknowledging something of the generosity of spirit that persisted in places like Corby. The other two losses were more personal, meanwhile: the death of my grandfather and the end of a relationship with someone not unlike Surinder. The challenge then was to mourn a loss without being mournful, to recall a relationship without becoming maudlin, and to achieve both within the linguistic and emotional range of a 15-year old boy, albeit an intelligent, sensitive boy.

It is, then, no surprise that I came so often to feel like the narrator of Paul Auster's novel *Leviathan*, who says:

> I have always been a plodder, a person who anguishes and struggles over each sentence, and even on my best days I do no more than inch along, crawling on my belly like a man lost in the desert. The smallest word is surrounded by acres of silence for me, and even after I manage to get that word down on the page, it seems to sit there like a mirage, a speck of doubt glimmering in the sand. Language has never been accessible to me in the way that it was for Sachs [his friend]. I'm shut off from my own thoughts, trapped in a no-man's-land between feeling and articulation.[7]

For every 'plodder' there will be a particular explanation, a unique set of causes. No doubt in my own case there are many reasons for my slowness, some entirely unrelated to class or the psychology of entitlement. I have by now been 'trespassing' in the language long enough to have gained some sense of my freedom to roam, and yet I continue to struggle; I remain a plodder. Circumstances will vary, but for each of us, the effort to achieve a plausible narrative voice, and then to maintain that voice across the daunting, desert-like expanse of a novel, will be the effort to emerge from the no-man's-land between feeling and articulation. And it *is* an effort. Even if it does not involve crawling in the sand, we should expect it to be an effort – firstly to find the words that will crowd out the silence of the page, and then to resist the temptation of saying 'this will do', and the yet more insidious temptation of saying 'it won't do, nothing will ever do'.

Notes

1. C. Bigsby (ed.) (2001) *Writers in Conversation: Volume Two* (Norwich: Arthur Miller Centre for American Studies), p. 158.
2. J. Cameron (1995) *The Artist's Way* (Basingstoke: Pan Macmillan), p. 120.
3. A. Cowan (2011) *The Art of Writing Fiction* (Harlow: Pearson), p. 46.
4. R. Williams (1977) *Marxism and Literature* (London: OUP), Ch. 9.
5. A. Cowan (2011) *The Art of Writing Fiction* (Harlow: Pearson), p. 58.
6. V. Woolf (1977) *A Room of One's Own* (London: Grafton), p. 69.
7. P. Auster (1993) *Leviathan* (London: Faber & Faber), p. 49.

11
Knots and Narrative

Jane Rusbridge

When I began writing *The Devil's Music*, there were fewer than ten short stories to my name, plus a slightly larger number of poems. Although already in my early forties, I was a beginner, a late starter filled with euphoria at discovering my writer's 'voice'. It was all new. As I will explore here, issues of 'voice' were to preoccupy me throughout the writing of my first novel, but the process began, quite simply, with two related issues: my strong reaction to one voice and the absence of another.

For me, *The Devil's Music* is 'about' Andy, a little boy whose character sprang, pretty much fully formed, from a case-study extract I chanced upon in the library which outlined the Squiggle Game, a test used by the psychologist D. W. Winnicott in the 1950/60s. One boy had responded by turning seven out of ten line drawings into objects related to string: a lasso, two whips, two crops, a yo-yo string, and a knot. I could see this little boy, his head bent to a ball of string as he tied together cushions and toys, door handles and the legs of chairs; even weeks later his image haunted me. Curiosity drove me back to the library to read the full paper, 'String: A Technique of Communication'.[1]

Winnicott states that the boy's preoccupation with string is a response to a denial of separation from the mother which 'could grow into a perversion'. The diagnosis was a shock. Delivered in the authoritarian voice of a doctor, as if unarguable, it slammed a door on questions which had drawn me to the boy; questions about the power of the imagination to create a reality more potent than 'real' life. In retrospect, I see that Andy was already 'real' in my imagination. I was possessive and protective of the child whose love of working knots I believed to be crucial, in some way and for some reason, to his survival. Moreover, the boy's voice was missing: where was his point of view? All this had me needled.

When I read the case study now, it's strange to recall the fury which drove me to interrogate Winnicott's text. I was determined to open up spaces for alternative interpretations: why might a little boy turn a line into a lasso, or a whip? Did he watch the cowboy and Indian films I'd loved as a child in the 1960s? Did he want to be a cowboy? I wrote my very first sentences: 'I wore my cowboy outfit when they took me to the clinic: waistcoat, chaps, bandanna, holster. The Lone Ranger galloped and hollered through my head.'[2]

I picked apart Winnicott's language. The boy's fascination with string is labelled a 'preoccupation', from the Latin *occupare*, 'to seize'. Also a traditional nautical term, I discovered 'to seize' means to fasten or attach by binding with turns of yarn. Seizings are used to secure together two parts of a rope so that neither will give nor slip when under strain. If seizings make safe a join, might not a mental 'preoccupation' perform a similarly protective function for a mind under strain, rather than turning into perversion? This is what I wanted for 'my' little boy, Andy. I wanted him to be safe.

The Devil's Music explores what happens to a family faced with the question of what to do when the youngest child, Elaine, is born in 1958 with severe disabilities, and is destined to remain forever mute and as helpless as a baby. The novel weaves between two time strands: the late 1950s/early 1960s, narrated by Andy and his mother; and the 1990s, narrated by Andy as an adult, now called Andrew.

The novel opens with Andrew begin called home by his other sister, Susie, after their father's death. She wants help to find their mother, who disappeared when they were children. Andrew is a drifter, a loner who avoids responsibilities and commitments. After 30 years of self-imposed exile he returns to The Siding, the family's seaside holiday home where, as a child of nine, he was left in charge of baby Elaine with seemingly tragic consequences. Now, Andrew is forced to face the past that he has spent his adult life trying to escape, which include memories of guarding Elaine's cot each night after overhearing his parents argue about sending her away. Refuge from his mother's grief and his father's bullying came from time spent with his grandfather, Grampy, who called him '*My Treasure*'. Grampy recounted stories of the great escapologist, Harry Houdini, while teaching him how to work knots; knowledge which was to remain one of the few constants in Andrew's life.[3]

Research into rope and knots made me aware of everyday phrases which link story-telling and rope-making, for example 'to spin a yarn', 'to tie up loose ends', a 'twist in the tale', narrative 'strands' and even the 'line' of words on a page. This influenced the way the novel as a whole emerged, strand by strand, one voice at a time. The narrative is not chronological, but loops and crosses between the two eras and three voices. Reviewers note the novel's 'texture', the rope-like form with, at its core, 'the mind's interpretation of events and the impact of that internal reality on how a life is lived'.[4]

From the start I was looking for the right way to tell *this* story, to find a good fit between form and content. Bringing the three voices together involved much experimentation, with constant reconsideration of where to place each narrator in relation to the others, and the consequent effect on tension and reader empathy. My starting point, however, was straightforward. I began with one voice, the one missing from Winnicott's case study: the little boy's.

Andy, the child's voice

I had no ending in mind. No starting point, even. I wrote into darkness, the plot concealed within characters as yet not fully imagined. Freedom to write into the unknown can be frightening but also exhilarating; I find the chaos of this part of the process essential to allow the 'wild mind', as Natalie Goldberg describes it, the freedom to range. As I wrote, the secrets of Andy's story were uncovered, as if by accident, through the combined acts of writing and research.

Rudyard Kipling advises writers to 'Drift, wait, obey.'[5] I drifted; waited. There were weeks, months sometimes, when life intervened and I didn't write anything, but I slowly amassed, over a year or so, several thousand words in the form of notes and random scenes, mostly set on an English beach similar to those I knew in childhood, and close to where I now live. The choice of setting so early on was probably because the seascape provided something familiar in this unfamiliar process, something I *did* know. As I wrote, I began to understand how the difficulties of Andy's home-life set him apart from his peers. His father, a character partly inspired by Winnicott's authoritative voice, is a consultant, used to giving orders and being obeyed, both at the hospital and in the patriarchal 1950s home. A somewhat solitary child, Andy develops a close sensory relationship with his surroundings, especially at The Siding, the family's seaside holiday home, where he is free from his father's rules and restrictions:

The sky is huge and high, up from the sand and up from the sea. Wind and sky rush in my ears. I can breathe in whole sky. I run, stop, fill myself up with sky to the very top until I am full and fat like a balloon. Then I shout it out. Susie copies. We can shout at the tops of our voices and still the sand and sky go on being big and flat and happy.[6]

Aware of the dangers of allowing a child's voice to grow 'cute' or 'twee', I pushed Andy's point of view towards a more poetic language where possible ('Father is burning our dreaming waves'[7]). His synaesthesia and acute awareness of texture and colour enabled me to manipulate the power of suggestion through imagery, and to enrich his voice with metaphor ('The vicar's voice is old and stony, like the walls'[8]). The delight in words common to young children gave me the opportunity to 'play' with language. ('It's like being in a whale's belly. Like Jonah. Belly is a wobbly word.'[9])

This was the first time I'd written a child's voice, but I was aware of the buoyancy and tension – sometimes humorous, sometimes poignant – which arises from the difference between a child's misinterpretations of the adult world and a reader's perception. At times, Andy's understanding is very literal. When his grandfather says Elaine is 'not quite all here',[10] Andy believes this means a part of Elaine is elsewhere, perhaps even dead like Granny. He is terrified Elaine will disappear completely which, eventually, she does, the phrase foreshadowing events which were to become the core of the narrative. This only became clear once I was about 60,000 words in, searching amongst a mass of random scenes for a thread of cause-and-event. Everything came together in a heated rush of excitement, an experience Aminatta Forna describes as the 'perfect storm':[11] I knew Elaine was the key to unlock the plot.

Andy's special name for Elaine is 'Jelly'. Being mute, Jelly has no voice at all in the novel, but her character – fluid and ghostly – is central to the tension which holds the combined narratives together. In an era when disability was largely hidden, the instability in the family arising from Jelly's birth sparks Andy's interest in the steadfast knots on which he comes to rely, and fuels his sometimes dangerous identification with Houdini. When Elaine is sent away, Andy hears 'The Voice' he has longed to hear. It is 'The Voice' Houdini listened for, to tell him when to jump, and is the voice which, at last, enables Andy to express clear defiance against his father:

'*Now!*' The Voice says.
I breathe very deep into my lungs, and I am
HOUDINI THE HANDCUFF KING!
I can bend over backwards and pick up pins with my eyelashes.

I'm in the hallway, almost at the kitchen door.
'*Now!*' The Voice says, '*Now!*'
(. . .) I pull open the door of the cupboard under the stairs
    and climb inside, shutting the door behind me.
Straight away, Father opens it again. My eyes are screwed up tight,
    my arms around my knees.
'A word with you, young man, Out!'
I screw my eyes tighter, press my fingers to my eyelids. The Voice
    is fading.
'Do you hear me? Out!'
Rolling over, hands flat over my ears to get rid of HIS voice, I curl
    into a ball.
Father grunts. His hand grips my arm, my ankle, pulling at me.
'Do as you're told, Andrew!'[12]

If Andy's passion for knots was to keep him safe from mental breakdown, I needed to know about the adult he became. Once several
thousand words were written in the child's voice, I tried some scenes
from the adult perspective, but Andrew's head was impenetrable. I could
not find a way in. In the meantime, Andy's story had grown beyond the
scope of the child's viewpoint, and it felt natural to shift to the mother's
story, already beginning to show its shape in Andy's awareness of her
grief:

Mummy is lying on her side on the counterpane. I can only see her
back. She has all her clothes on except her shoes. She does not move.
The black shiny phone by the bed begins to ring. It rings and rings.
I look at Mummy's back. The round bottoms of her toes are squashed
in the stockings.[13]

In order to write myself into the heart of Andrew's character both 1950s
strands of the novel had to be written; the mother's and the child's
perspectives had to be seen. A view of the novel's direction gradually
became clear, but not its structure. To counteract my sense of wandering about lost, I read one or two 'how to' books for suggestions on how
to plot. The detailed advice given in Raymond Obstfeld's *Crafting Scenes*
was helpful. He calls the method 'aerial mapping', a 'visual method of
"seeing" your scenes'[14] and suggests recording for each chapter, point
of view, characters, setting, plot, key information and page numbers.
I put these details on index cards and pinned them to a notice board.
This helped with thinking about cause and effect and 'cutting the fat',

as Obstfeld calls it, to improve pace. Being a lover of detail, 'cutting the fat' is something I need to do regularly. Obstfeld's aerial mapping technique enabled me to handle large chunks of writing and the movement of scenes without getting bogged down with reading page after page every time.

The Mother's Voice

I'd never written in the second person before, but it was an instinctive choice for the mother. I loved the slow, introspective pace, a contrast with the boisterous first-person narration of the child:

> You step into the cool of the larder with the butter dish in your hand and stand for a moment in the half light, listening to the distant rattle and pause, rattle and pause of a lawnmower: yet another summer afternoon (. . .) There's a weight of slowness. Sometimes you just sit.[15]

The second person can make a highly individual experience feel more universal. Perhaps this was the unconscious reason behind my choice, because I had an idea the mother might leave her family, a taboo even now, and considered unspeakable in the 1950s. I read and re-read short stories and novels which make use of the second-person viewpoint in different ways, and learned that it carries a sense of detachment from the self even while pulling the reader more intimately into the story to become the character whose perspective it represents. When a loved one dies, we address them in our thoughts as 'you'; similarly, those suffering trauma may speak about themselves in the second person. This tension between intimacy and absence was what I wanted.

At the beginning of the novel, the mother is a passive rather than active character, dominated by the will and wishes of her husband. Further into the story, she suffers from depression, falls in love with another man and leaves the family home. Any or all of these things might threaten reader empathy, so I needed a way to tug the reader in close. Emma Darwin highlights John Gardner's useful term 'psychic distance'[16] to describe the distance readers feel between themselves and the character, the second person being the most up close and subjective. This is illustrated well in Iain Banks' novel *Complicity*. His very occasional use of the second person 'you' for the murderer's viewpoint hauls us close to shocking events and makes us 'complicit'.

All these qualities made second-person narration a good fit for my purposes but, even so, uncertainty remained. The problem, pointed out to me several times, is that it can alienate readers. This was my first novel. Could I trust my instincts? Why not use third-person narration? I was asked more than once, by experienced writers. It was sensible to consider their advice. A few months before I sent the novel out to agents, my mentor, Kathryn Heyman, and I were talking over issues related to the complexity of structure of *The Devil's Music*. Part of the problem was the extreme difficulty (for a novice) of juggling two time periods with three narrative strands in three different voices and two different points of view (first and second person). In an attempt to create more unity, I set about rewriting the entire novel in the third person. An interesting learning experience! The switch from first to close third was a reasonably good fit for Andy and Andrew's narratives, but when it came to translating the second person into third, the mother's voice was dead in my hands. Only through such trial and error could I grow to have confidence in my intuition.

Second-person narration can often be aggressive, a side effect I didn't want. Reading other authors' use of 'you', alongside my own experimentation, revealed the less often the word 'you' is used, the less obtrusive the point of view. Consequently, one entire line-by-line redraft was spent altering sentences to avoid using 'you' wherever possible. I enjoy this kind of time-consuming editing. Less terrifying than facing blank pages, it also satisfies a desire to labour at the improvement of my writing.

Oddly, after writing many scenes from the mother's perspective, I knew her intimately but had no idea of her name. I hadn't even thought about it. Then I realized: leaving her unnamed for most of the novel echoes her loss of identity within the stifling confines of her marriage. In the postscript, narration moves into third person and, as the reader learns of the cathartic changes she has made to her life, the mother is named:

> Helen wakes in the half light. Curled on one side, cheek on his pillow, she listens for a moment to the familiar sounds of Ian's movements downstairs. He must be whisking sugared milk and eggs in a bowl, she decides, making *torrijas* for breakfast: her favourite.[17]

Andrew, the adult's voice

Even once the 1950s narratives were more or less complete, Andrew remained in the shadows. In the postscript Helen, who hasn't seen him since he was a child, describes a photograph which shows him as 'a tall, gaunt man caught half turning in a doorway, entering or leaving it's hard to say, not smiling but frowning at the camera (...) almost a stranger'.[18] Worryingly, this is how Andrew still appeared to me, although I had written thousands of words and placed him in many different situations and scenes, written and crafted, but ultimately discarded. At one point I considered cutting the adult viewpoint altogether, but since the original impetus for the entire novel was to make sure Andy – that little boy I'd first imagined with his head bent to a ball of string – was going to be safe, I had to persevere.

Many readers assume Andrew is autistic, even praise my portrayal of autism. I never thought of him as such. Andy is an ordinary boy with a vivid imagination. His hobbies include learning about knots from Grampy and reading about his hero, Houdini, until his childhood world is devastated by traumatic events which occur more or less simultaneously: the loss of his much loved baby sister Jelly, Grampy's death, and his mother's apparent abandonment. Andy's father never speaks of what has happened to Elaine, nor does he explain his wife's sudden disappearance. For Andrew, in consequence, these events are not only distorted by memory and guilt, but shrouded in silence. This silence, amplified by the 30-year gap between the two time periods in the novel, needed to be explored before I could give voice to a man as reticent as Andrew.

Many writers talk of 'hearing' the voices of their characters; I used to worry that this is not my experience, especially as writing dialogue doesn't come easily to me. I worry less now. The characters I'm drawn to write about can't, or don't, talk easily. Perhaps I don't hear their voices initially because their stories are difficult for them to express, due to taboo, shame or fear, but I'm inside their heads, looking out, thinking their thoughts, inhabiting their bodies. I know whether they are long-limbed, or have strong hands, whether their skin is freckled, how they move and what they notice and think about the outside world. All of these elements help to build the 'voice' of a character, above and beyond simply the way he or she speaks. 'Becoming' my character in this way often reveals how he or she expresses him/herself, but everything was back-to-front with Andrew: I saw him largely from the outside.

Andrew doesn't talk much to anyone. He fights the thoughts and memories which threaten to take him back to the chaos of his emotions at nine years old. His obsession with knots is a form of self-expression. But because those knots fill his head, I couldn't see beyond them to fully inhabit his mind. 'One writes', Ted Solaratoff says, 'mainly to rewrite',[19] so I kept writing, striving to make Andrew less of a stranger. I had both

Helen's and Andy's stories, and an idea of the shape of the novel, so I stopped fussing over crafting every sentence and forced myself to write with plot in mind. Andrew had to return home. Start there. Write about him returning home. Who's he going to meet first? His sister, Susie. Write about him meeting Susie.

It was thin writing, at first, but it was better than nothing, and the strong, rope-like structure helped considerably. The child's narrative was already written, enabling me to 'grow' the adult story alongside it. As a boy, shut in the under-stairs cupboard by his father, Andy finds comfort when he imagines Grampy's voice instructing him how to tie a Reef Knot – 'Left over right, right over left and under, his fingers on my fingers.'[20] I knew the adult Andrew would too.

Ongoing research allowed me to find my way into Andrew's psyche. I came across a soldier's account of what it was like to suffer posttraumatic stress disorder. The soldier wrote eloquently of the way his mind and body reacted, totally beyond his control, to the sound of rain. He'd do almost anything to avoid a situation which would call up this panic. This story moved me. More importantly, his words gave a little insight into what life might be like for Andrew. As I read about memory, recurring dreams, about fear and the amygdala, which houses memories of fear, it dawned on me that Andrew – even more so than when he was a boy – needs the enchantment of knots to keep him safe from his fears, and to prevent his thoughts from wandering onto the treacherous wet sand of his last memory of Elaine at the beach.

I pressed on with this thin, plot-based writing and inched closer to Andrew. Reading *Ashley's Book of Knots*, the book Grampy gave to him as a child and which he always keeps close, I wrote about the knots Andrew created. Terse, incomplete sentences arrived. They had a hesitancy to them, caused by Andrew's reliance on knots, rather than speech, as a means of expression. As the sentences built they developed a rhythm of their own that was, at last, Andrew's voice: 'Wet sand: gleaming and ridged for miles and miles. The smear and squelch of it, thick as wet paint. Adrenaline flares. My body wants to be far away. Fast.'[21]

Andrew's reactions to walking on the beach he once loved express the fear that Jelly had drowned when he left her by the pool he'd dug; a memory conflated with that of his mother leaving. He has never spoken to anyone about this incident, which forms the pivotal scene and is told fully in the child's narrative. This scene is also briefly recalled by Andrew at the novel's opening, and was the last section to be written. To express a child's perception of events, couched within the more adult and concentrated language of memory, was another challenge – one which reminded me that a character will have many 'voices', as we all do:

> My mother reaches the pool. She stands rigid. The ice creams topple and fall. She bends to scoop Jelly from the sand and wraps her arms around her. My mother lifts her face to the pale sky, her mouth wrenched open.
>
> And that's when I hear the high-pitched sound, a keening that goes on and on and doesn't stop. It doesn't stop when the lugworm man throws his spade to the ground and begins running, doesn't stop when the bucket drops at my feet, doesn't stop when I'm crouched low, hands covering my ears.[22]

There are no novels under my bed; *The Devil's Music* is literally my first, though during the six or seven years of writing, it went through many shapes and forms. Thinking over that long creative journey, it's fitting here to mention Clifford Ashley, whose book and passion for knots was constant inspiration. Ashley says, 'To me the simple act of tying a knot is like an adventure in unlimited space (. . .) which provides an opportunity for an excursion limited only by the scope of our own imagery and the length of the rope-maker's coil'[23] – an apt description of my experience of writing *The Devil's Music*. Ironically, my 'adventure' took me, via a circuitous route, back to Winnicott's diagnosis of 'separation anxiety', but the mystery and magic of the imaginative process created space for three narrators to tell their stories, and gave them life and pulse.

Notes

1. D.W. Winnicott (1960) 'String: A Technique of Communication' *Journal of Child Psychology and Psychiatry*, 1, 49–52.
2. J. Rusbridge (2009) *The Devil's Music* (London: Bloomsbury), p. 234.
3. I. Costello (2011) Review of *The Devil's Music*. http://isabelcostelloliterarysofa. com/2011/11/04/book-review-the-devils-music-by-jane-rusbridge/
4. T. Nicholson (2011) 'The Devil's Music: A Review'. http://trishnicholsons wordsin thetreehouse.com/2011/09/23/the-devils-music-a-review/.
5. R. Kipling (1937) *Something of Myself: For My Friends, Known and Unknown* (London: Macmillan and Co. Ltd), p. 210.
6. J. Rusbridge (2009) *The Devil's Music* (London: Bloomsbury), p. 19.
7. Ibid., 27.
8. Ibid., 53.
9. Ibid., 53.
10. Ibid., 57.

11. A. Forna, Interview on Bat Segundo Show. http://www.edrants.com/segundo/aminatta-forna-bss-383/, date accessed 17 June 2011.
12. J. Rusbridge (2009) *The Devil's Music* (London: Bloomsbury), p. 223.
13. Ibid., 53.
14. R. Obstfeld (2000) *A Novelist's Essential Guide to Crafting Scenes* (Ohio: Writer's Digest Books), p. 183.
15. J. Rusbridge (2009) *The Devil's Music* (London: Bloomsbury), p. 59.
16. E. Darwin, 'Psychic Distance: What it is and How to Use it' http://emmadarwin.typepad.com/thisitchofwriting/psychic-distance-what-it-is-and-how-to-use-it.html, date accessed January 2011.
17. J. Rusbridge (2009) *The Devil's Music* (London: Bloomsbury), p. 297.
18. Ibid., 303.
19. T. Solaratoff (1985) 'Writing in the Cold', *Granta 15*, Spring 1986, 274.
20. J. Rusbridge (2009) *The Devil's Music* (London: Bloomsbury), p. 28.
21. Ibid., 25.
22. Ibid., 4.
23. C. Ashley (1944) *The Ashley Book of Knots* (Great Britain: Faber and Faber), p. 8.

12

'Voice' and the Inescapable Complexity of Experience

Isabel Ashdown

In life, we don't have the luxury of choosing our closest family members, and yet we live together in close proximity for many years. Extended members – in-laws, step-siblings, half-siblings, step-children, boyfriends, girlfriends – are at best warmly welcomed into, at worst inflicted on, the existing family unit, bringing with them all the complexities of their own existence. As a reader, I am most interested in the complicated dynamics played out between family members. I am endlessly fascinated by documentaries which reunite separated siblings, explore genetic similarities or uncover secrets from the past. Secrets, if spoken aloud, have the power to unite or destroy families, for while knowledge is an enlightening thing, it can also be dangerous and destructive. It is my fascination with consequence – the compulsion to see what happens next, to explore how a family copes with new and potentially life-changing knowledge – that drives me forward as a writer.

At the earliest stage of writing the short story that would eventually become my first novel, *Glasshopper*, I was inspired by a television show in which a young man was waiting for DNA test results which would reveal the identity of his biological father. I was halfway through a Creative Writing degree and gripped by this idea of ambiguous parentage, and the secrets that must surround such a complex scenario. I started work on a short story in which the question of paternity is unexpectedly raised. What would happen to a family in receipt of such a deeply significant revelation? How would it affect the child, the mother, both of the possible fathers?

After a number of early drafts and redrafts, I found I was struggling with the structure of my short story, so I booked a tutorial with my Creative Writing tutor, hoping he might have a few ideas to help me make sense of it. He took one read through and said, 'I think this is actually the start of a novel.' There was simply too much material to squeeze into the constraints of a short story, and so, now granted the space to breathe and expand, I was able to start thinking more freely about what this story was *really* about.

My earliest instinct was that this would be the story of a teenage child growing up in 1980s Britain with an alcoholic mother. With some personal family experience of alcoholism, I was dealing with certain themes that were unsettling to me but, I knew, entirely necessary to the story if it were to succeed. I felt a strong compulsion to express and explore elements of my life/self through a fictional world, but at the same time, was slightly afraid of what I might unearth. It troubled me enough to stop me writing for a while, but all the time I wasn't writing, I was constantly thinking about it. For the first time ever I suffered with insomnia, waking in the night with this faceless adolescent on my mind. On the school run, I'd hear this youngster in some small thing the children might say from the back of the car, or in the world-weary posture of a teenager seen beyond the windscreen, on their solitary walk home. My fictional character had possessed me, and I had to concede that this really was a story that wanted to be written.

When I finally threw myself into the early stages of writing, I instinctively wrote in the present tense, and the adolescent who emerged, was, to my surprise, a male called Jake. At once my writing was liberated and afforded greater honesty, as I gained a sense of distance from my own personal experience. Jake's story would undoubtedly draw on certain emotional cues from my own life, but via a simple switch in gender, any fear of mirroring real events had vanished. In *The Way We Write*, Graham Swift discusses the constraints a writer can feel when writing from life:

> When I have talked about writing in the past, I have possibly overstressed the fact that my own life, my biography, is not the stuff of fiction. I have said things like, 'One writes fiction because one doesn't want to write fact', and I do feel that you need to keep your subject matter at a distance from you, so that your imagination can take flight to it.[1]

My liberation was certainly borne out of the 'distance' that Swift refers to, as I allowed my imagination to take flight, to reveal a character with a unique voice, in what seemed to me a very real world.

Jake is fascinated by Greek mythology, holds down a Saturday job at the corner shop and tries to rationalize events in his family with pragmatic naivety. Jake's father has recently left the family home. He's still a part of Jake's life and he still loves his wife, but he can't cope with her drinking any more. Meanwhile, Jake's older brother has also flown the nest, and Jake is now the nearest thing to a responsible adult in the household. And he feels responsible, maybe more responsible than he should, for his fragile mother, and for his younger brother. A trip to meet Aunt Rachel and his cousins for the first time provides Jake with the uplifting comfort of extended family, yet out of this reunion family secrets emerge relating to Jake's paternity, which ultimately lead to tragic results.

I knew Jake's story would be sad yet, surprisingly, the voice that came to me was vibrant and energetic; it was a voice full of optimism about the world around him:

> I love November. I love the frosty grass that pokes up between the paving slabs, and the smoke that puffs out of your nostrils like dragon's breath. I love the ready-made ice rink that freezes underneath the broken guttering in the school playground. And I love the salt 'n' vinegar heat inside a noisy pub, when everyone outside is walking about under hats and gloves with dripping red noses.[2]

In order to portray the dilemmas presented to a child of an alcoholic parent without being either sentimental or overly dramatic, I suspected that the right choice of voice and viewpoint would be critical to achieving my aim. From the outset, I had written in the first person, and for 13-year-old Jake it felt like a natural fit. In *The Art of Writing Fiction*, Andrew Cowan says, 'One of the main effects of first person point of view is to personalise and particularise a story and thereby draw the reader into a relationship of apparent intimacy with the "speaker" and the world she inhabits.'[3] The intimacy between Jake and the reader is crucial, as his teenage viewpoint – with its limitations and naiveté – tends to focus on the stark 'telling' of what's happening. His humour and cheery exterior is the facade he adopts as he attempts to cope with his difficult home life, yet, as readers, our close proximity to him means that we are able to interpret the inconsistencies in his character.

In *Adult Children of Alcoholics*,[4] Janet Woititz discusses how lying is basic to the family system affected by alcohol. Lying, borne out of devotion, masquerades in part as overt denial of unpleasant realities, covering-up broken promises and inconsistencies which might alert the outside world to the problem. It was this futile sense of loyalty that I aimed to convey through Jake's story. He is a teenage boy, growing up with the reality of his mother's addiction, and yet, despite its huge presence, the problem is something to which the family are unable or unwilling to give voice. In one important scene, Jake's mother lays down the 'rules' of loyalty after collecting his older brother, Matthew, from their grandmother's house after the school have alerted her to his absence. When she arrives, they argue and Matthew calls her a 'pisshead'. As soon as they are out of sight of Gran's house, Jake's mother pins Matthew against a wall:

> We need some rules, darling. And the most important one is about loyalty. We're a family and we do not, ever, go around telling lies about each other. To anyone. What you said to Gran back there – it was a lie. You know it, and so do I.[5]

Denial and cover ups thread through the whole novel, and in moments of crisis Jake alternates between baffled onlooker and frustrated participant in events beyond his control. We witness Jake's lack of agency, and often, his subsequent lack of voice. Early in the book there is a moment when he is confronted by his mum's drunken behaviour outside his father's local pub. Embarrassed, he only looks towards her when his friend has left: 'For a moment, I'm stuck to the spot. I just stand there and stare at the back of her head. She's like a gorgon, and I have turned to stone.'[6] Should he pretend he hasn't seen his mum or go to her aid? Finally, he does what he knows is the right thing: 'Quietly, I walk over and slip my hand into hers, and lead her away from the pub.'

Jake's actions express his true character far more effectively than words ever could. As the story developed and Jake's presence became more established, I knew that in order to bestow on him a truly authentic teenage voice – and to give texture and depth to the narrative, itself – his unspoken emotions would be as important as those he could articulate aloud.

When I began *Glasshopper*, I was wholly certain that this was a story for adults. As Jake's voice and viewpoint developed, however, sudden uncertainty left me creatively grounded. Thirteen-year-old Jake's daily interests and preoccupations had obvious appeal for a younger readership and this made me pause to ask myself two significant questions. Firstly, was I actually, without realizing it, writing a book more suited to older children? Secondly, could teenage Jake's intimate first-person narration – limited by his knowledge and understanding – satisfyingly convey to adult readers what is at the heart of the story? That is, the far-reaching consequences of long-buried family secrets.

The categorization of adult and teenage fiction is a topic regularly debated, and so I was aware that the question of audience was certainly an important one to consider. During this period, I read a related essay by Myles McDowell, in which he sets out to make certain distinctions between adult and children's fiction, summarizing succinctly: 'a good children's book makes complex experience available to its readers; a good adult book draws attention to the inescapable complexity of experience'.[7]

When I'd written a few more chapters containing scenes with both Jake and his alcoholic mother, I realized, with absolute clarity, what was causing me to question the strength of my single narrator. Mary needed a voice too. There was more than one story at work, and by focusing on Jake to the exclusion of others, I was at risk of simplistically casting characters as either victim or aggressor; of making something that is deeply complex too readily available. I realized that, in spite of her behaviour towards her children, we could only really understand Jake's and the family's situation if we were also able to see the world through Mary's eyes.

After penning the first 'Mary' chapter, contentment washed over me – Mary's narrative had been there all along, waiting quietly but insistently inside Jake's story; I just had to recognize her voice and let her speak. The initial chapter I wrote for Mary, by instinct rather than design, told of the moment she met Billy, Jake's father, as a 19-year-old student in 1966:

> The first time I see him, he's standing in the kitchen window of my student halls and I know he will be my one great love. I want to ask him his surname, to know if it suits me. Somehow, I recognise his steady brown eyes, his slow smile, his broad hands with their deep set nail-beds. He's replacing a broken pane of glass, and he's framed in the high window, looking down at me, a tape measure gripped in his tanned fist, a stub of pencil between his teeth.[8]

From this opening chapter I worked backwards to the child Mary had once been, and forwards to explore key moments in her life that have led her to become the person Jake knows. From her genteel beginnings in 1950s Hove to the prolonged estrangement from her family and the break-up of her marriage, Mary's story begins to make sense, and she emerges as a woman who has suffered loss and a profound sense of being misunderstood. In Jake's world, she is a woman who swings from sobriety and joy in her peaceful moments to depression and alcoholic bingeing when life overwhelms her. As Mary's story draws alongside his, her decline has been so subtle and slow-burning that we are still able to recognize in her the hopeful young woman she once was. By sympathetically exploring Mary's voice and motivations as a person quite separate from Jake, I was effectively able to move away from the stereotypical or clichéd portrayal of 'the drunk'.

The two narratives not only help to establish different viewpoints on the same family situation, but also highlight the class divisions that are integral to *Glasshopper*. Mary's background is certainly more moneyed than Billy's. When Billy meets Mary's mother for the first time it is clear that Mrs Andrews does not think Billy is 'their kind of person'. Ultimately, it would be these differences that alienate Mary from her family, and which present her to the reader as a character for whom we can afford a degree of empathy.

While Jake's story covers less than a year, Mary's takes her from childhood to adulthood, until their stories eventually converge in France, when long-buried family secrets come to a head in the Dordogne. Eudora Welty says that location 'is the ground conductor of all the currents of emotion, belief and moral conviction that charge out from a story'.[9] In *Glasshopper*, location was fundamental to the plot for heightening and suggesting the central characters' fraught emotions. It is in a remote farmhouse, in the intense and claustrophobic heat of August, that the two stories collide and Jake finally discovers the truth about his paternity.

Overall, the novel took five years to write and shifted, quite naturally, from the starting point of a single first-person narrative set in a single time zone into something more complex: a novel of two first-person viewpoints spanning four decades from the 1950s to the 1980s. With two distinct voices and shifting time zones, the writing of each narrative strand served to create new depths within the other, to create a story that would, I hoped, draw attention to the 'inescapable complexity of experience'. With the introduction of Mary, there now seemed no question over the target readership. This was indeed a work of adult fiction, as each voice played a vital role in revealing the way in which past events shape and affect the present.

A few months before I finished writing *Glasshopper*, I received the news that an early extract of my novel had won *The Mail on Sunday Novel Competition*, judged by Sir John Mortimer and Fay Weldon. Naturally, I was overjoyed, but most importantly the announcement spurred me on to complete my novel and send it out in search of an agent. My fascination with one family's story had driven me towards the finishing line; *I* wanted to know what would happen to Jake and Mary. But, in reality, and out in the wider world where thousands of new titles hit the shelves every year, would others share my interest? I posted off my agent submissions, and I waited. Within a few weeks an agent responded, followed by two more, and I signed with one whose faith in *Glasshopper* was both encouraging and infectious.

As we went through the process of submitting and signing with a UK publisher, I set to work on my second novel, in part as a way of distracting myself from the uncertainty of impending publication. In contrast to *Glasshopper*, I had the comfort of writing my second novel more consciously. From the outset, I knew my material required the space and breadth of a novel. I also knew there would be uncertainty, at times, as to whether my fascination was leading me up a blind alley. I knew I would lie awake at night questioning where on earth the story was heading, or fretting over the chaotic disorder of my thoughts and the words on the page. And I knew I would experience the wonderful rush and euphoria of those unexpected moments of synchronicity, when the imagined world becomes more unified and concrete, the characters more real. This time round, I was able to recognize the agonies and ecstasies for what they are: just a necessary part of the creative process, essential to the organic and sometimes mysterious development of a new story, a new voice.

Notes

1. G. Swift (2006) untitled essay in B. Baker (ed.) *The Way We Write* (London: Continuum), p. 178.
2. I. Ashdown (2009) *Glasshopper* (Brighton: Myriad), p. 5.
3. A. Cowan (2011) *The Art of Writing Fiction* (Harlow: Pearson), p. 132.
4. J. Woititz (1983) *Adult Children of Alcoholics* (USA: Health Comms Inc).
5. I. Ashdown (2009) *Glasshopper* (Brighton: Myriad), pp. 271–2.
6. Ibid., 13.
7. M. McDowell (1976) 'Fiction for Children and Adults: Some Essential Differences' in G. Fox (ed.) *Writers, Critics and Children* (London: Heinnemann), p. 143.
8. I. Ashdown (2009) *Glasshopper* (Brighton: Myriad), p. 83.
9. E. Welty (1991) 'The Sense of Place in Faulkner's Spotted Horses' in A. Charters (ed.) *The Story and its Writer* (New York: St. Martin's Press), p. 1537.

Part IV
Form and the Novel

13

Giving Shape to One's Universe

Helon Habila

I wrote most of my first novel, *Waiting for an Angel*, in Lagos, Nigeria, and if you have been to Lagos the fractured, discontinuous style of the narration would make sense to you immediately. Lagos in the 1990s, under the military dictatorship, was a large, sprawling suburb of hell – this is not an exaggeration. There were dead bodies lying for days by the roadside; there were traffic jams that went on for hours, trapping you in old, overcrowded molue buses where you were pinned between sweaty bodies as you hung on to the top railing for balance with one hand, and with the other hand you held on tightly to your wallet. Do I need to mention that when you finally got home from work, sometimes around 9 p.m., it was guaranteed that there would be no electricity? In my particular neighbourhood of Ketu we had had no power for months, at exactly the time I was writing my novel. Chinua Achebe, asked at a reading to say something about Lagos, said that his only advice to anyone who found himself in Lagos was to get out as soon as he could.

Lagos is a much saner, better organized place now, but this is now and that was then. Living in Lagos then, I found it hopeless to try to write my novel in a linear, continuous way – I just couldn't see that far into the future. Every day had to be lived fully, to be brought to a closure because there was no guarantee it wouldn't be the last day. So I wrote my book as a series of autonomous but structurally and thematically linked short stories; each story was also a chapter in the novel. Writing mostly at night by candle light, I wrote each self-contained chapter as quickly as I could, putting yet one more day and one more chapter to bed, and going to bed myself at three or four in the morning with a sense of achievement, a sense of closure. At least for that day. I am not saying that each story in the book took exactly a day to write, but each took a bearably shorter time to write than a novel would have taken.

Years later, after my book was published, reviewers and critics would often comment about my deliberate use of fragmented narrative style as a tool for capturing the urban chaos that was Lagos, and Nigeria, in the 1990s. A style described as 'typically postcolonial' or 'postmodern'. As if I had sat down in a state of Wordsworthian tranquillity or visited an arty coffee house and decided to structure my book like I did. All I wanted was to finish my book as painlessly as possible.

Form, which at a basic level can be described as the structuring of narrative, or, as Edith Wharton puts it in her succinct style in *The Writing of Fiction*, 'the order in time and importance, in which the incidents of the narrative are grouped',[1] can be circumstantial, dependent on the time, place, or situation the author happens to be in when he or she is writing the book. If I had written my novel in Bauchi, where I used to live before moving to Lagos, and where life is more tranquil and more predictable, it is doubtful whether the book would have ended up in the form it is in now. Certainly, Virginia Woolf's *Mrs Dalloway* and her other Stream of Consciousness novels couldn't have been written before World War I, or set anywhere else but in post–World War I London. A modernist novel can't be written before the advent of modernity. Art, and most especially the novel, is always a product of its time and place. The omniscient, minutely detailed and linear style of the Victorians was a reflection of their worldview, their simple, agrarian life style. I call these the external or even accidental influences that do sometimes determine the form or shape of a novel. They are presences hovering by the writing table, guiding your hand, and most of the time you are powerless against them. This is especially true with earlier works, when the writer isn't yet skilled enough to be intentional, to force his design on his work regardless of the situation. Often, sitting in my room, writing, I felt as if only the circumference described by my candle light existed. The real world, everything outside of that, was shadows. There was a feeling of blind terror, for I wasn't sure what I was doing. I wrote by instinct, without thinking too much. A lot of writing coaches do encourage this kind of writing, especially for the first draft. Write, they tell you, just get everything down on paper. Don't think. This is good advice, especially with longer pieces, like a novel. I felt my way through my characters and my instinct for conflict. I let character interact with character, always making sure not to resolve conflicts too soon, always delaying the payoff moment. Gradually, the circumference of light expanded as each character developed. Perhaps it helped that I didn't sit down to write with a lot of answers, but with questions. In a way, writing a novel is about articulating for oneself what one already senses through experience and instinct, but the truth of which one is still not sure about. In giving shape to a novel one is also giving shape to one's universe.

I was working as a journalist while writing *Waiting for an Angel*, the story of Lomba, a journalist and aspiring novelist, imprisoned for two years without trial during the repressive Abacha regime of the 1990s. Later, I realized that in writing about Lomba I was also asking myself: how far was I willing to go for the 'truth'? Did I believe in what I was doing, as a journalist? How would I behave if I were arrested and imprisoned without trial? Suddenly the story became more personal. My circumference of candle light became much enlarged. In writing Lomba's story, I was also writing about the politics and violence going on outside and how it affected bystanders like myself. I was involved, whether I liked it or not, and so threw everything I knew into the book: journalism, poetry, desire for love, anger and hope, above all else. I realized how brave ordinary Nigerians were; people like Auntie Rachael, who every night came back home alive and 'pushed aside the darkness'[2] from their faces, at least for that night. I realized that in Nancy's obsessive graffiti scribbling on her bedroom wall there is an echo of the Nigerian youth silenced, desperately trying to discover a voice to emerge. In every one of our characters there is a bit of us, and if we can identify what it is, we can use it as a handle to really make that character come alive.

But, as much as I acknowledge how much circumstance and the accident of my being in Lagos helped me to get a form for my novel, it is not always that chance and serendipity work to give a book the desired shape. A well-written story is an artificial thing, a made thing. Talent and instinct and empathy can only take you so far, and no more. The beauty of the novel is that it gives you the space, within a single story, to evolve and grow from ignorance to awareness, especially since some novels take years to write. After a few drafts I knew which chapter had to follow which, and I decided on arranging the stories in reverse chronological order because it strengthened the theme of confusion and uncertainty I was aiming for. The silences and spaces between chapters also worked out well for me, as each silent space that surrounds each story seemed to mirror the gaps felt in a country on its knees. Nigeria is a country where information is repressed, where people are beaten for knowing things, where people disappear for knowing things. The dead bodies I saw by the roadside, well, one of them could be the youth I depict running from a mob and who is bludgeoned and set on fire. Without a history, he appears and dies. We know nothing more. Nabokov says there is no reading a book, only re-reading it, in the same way I believe there is no writing a story, only re-writing it. In revision everything becomes clearer.

How, then, do we impose a suitable form on a novel? How do we hold a story together, not so rigidly that it feels like a block of ice, not so loosely that it lacks form, but fluidly, pulling and pushing, rather like a balloon filled with water? The first thing to note is that everything that goes into a novel can contribute to its final form. All the elements are interconnected – plot, character, dialogue, setting, point of view – and any separation is really artificial, for the sake of analysis and discussion. As James Wood, the critic, points out in the preface to his excellent book on craft, *How Fiction Works*: 'When I talk of free indirect style I am really talking about point of view, and when I am talking about point of view I am really talking about the perception of detail, and when I am talking about detail I am really talking about character.'[3] In the same vein, Henry James asks rhetorically: 'What is character but determination of incident, what is incident but illustration of character...?'[4]

Although here I want to focus on conflict and character, in talking about them I will also be talking about everything else. Because my early writing career was surrounded by conflict, I am convinced that in a story, as in life, the more conflict there is, the more interesting things become. In fact, a narrative could be said to be nothing but the introduction of conflict, the complication of conflict, and finally the resolution, or at least a recognition or containment of that conflict. The question, then, is at what point in the story do we introduce conflict; introduce it clearly, unequivocally, so that the reader knows that this is the story's major conflict? The answer is simple: at the beginning. But we all know there are three types of beginnings, as suggested by Aristotle: a beginning that begins at the beginning, one that begins at the middle, and one that begins at the end. Of course, every beginning also has a beginning, a middle, and an end; so does the middle, and so does the end.

In *Waiting for an Angel*, I decided to open with Lomba in prison. This event occurs at the beginning of the end of the novel. Structuring my novel in this way helped me to achieve two things simultaneously. Firstly, I was immediately introducing the central conflict of the story, which is freedom versus repression. A journalist is imprisoned for daring to join words 'together to form a sentence'.[5] I localized the conflict and contained it within a single setting, the prison, and confined it to the interaction between two people: the protagonist, Lomba, and his antagonist, the Superintendent. The second thing I achieved, is that through opening at this point of high tension, the reader's attention is immediately grabbed, more so than if I had opened at the 'beginning' with a long passage of description or background information. Opening with the ending directs the reader's gaze backwards, through the chain of events which lead to that point. It offers the reader a chance to see retrospectively those choices the character made under pressure, the moments that determine the character's path and final fate.

Nothing illustrates character better than conflict. Conflict need not be momentous as in Homer's *Odyssey*, with Achilles in conflict with King Agamemnon against his sense of duty, and with his mortal half against his superhuman, egotistical other half. Conflict can be found even in the most mundane of situations, for instance in the decision at breakfast to choose between the healthy brown wheat bread, or the tasty but less healthy potato bread, the resolution of which can tell us more than words can as to what kind of character we are dealing with. Here is an example, again from James Wood, describing a character: 'This man, let us say, is curious, because the top half of him is expensively turned out – a fine pressed shirt, a good jacket – while the bottom half is slovenly: stained, creased trousers, old unpolished shoes.'[6] Wood is here suggesting the use of dissonance, or conflict, in the appearance of a character, so as to make him immediately striking. Not just to introduce a character, but to 'launch' the character. In life, as in stories, nothing develops character like a little opposition.

In the right dosage, conflict can make a story taut and tense. It gives a focus to stories that would otherwise meander aimlessly. Most of all, it makes a reader immediately sit up and take notice; it makes a reader realize that this writer really means business. It has to be in the right dosage, mind. A common caution against an overdependence on conflict is that it can cheapen a story. This happens when it is used mainly as an external plot device; a gimmick to propel the story forward and nothing more. At the other end of the spectrum is the almost total absence of conflict, and it is hard to say, between the two, which one is worse.

I have just finished reading Amit Chaudhuri's *The Immortals*, an ambitious book about music in particular and art in general, and the sacrifice necessary to pursue excellence as a singer, and the artistic immortality that might come with mastery. A beautifully written story, but one that lacks conflict. The talented but undriven Mrs Mallika Sengupta, the character through whose experience most of the story is told, too easily accepts the middle-class life and the material comforts that her marriage to a company director confers on her. Her teenage son, Nirmalya, something of a purist, wants her to be more dedicated to her singing, whereas her husband doesn't really care:

> There was no quarrel between Nirmalya and Apurva Sengupta about this; they wouldn't even have been aware of the difference of opinion – but while one wished to always listen to his wife sing, and that she should be heard, somehow, by a few others, the other wanted her – it was never clear in what way – to be true to her talent. She, in the middle of this, could take neither Apurva Sengupta's comfortable faith nor her son's impatience seriously; compromise was necessary to lead a life even as unreal as this on an even keel – compromise, which engendered but also tempered disappointment.[7]

Does Mrs Sengupta fully understand or care enough about what her talent means, what she might have become? We do see her reflecting on this many times, but we want her to make a choice, an attempt, or to at least show some regret at what she is giving up. The conflict fizzles out even as it is introduced, and we know she is never going to do anything drastic or surprise us in any major way, and so our interest in her lessens. In the hands of a lesser talent the narrative would have fallen apart – but Chaudhury keeps you reading simply by his great style, though his work would have been made easier if he had injected more conflict, possibly. It is Kurt Vonnegut, I believe, who advised that you must make your character want something from the start of the story, even if it is only a cup of water. Well, he should have also added: 'Make him want it bad, then make someone try to stop him from getting it.' Mrs Sengupta's love for music is never seriously tested or challenged in the story. It is simply something she does.

What conflict does is to give balance, push and pull – Dr Jekyll is opposed and thus balanced by Mr Hyde. Authors use this device all the time. I am not talking merely of foiling, or counterpointing, though both techniques can be developed through conflict, but also of localizing conflict. It is not enough to present conflict, it is important to develop it, and one way of doing that is by containing it, and managing it; if this is done well a story is raised beyond its basic meaning to a more complex, figurative level. I could use the word 'allegory', but that is not exactly what I have in mind – I don't want the reader to think of *Pilgrim's Progress*, or *Animal Farm*. I am particularly concerned with character and conflict, and how the two working together might be used to enhance a story's form.

Almost all of J. M. Coetzee's novels work this way. But I think he uses this technique best in *Waiting for the Barbarians*. This is the story of a Magistrate, a loyal servant of the Empire, posted to a remote frontier district of the Empire, who finally revolts when he becomes uncomfortable with the treatment of the natives, or Barbarians as the colonizers call them, by the soldiers of the Empire led by Colonel Joll. After the introduction, where Coetzee establishes the broader conflict between the Empire and the Barbarians, he immediately turns our focus to the Magistrate and a certain prisoner, a Barbarian woman, captured and tortured and imprisoned by Colonel Joll. Now she can hardly walk, her ankles have been fractured, her eyes partially blinded by her torturers. The Magistrate, in the grip of conscience, takes her in and, in a way, turns himself into her servant. He wants to make amends and in an elaborate ritual of self-abasement which he performs daily, he washes her feet with water and kneads and massages them until he falls asleep, exhausted. He becomes obsessed with her scarred and mutilated body, which he wants both to heal and to possess. 'It has been growing more and more clear to me that until the marks on this girl's body are deciphered and understood I cannot let go of her.'[8]

He understands, in ironic reversal, that he has become her prisoner. In washing her feet and in seeking to own her, he is being a supplicant as well as re-enacting the role of torturer. And so for the time being, and for a large portion of the novel, the focus has been reduced to just two people, their thoughts and actions and dialogue imbued with much meaning, raising the whole story to a more complex level. At once we are dealing with an older man's sexual desires and frustrations – which he is trying to control under the guise of penitence – aimed at this woman's broken, lumpen body. The woman's body has become a theatre where the novel's central conflict is dramatized and highlighted.

J. M. Coetzee is often compared to Franz Kafka, and it is to Kafka I want to turn for my last example of localizing, or containing conflict. Kafka's excellent short story, 'In the Penal Colony', has many similarities to Coetzee's Barbarians, even though the former is a short story. It is also set in a distant outpost of an unnamed Empire, a European power, and its theme is also on justice, power, and powerlessness.

The story opens with the arrival of the protagonist, the Traveller, or in other translations, the Explorer, who has arrived in time to witness an execution. A rank and file soldier has committed the crime of insubordination and is going to die for it. A Colonel, who is the executioner, carefully explains to the Explorer how the machine works. It is a medieval torture contraption, and once the prisoner is tied to it, it takes all of 24 hours to carve the name of his crime on his body before he finally dies. The machine, from the opening of the story, is clearly the location of the conflict because it is the embodiment of an archaic justice system where the accuser is also the judge and the executioner. The Colonel is fighting to preserve it, because it was designed by the previous Commandant to whom he is very loyal. He hopes the Explorer will put in a word for the continuation of the old system with the present Commandant, who wants to scrap it. The Explorer says no. And then, in one of the most beautiful moments of reversal and poetic justice, the Colonel sets the prisoner free and executes himself on the machine. For the story to achieve harmony, conflict is resolved. Yet conflict is not always resolved. Sometimes it is enough for it to be identified or acknowledged, especially in epiphanic short stories where the resolution is not as necessary as in a novel. In a novel, not only is conflict resolved, it is often taken to a denouement – that is, we are shown a consequence of that final choice that resolves the conflict. For example, boy wants girl, father opposes boy, boy tricks father and gets girl – the denouement is boy has to live with the fear of discovery of his trickery. This, of course, does not need to be illustrated and fleshed out, it just needs to be acknowledged and recognized.

My experience of writing my first novel in Lagos has taught me never to worry about linearity when writing the first draft of a novel. I begin wherever I want to, wherever I can see most clearly and truthfully; as a result I have never experienced writer's block. Some people see writing as a contest between their minds and the narrative. They have to start from point A and move on to B then C and so forth, until they reach the end. I don't. When I get stuck I simply move on to another point, another character, another scene, and when all the scenes are down, I begin to join them together with transition passages. It jars in the first and second and maybe third draft, but by the fourth draft it flows as if it had been originally written in a linear fashion. And nowadays, with cut and paste, anything is possible. The important thing is to trust in the revision process – you can never be a good writer if you don't. Of course, as one grows older and more conversant with the writing process, and now that one's chances of returning safely in the evenings are better, it is easier to predict – even from the ideational stage – where a story is going, or what a character might or might not do. At times, I find I miss the accidental, puzzling and challenging process of writing my first book, when I had to, as it were, invent everything from scratch.

Notes

1. E. Wharton (1997) *The Writing of Fiction* (New York: Scribner), p. 28.
2. H. Habila (2002) *Waiting for an Angel* (London: Penguin Books), p. 180.
3. J. Wood (2008) *How Fiction Works* (London: Vintage), p. 3.
4. H. James (1996) 'The Art of Fiction' in D. H. Ritcher (ed.) *Narrative/Theory* (New York: Longman), p. 50.
5. H. Habila (2002) *Waiting for an Angel* (London: Penguin Books), p. 195.
6. J. Wood (2008) *How Fiction Works* (London: Vintage), p. 77.
7. A. Chaudhuri (2009) *The Immortals* (New York: Vintage Books), pp. 97–8.
8. J. M. Coetzee (1980) *Waiting for the Barbarians* (New York: Penguin Books), p. 31.

14
Another Fine Mess
David Swann

Sometimes when teaching the craft of short fiction, I show my students the old one-reeler *Our Wife* in which Oliver Hardy's optimistic attempts to elope are frustrated by the tiny car that Stan Laurel has hired for the getaway.[1] When Stan tries to squeeze himself, Ollie and his lover, and all of their suitcases into a matchbox-sized vehicle, I hope the students will laugh while also detecting what a decent story needs: characters struggling against their flaws to meet difficult goals, and not giving up easily, no matter how great the odds. And I hope they spot the parable I've smuggled in about short stories – namely, that you can't take *everything* with you. Unless you leave behind most of the backstory, you risk the fate suffered by Ollie, whose dreams eventually lie crushed on the asphalt.

I'd had success with short fiction and poetry after finishing three novels that failed to live up to my expectations. But the longer form always drew me back – and when I found myself unexpectedly working on an historical novel, *The Advocates of Darkness*, I was excited again by the prospect of a bigger car and a longer journey. Yet I wasn't under any illusions about the difficulties, and recalled Flannery O'Connor's observation that a novel is a 'dark wood'[2] while a short story is a forest clearing containing a wolf.

Laurel & Hardy. The forest & the wolf. For some reason, I'm drawn to double acts. Set in 1812, during the early Industrial Revolution, my novel focuses on the odd couple of Mollie & Tom, orphaned 'apprentices' employed in a remote cotton mill, where crippled youths toil in dreadful conditions. Although it tackles child labour and industrial sabotage, the book is primarily an adventure story which draws on my love of the wilderness, where the two protagonists are forced to seek shelter after they flee a terrible act of self-defence. At its heart, I believe the book is about the search for home and belonging.

Right from the start of the five-year drafting process, the novel began as two intertwined dramatic monologues, one narrated by Mollie – a beautiful and optimistic girl dispatched from a London workhouse – and the other by a tormented lad named Tom, who performs the dirty work for his corrupt Master in the Cripples' Mill in Lancashire. I was interested to see what would happen when a creature of darkness collided with a disciple of the light. I was also excited by the formal challenge of bringing variety to the monologues while simultaneously attempting to maintain a unified narrative flow.

Well, the road I travelled in this latest fine mess turned out to be slightly smoother than the gruelling treks I'd experienced on three previous failed novels, and I'd like to spend the rest of this chapter speculating why, in the hope that this will be of help to aspiring novelists who are struggling to steer their own jalopies down that bumpy road towards completion.

As best I recall, the seed for the novel's form was planted a decade ago on a visit to the dented cotton town where I was born. I was hoping to find out more about the discovery of a mysterious old book that had been dubbed *The Accrington Antiphonary*. My trip coincided with ethnic riots in nearby towns, and one night I heard racists taunting Asian lads in the street. As their voices hung on the wind, I was struck by how the two communities – chanting at each other from opposite sides – reminded me of the antiphonal psalms that are chanted by choirs on either side of a church.

I ended up writing a poem that meandered between the ancient book and the contemporary trouble. The poem turned out to be rubbish, but it started a process of thought in which I pictured two figures singing to each other across a dark gulf. And this, in turn, led to the light-bulb moment when I discovered that our word 'tragedy' is a Greek compound, made of 'tragos' (goat) and 'oidos' (song/poem). Hence: 'the song of the goat'. According to some scholars, the word is rooted in an ancient agricultural practice. After kids were separated from the mother-goat, they'd sing across the gulf between Greek islands. Seen this way, tragedy requires separation.

I remember hearing once that Stan Laurel continued writing sketches for himself and his sidekick even after Ollie had gone to his grave. For me, there was something unbearably sad and beautiful in that. And maybe I had the finality of such a separation in mind when

I considered the various gulfs that might separate a double act consisting of two orphans.

Meanwhile, I was also drawing on memories of my days living beside Morecambe Bay in northern England, where I'd wasted many pleasant hours gazing across the sea towards the alluring hills of the Lake District on the other side. One night, when my flatmate had found me staring into the darkness again, he asked what I was always looking at, and I pointed at the light that was flashing far away in the waves. 'I keep thinking of Daisy in *The Great Gatsby*', I confessed.

'But that's the warning signal on the sewerage tower,' he said.

It occurred to me that a novel consisting of twin voices had the potential for this sort of 'double vision', where two characters look at the same thing yet interpret it in wildly different ways, to both comic and tragic ends. I think that's when I decided that my characters would 'sing' from the northern shores of Morecambe Bay (incidentally, not far from the birthplace of my hero, Stan Laurel). Also, I was excited by monologues, generally. They have an in-built capacity for dramatic irony, with characters serving as vessels for two stories: the one they know they're telling us *and* the one that leaks out beyond their knowledge. This *other* story – unspoken and unconscious – is what I find really exciting, since it has the potential to involve the reader at a deep level, allowing discoveries that aren't written on the page. In wearing the murderous mask of Tom, I found that I was also able to put forward 'the impossible case',[3] an argument that would otherwise prove difficult. As his voice increasingly came to use me as its channel, the case for violent revolution seemed less my own feeble polemic than the logical outcome of Tom's experiences at the hands of his masters.

My obsession with the characters' voices is probably a sign that the book was in its early stages. It's a common flaw in early drafts for characters to wander around aimlessly while also *talking* for page after page (as the writer tries to home in on the key struggle). Hence, the project floundered for a while, partly because I was searching for a pattern in the dramatic action, and partly because I was working on smaller projects that seemed closer to fruition. Meanwhile, I continued to research the early Industrial Revolution, hoping I was preparing my mind for a creative accident – and trying to forget I was hoping for anything at all.

The research allowed me to view the past from a new angle, bringing home the savagery of an age that most of my school teachers had described as an innocent series of ingenious Lancastrian inventions. In John Waller's *The Real Oliver Twist*, I discovered the extent to which early cotton barons had depended upon slave labour performed by children, many of them orphans brought up from London, some of them cripples put to work by employers 'unrestrained by either law or human decency'.[4] In Robert Reid's *Land of Lost Content*, I learned about the mysterious Luddites who struck back against this industrial savagery – and met with a vicious military response from the British Government, which assembled an unprecedented force 'of upwards of 35,000 men'[5] to quell the risings.

The research allowed me to understand why the book seemed to demand first-person narration, a valuable formal insight. What I wanted to write about – what I *always* want to write about – is the margins of our society, and the people who struggle to exist in them. I agree with the novelist Iain Sinclair, that these 'unwritten places'[6] are where we discover most about the health of our democracy, and where we also find the true heroes: those embattled souls who go on dreaming and striving despite hardships and injustice. By the very nature of their marginal position, those people can't have access to the whole story. Hence, the partial view of a dramatic monologue seemed perfect for my purposes.

I kept in mind the historian Johan Huizinga's warning to maintain 'an indeterminist point of view'[7] towards my characters' monologues, so that I avoided the perils of hindsight. Or, as Huizinga, put it: '[The writer] must constantly put himself at a point in the past at which the known factors still seem to permit different outcomes.' The challenge is to judge the level of knowledge shouldered by the characters, and also to resist burdening them with information that's simply convenient for the plot. How much would a dispossessed teenage orphan know about Napoleon's retreat from Moscow? Would he care that 1812 was one of those weird years in Britain's history when everything happens at once? The only assassination of a British prime minister? The Luddite rising? Assizes and hangings in York? Whatever I decided on any of these issues, I tried to avoid using my ignorance as an excuse. I went on researching the historical facts while also trying to write the scenes that are the basic unit of good dramatic writing (and which reduce a novel to less frightening dimensions).

Most of the scenes were fragmentary, written in a strange otherworldly language, rich in dialect but cut back to the bone. As an admirer of Russell Hoban's novel, *Riddley Walker*, I saw potential for the voices to turn yet more weird and minimal, allowing the novel to transform itself into a vision of the far future rather than the days of the Prince Regent. The other half of my mind, however, insisted upon a more traditional, historical approach, less splendidly bewildering than Hoban's unique experiment in medieval sci-fi.

My struggle to find links between these disconnected scenes became more frustrating when I suffered a spinal injury, which made it impossible to sit down for ten months. For many weeks, I struggled to write anything at all until, one strange afternoon, it struck me that the experience had come to help me understand my crippled girl, Mollie. Rather than risking exhaustion by opposing the pain, I channelled it into my fiction and found new depth in my character. That was one of those strange turning points that many novelists report, and it taught me a valuable lesson: these days, rather than punching against my blocks, I work hard to incorporate them.

Apart from that breakthrough with Mollie, the writing remained a slow and fragmented process, often interrupted by the mundane life-pressures which writers hate, yet find utterly necessary (after all, if you didn't have a life, what the hell would you write about?). Also, I was torn up about precisely how experimental I wanted the writing to be. Sometimes I cursed my original design for the book, those twin-monologues that made the shaping of the plot so difficult and time-consuming. Both of the voices had to be dramatically dynamic in their own right, but they also needed to dovetail with each other and move the story on, maintaining a narrative flow. I tried to re-write the book, experimenting with a detached third-person voice that I imagined would make my job easier. None of the re-jigs worked. At first this was maddening, but I eventually started to take it for a good sign. The content and the form seemed to be bound together in a close relationship that didn't want to be disturbed. Nevertheless, there were days when I felt like Stan & Ollie trying to get a piano up an endless flight of steps. The big fella was pulling me uphill while the little guy dragged me back down, and sometimes I retreated towards the short fiction and poetry that seemed more familiar and immediately achievable.

That was how I ended up in the reading room at Manchester City Library, hoping to research haunted factories for a stalled poem, yet sidetracked by books on the city's first gaslights. Exasperated by the distraction, but unexpectedly fascinated that the lights had been criticized in some quarters as an affront to God's darkness, I solved the problem by distracting myself further, picking out books on the folklore and natural history of my old home, Morecambe Bay.

Then, finally, with several nature books lying on the desk alongside articles describing England's first gaslights – something clicked! Without any thinking or planning, the gaps between the fragmentary scenes wrote themselves. Almost too fast for my pen to record, the novel's plot emerged in a complete thread, its monologues sprinting on in a linear series of scenes. It was an uncanny experience, giving me a feeling that the plot already existed in some other dimension. It seemed to have hardly anything to do with me. After four hours, the dictation was done, and I stumbled into the Mancunian drizzle, not sure where I was, or where I had just been.

Looking back, I can see that the plot arose from a set of double acts created by my chaotic reading: the wilderness and the city, the sea-kelp and the gas-lamps. In striking together those opposites in my research, I had somehow kindled a spark, and the light of that little flame had helped me to move beyond the two talking heads with which I had begun. Rather than just hearing voices, I now had enough illumination to *see* two children slaving away in a crumbling cotton mill – and stumbling downstream to escape.

Later, it struck me as interesting that research influenced form as well as content. More important, there was something strange and new stirring inside my imagination: a sense of optimism that I could finish the book. And what seemed to make the crucial difference was the ending which had rushed at me in Manchester City Library, a visual image of precisely *where* the main characters would wash up at the end of the book. In three previous failed novels, I had always felt I was stumbling through fog-bound quicksands, no end-point visible. In all three, the ideas had possessed a fair bit of depth in characterization, but little plot-direction.

Depth and direction, another double act. The way I see it now, a novel is a brawling river that the writer must somehow cross. If you develop a rough idea of the place on the other shore where you'll eventually scramble ashore, you gain confidence and motivation, even if the end-point ultimately shifts. But you'll also need stepping stones in mid-river – the crucial scenes which give the crossing a sense of purpose. The trance-plot that had visited me in the library had revealed the stepping stones that would supply direction: the children's blizzard-swept escape along the millstream...their stormy boat journey to a nearby island in the bay...the struggle to grow crops...their disturbance by intruders...In scene after scene, I had found the dramatic action which would give substance and grounding to the voices.

Rivers were much on my mind. As well as the millstream in the novel, I was thinking about the roots of Hoban's inspiration for *Riddley Walker*, a painting in Canterbury Cathedral which depicted a saint being torn apart by wild animals while stranded in mid-river. This, Hoban suggested, was how he'd felt emotionally following the break-up of his marriage.[8] I was reminded of the enormous metaphorical power generated by rivers, and of their use as story-channels in some of my favourite books: *Huckleberry Finn* by Mark Twain, *Greybeard* by Brian Aldiss, *Heart of Darkness* by Joseph Conrad. And I was struck by the inbuilt narrative of *any* river, with its waterfalls and rapids, its pools and meanders. Always changing, always the same... like a well-made story, its end implicit in its birth, the spring destined to become delta...

At around about the time when I was dreaming up my mixed river metaphors, I had the good fortune to become friends with the writer Henry Shukman, whose novels often feature remarkable set-pieces in which the characters become lost in the wilderness. He proved to be an inspiring mentor, reminding me of my faith in landscape as the key to narrative – and calming me when I was in danger of striking down the wrong trails. 'If you have a journey', he said, 'then you probably have a plot'. I liked that, and trusted Henry's instincts, a powerful factor in my increasing confidence. For it's hard to cross a river alone, as I knew from past experience.

There were other companions who made the crossing easier, one of them the writer Jemma Kennedy, whose novel *Skywalking* succeeded in soldering together monologues by breaking them off in mid-sentence, but then continuing them in the voice of another character in the following chapter. This gives the book a fluidity sometimes lacking in multi-person narration. It provided me with a glimpse of how I could pattern my novel, so that the characters inherited the narrative baton, allowing the action to remain continuous.

Now it became easier to shape those tricky dual monologues. I visualized my novel after the manner of E. M. Forster, who likened the shape of various novels to 'hour-glasses... and... a grand chain'.[9] When I shut my eyes in search of 'patterns so definite that a pictorial image sums them up', I saw two streams rushing towards the sea, their paths crossing before kinking away again. It struck me that these twin streams/characters made the shape of an 'X', two lines meeting in the middle before being gathered up and fired off in contrary directions. This, I think, was the moment when I understood that the novel's central theme was the search for belonging. The crossing point at the centre of the 'X' marked the spot where Tom & Mollie would meet in the fullest sense – and come closest to finding a common home, even if they themselves never understood that.

Writing short fiction, the temptation is usually 'to start late', as screenwriters sometimes put it, cutting any cumbersome lead-in at the opening of the tale. But now I realized that my novel had started too close to the crossing point at the centre of the 'X'. If I didn't go back down the trail and start earlier, the plot would risk being lopsided, unshapely. So I began writing scenes that, until now, I had merely implied: Mollie in the London workhouse... Tom hunting down runaways for his Master... Mollie travelling north...

This felt exciting, but risky too. I was wary of slowing the opening with unnecessary exposition – another common flaw in the work of first-time novelists. Yet I knew I wasn't simply adding material for the sake of it. And it was my new-found knowledge of the book's theme that allowed me this confidence, for, as Lajos Egri reminds us: '*You must have a premise*... If you have no such premise, you may modify, elaborate, vary your original situation, or lead yourself into another situation, but you will not know where you are going.'[10] Having discovered what lay at the core of the narrative, I could now travel backwards towards the story's source, since I saw an opportunity to dramatize the orphans' *experience* of abandonment – a crucial ingredient in a book about the search for belonging.

It seems to me now that Egri was right when he said that 'a synopsis unrolls itself'[11] if you manage to clarify what your work is actually about. Most writers need to labour long and hard before uncovering that underlying principle (since very few of us *begin* with theme), but it's surely vital that we work towards that point. I suspect that an unfinished novel hidden underneath someone's bed has usually been abandoned because its writer never managed to uncover the central theme that would help to organize and shape the narrative.

While visualizing the novel in terms of landscape and journey, I did my best to make the writing itself a physical experience. I was helped by the example of Karyn Langhorne, an American writer whose minimum aim is to write three pages and walk three miles every day.[12] It struck me as good advice, and that's what I did. Three pages, three miles. Ninety pages a month. And every day for four months. When you work like this, a rhythm has a chance to steadily establish itself. Pages pile up, and you gain confidence from the accumulation, until you're writing beyond your target, as was the case with *The Advocates of Darkness*, which, after years of toil, suddenly became the swiftest and most pleasurable experience of my writing life!

In time, I grew enraptured with the mysterious relationship that D. H. Lawrence described in his short poem, 'The Third Thing' – not the double act of hydrogen and oxygen in water, but the invisible 'third thing that makes it water/and nobody knows what it is'.[13] Here, Lawrence seems to have been referring to the unseen connections and tensions between those two elements, the constant, interactive stream where he located nature's baffling life force. Ultimately, I think this helped me to understand how a successful double act works. The characters are programmed from the start to generate a third force, the one that binds it together, and keeps the partnership in tension. The odd couple of Laurel & Hardy are destined to squabble forever, but they go on singing to each other across the gulf because a common optimism binds them.

That's exactly the bond I was looking for between Tom & Mollie. They don't carry around comedy planks or pianos, just an optimism that they'll survive (although in differing ways), and it's this that directs them. I tried to imagine a dynamic relationship in which Tom & Mollie became a single opponent of the Industrial Revolution, while also retaining their individual identities and the struggles inside themselves and between each other.

Yet I knew there would have to be an important *change*. In tragedies, the characters recognize their errors (whereas comedy figures like Laurel & Hardy can go on bickering, none the wiser). And I began to learn that the novel's 'X' contained fertile ground for a crossover in sentiment, with Mollie's quest for enlightenment giving way to a new-found trust in the darkness – while that child of the night, Tom, was driven away towards revenge by joining the Luddites in the blazing cities.

The two monologues, patterned together into the shape of an 'X', had carried the book in a direction that felt predetermined. But there was one big change that I consciously controlled. This was the decision to re-cast the novel in the past tense, a relatively late switch that had a big effect on the book's tone. Previously, I had felt that the present tense sat well with the novel's roots in the minimalist, elliptical tradition of *Riddley Walker*, perhaps because the pared-down language had suited the story-world. Now, however, the form had determined a more conventional historical saga, and the present tense struck me as an evolutionary leftover. Also, I had been having a few reservations about the thinness of the present tense in some contemporary fiction, doubts soon afterwards expressed by Phillip Pullman in an influential *Guardian* article.[14] The switch made an immediate impact on both the prose and my confidence, allowing in an elegiac tone that I'm a sucker for in works like Cormac McCarthy's *The Crossing*, a novel which inspired me with its vision of the wilderness as a source of both elemental beauty and elusive mystery: 'The wolf is made the way the world is made. You cannot touch the world. You cannot hold it in your hand for it is made of breath only.'[15]

Wolves, again! Since I mentioned those creatures near the opening of this chapter, perhaps it's fitting that I should close with them. But before I dust down my road-worn shoes and restore the dented bowler to my head, I feel I should turn towards the camera and record a confession. The final draft of *The Advocates of Darkness* was finished only a few weeks before the editorial deadline for this book. Hence, the project's fate now lies in other hands, and it is possible that I am writing about a novel that is never published. Nevertheless, I hope these reflections may help to instil optimism that the gleaming delta can eventually be reached, no matter how hard the journey from that remote moorland spring where our ideas first bubbled up out of the rock.

Notes

1. J. W. Horne (director) (1931) *Our Wife*, MGM.
2. S. & R. Fitzgerald (eds) (1972) *Mystery and Manners: Occasional Prose* (London: Faber & Faber), p. 77.
3. R. Langbaum (1985) *The Poetry of Experience: The Dramatic Monologue in Modern Literary Tradition* (Chicago and London: University of Chicago Press), p. 86.
4. J. Waller (2006) *The Real Oliver Twist – Robert Blincoe: A Life that Illuminates a Violent Age* (Cambridge: Icon), p. 384.
5. R. Reid (1986) *Land of Lost Content: The Luddite Revolt, 1812* (London: Cardinal), p. 152.
6. I. Sinclair (2010) 'Life on the Margins', http://www.guardian.co.uk/books/2010/may/29/iain-sinclair-richard-mabey-rereading.
7. J. Huizinga (1970) 'The Idea of History' in F. Stern (ed.) *The Varieties of History*, 2nd edn (London: Macmillan), p. 292.
8. Interview with Hoban by Edward Myers, http://www.ocelotfactory.com/hoban/rhint1.html, date accessed 8 October 2011.
9. E. M. Forster (1990) *Aspects of the Novel* (London: Penguin), p. 134.
10. L. Egri (2004) *The Art of Dramatic Writing* (New York: Touchstone), p. 6.
11. Ibid., 15.
12. K. Langhorne, 'Plodding on to self Discipline' http://absolutewrite.com/forums/archive/index.php/t-4412.html, date accessed 15 September 2011.
13. V. Pinto and W. Roberts (eds) (1972) *The Complete Poems of D. H. Lawrence*, Vol. One (London: William Heinemann), p. 515.
14. P. Pullman (2010) *Philip Pullman Calls Time on the Present Tense*, http://www.guardian.co.uk/global/2010/sep/18/philip-pullman-author-present-tense.
15. C. McCarthy (1995) *The Crossing* (London: Picador), p. 46.

15
Man of Letters
Soumya Bhattacharya

In the summer of 2006 I published my first book, a memoir about being an Indian cricket fan. *You Must Like Cricket?* was actually a book not so much about as around cricket; it was a book about India, and about how one game has come to define a country of more than a billion people. On its publication, the book garnered enthusiastic reviews (particularly in England and Australia), was nominated for a couple of prizes, and was a book of the year for Britain's award-winning *Observer Sport Monthly*.

Accompanied by my family, I came to England from Bombay for the promotion of the book. For a number of reasons – some too dull to go into here – the book was published nearly two years after I had handed in the manuscript. But before that, my wife, our daughter – then four years old – and I went on a longish trip to the south of France. Those were heady days of swimming in the azure of the Mediterranean (not for nothing is the area known as the Cote d'Azur of eating oysters and drinking champagne; of the crystalline blue of Mediterranean skies and the pure glare of its sunlight.

By the time I arrived in London, to be greeted, as my publisher noted with delight, by a very generous review in the *Times*, I was beginning to feel that I was at the end of something and my mind was already working on new ideas. *You Must Like Cricket?* had had a long gestation: it had taken me, then a new father with a demanding day job, several years to write. I had not at the time become – as I later would – used to the notion of being a schizophrenic, of being able to keep my day job as a journalist and my other job as a writer in two separate compartments of my life. As I went from radio studio to reading, it seemed to me that I was talking about a former self who had written the book. This is always the feeling while talking or writing about a previous work. I am now writing about finding a form for my first novel, *If I Could Tell You*, but the self that decided on a form for it – in the winter of 2006 – seems somewhat removed from the self that is writing about deciding a form for it in the summer of 2011. But I digress. In the summer of 2006, I wanted to get on to something new. Now I was a published author who wanted to publish more, and I couldn't get away with calling writing a book a furtive game any longer. I returned to Bombay, returned to my day job, and began to build into my life the idea of being a schizophrenic to retain my sanity and get ahead with my writing.

I'm not sure exactly why, but the idea of fatherhood had always interested me since before being a father. But by 2006, it had turned from being an abstraction to a new reality that shaped my life, and changed it significantly, every day. What particularly interested me was the evanescent nature of the experience; how each moment of it was unique, unrepeatable; and how a father's life was torn between the thrill of enjoying those moments and the anxiety about their fleeting nature. The idea of how a child grew up, how it learned to relate to the world around it, how it acquired a vocabulary and a personality of its own, and how a father saw himself as central to this development fascinated me. If this was the material, then I wondered if I should write another memoir. But the form of the memoir did not seem to do justice to the material I thought I had. What I had, while containing my experiences as a father and my absorption in the life of a growing child, was anything but the raw material of my life. It was unsuitable to be dealt with as a memoir because – I came to realize – I was keen to write about a man who is *not* quite like me: it required a leap of the imagination.

I realized I wanted to write about a man who is obsessed with the notion of being a good father, and then fails to be one. He is a man who wanted to be a writer, and fails to get even a single article published in a newspaper. He is a man, orphaned when he was a child, who wants to be a good husband and makes a mess of his marriage. He is a man who is so wealthy because of his inheritance that he has never needed to have a day job; whose money multiplies as India's stock market goes up and up and then begins to get wiped out as, on the back of a scam, the market begins to tumble.

In short, I was obsessed with writing a study of spectacular failure; of how luck and chance and a twist in events can irrevocably alter a life; of how the economy of a new, aggressively consumerist India can make – and then break – on its wheel a man who wanted to be nothing more – and nothing less – than a writer, a good father and a decent husband.

One of the problems that a first-time writer faces with a novel is dealing with something that is so long, on a scale that he has not previously encountered. There are problems of structuring the thing, putting word after word, sentence after sentence, paragraph after paragraph, chapter after chapter until the work coheres and seems to be finished. Having already published a book, I was not faced with the daunting prospect of length and sustaining the endurance necessary for a longer piece of writing. But I had not written fiction before, and knew that the material necessitated a different approach.

The American writer, Joan Didion, who wrote both memoir and fiction, compared writing non-fiction to architecture, and that of writing fiction to painting, especially painting watercolours. In the former, it is a matter of research, of ordering the material, of structure and plinths. In the latter, it is a matter of bringing the whole thing into 'being'. Here there is the leap of the imagination; of creating a whole new plausible world inside one's head and then on the page for readers; of creating depth and shadow through characters and their actions, and a plot that witnesses those characters grow.

This is facile, and I don't entirely agree, but it's the closest I can come – as a practising writer in both genres – to bringing out the differences between the two kinds of writing.

And so, I was writing fiction. A novel, of a certain kind I knew; the kind that I, as a reader, would enjoy reading. So that's the answer to the standard, literary-festival, interview-circuit question: What kind of a reader do you write for? I want to write books that, as a reader, I would enjoy and be moved by. I have my literary pantheon – Bellow, Amis, Roth, Grass, Updike and Tagore – but I did not necessarily want to write a book like the ones my heroes had written. I wanted to write my own book: that's what *every* writer wants to do. But what form would it take? What form ought I to use to give shape to my narrative on spectacular failure? What form ought I to use to make best use of the material I had?

Writing a book (any kind of book, really) is about making a series of decisions to propel the narrative forward, and the decision about the form is one of those that comes right at the outset, even if it might change as the novel develops. Without making a decision about the form, there is no way in which the narrative can proceed. Without the form, one is simply stuck with the material, unable to fashion it into a story.

The novel, I decided, would take the epistolary form – a series of letters written by an unnamed narrator to his little daughter. This is the daughter whom the narrator loves so dearly, and this is – alas – the daughter he fails in the end. His relationship with his daughter would be the unwavering focus of the letters, which would speak of mislaid dreams and of trust betrayed:

> The story I shall tell you is about failures; it is largely a story of hopes thwarted, of promises broken. One of the reasons why I wanted to write these letters to you was to explain; but it was also, as though through writing them, I would come to understand. Through the writing, I hope to glimpse, before it is too late, some sort of pattern, some structure to the random events of the past few years. Words mean more than anything else to me. Perhaps they will to you one day too when you read this.[1]

The epistolary form is intimate and coexists well with non-linearity, with flashbacks and jump cuts. It allows for the kind of discursiveness I was aiming for. The narrator and author share the same literary tastes (if that is the only thing they do share), and the informality of the form let me – without sounding didactic or pedantic – make the narrator pay homage to some of the writers who reside in our pantheons.

Because the narrator's life is recounted through letters, it seemed natural to me to permit the sharing of secrets never shared before. The narrator tells his daughter – as he has never done before – of how his marriage went wrong, how his career as a writer never really took off, and why he has let her down in the end. The immediacy of the speaking voice, of a voice addressing a beloved daughter and telling her a story (although it is a very sad story) fitted perfectly with the nature of the epistolary form.

Most importantly, this form allowed all the events to be filtered through the point of view of the narrator, for everything to be refracted through the prism of his consciousness. We have here an unreliable narrator. What is more, we have a well-read, intelligent unreliable narrator who is acutely conscious of being an unreliable narrator. He alludes to this fact several times, and on one occasion, even likens himself to the unreliable narrator in Ford Maddox Ford's novel, *The Good Soldier*. The epistolary form allowed full play to this conceit.

It ought not to escape readers that the narrator addresses this confessional to his daughter largely because he wants to explain things to her. He is keen that she knows of his point of view. It would not be too much to say that he wants to be persuasive. He is looking for some sort of understanding and, more importantly, expiation. Given that this is his motive, it is hard to tell how much of what he says we should take as truth. In fact, at times, the reader should doubt whether any of what he says is the truth. There is neither a corroborative point of view, nor a contrapuntal voice; nothing is clarified by an omniscient author. All this, I felt, would create the inconclusive, elusive tone that I was aiming for, and would heighten the ambiguities that the novel is so full of.

Very early on, I decided that I wanted to make the epistolary form – or a subverted version of it – of a piece with the novel's wry postmodern subversiveness and irony. Only one character in the novel has a name. This is the little girl to whom the letters are addressed. She shares a name with my daughter, and for those readers who seek the writer in the writing, this point needs to be made. This is, if anything, an anti-autobiographical novel. I visited upon the luckless narrator the exact opposite of a lot of the things that have happened to me. So to name the little girl after my daughter was not to heighten the affinity between the narrator and the author, but to widen the distance between the two; to point out that *this* Oishi, the narrator's daughter, is *not* the Oishi who is the author's.

When the novel was published in India, I used to do a weekly column on fatherhood for one of India's largest and best-known newspapers. The column had a wide readership. So it was fair to assume that those readers of the column who had read the novel would be familiar with the author and his life with his daughter, and certainly his daughter's name. It was important for me, therefore, to suggest the distinction in the novel – although it was, I found out later, lost on the literal-minded.

The novel constantly riffs on the teasing interplay between life and art, and Philip Roth's line about life and art being distinct, and yet the distinction is wholly elusive. In this book, we have a narrator who is actually writing a confessional in the guise of a novel. We also have an author who is actually writing a novel in the form of a confessional. The epistolary form lent itself well to the confessional nature of the book.

Letters, the narrator keeps saying. But they aren't strictly letters. That is one of the conceits of the novel. Who, really, would write letters nowadays? And this is where the subversion of the epistolary form comes in. These are *seemingly* letters from a father to his daughter. The father does not even know if the daughter will ever read them. Towards the end of the novel, the narrator says:

> I shall print all the pages off (and I can see them already, double spaced, Times New Roman, twelve points, one thick stack, how, even now, I take a certain delight in pages stacked like that). I shall leave them for you to find one day. And perhaps to read and understand.[2]

But before he does that, after he has finished, he says he will email the whole thing off to a literary agent. 'Who can say what will happen after that? If it does become a book (a confessional in the guise of a novel rather than a novel in the guise of a confessional), I would have achieved my only real ambition in life.'

The inconclusiveness of all this – what happens to the narrator in the end is left uncertain, as is what happened to his wife – is another of the conceits of the novel, and is helped by the (subverted) epistolary form. So these aren't letters, no, not really. Well, given that we are reading the text that the narrator set down for his daughter, perhaps we should assume that the agent was impressed, and a publisher took it on? In that case, what of the author who created the narrator and his novel, *If I Could Tell You*, a book that conveys just the opposite of what the narrator intends?

In writing a novel in the guise of a confessional, my aim was to take the convention of the epistolary form and to splice it with the literary devices common to the postmodern novel in order to create something personal and intimate, but also self-reflexive; something that makes the reader aware of form and the writer's process, raising questions on art and life and 'truth'.

After the novel, I went back and wrote the memoir about fatherhood that I had toyed with before starting on the novel. And, as I wound up that book, I returned to fiction. I don't think of myself as a novelist; it seems constraining. I'd much rather think of myself as a writer – a writer of various kinds of prose. Writing a novel taught me that the material you have should dictate whether a book is fiction or non-fiction; knowing the material and making the decision is the key.

Notes

1. S. Bhattacharya (2009) *If I Could Tell You* (Delhi: Tranquebar Press), p. 17.
2. Ibid., 194.

16
Belief

Jane Feaver

In 1959 Sylvia Townsend Warner gave a lecture to the Royal Society of Arts entitled 'Women as Writers'. Early on she asks her audience to visualize literature as a palace – a place, she tells them which, if you happen to be a woman,

> you could only know from outside. Sometimes you hear music playing within, and the corks popping, and sometimes splendid figures came to an open window and spoke a few words in a solemn chanting voice... from time to time you met someone who had actually been inside... it was always a man...[1]

Although Warner doesn't cite him, Henry James provides a case in point. In his preface to *Portrait of a Lady*, he outlines, with great confidence, his vision for the novel: 'I would build large – in fine embossed vaults and painted arches...', describing 'the neat and careful and proportional pile of bricks that arches over it and that was thus to form, constructionally speaking, a literary monument'.[2]

Men, as Warner points out, are likely to be weighed down with the 'heavier equipment of learning and self-consciousness'. But rather than bemoaning or decrying the situation – which she characterizes as one of 'circumstance' rather than 'sex' – she finds a way of playing the game. The building may seem exclusive and impenetrable, but, 'one day', she says, 'you discovered that you could climb into this palace by the pantry window'. Then, 'Even at the risk of being turned out by the butler, rebuked by the chaplain, laughed at by the rightful guests, you'd climb in.' You had 'entered literature – breathless and unequipped'.

Writing is a solitary and lonely business and it helps to find allies of the calibre of Sylvia Townsend Warner. Her image, as well as offering encouragement to the meek, also serves to illustrate how intrinsic 'form' is to 'literature'. And how important it is, in countenancing this edifice, not to be intimidated, to cultivate a sense of fearlessness.

When I began, towards the end of the 1990s, writing the bits and pieces that would eventually find their way into my first novel, *According to Ruth*, I confess I gave little thought to structure. About five years passed before I had amassed enough material to even begin to consider that I might be working towards a novel. Then my preoccupation with form did not extend further than to make a word count of the shortest and best books I could find on my bookshelves. The fact that I had studied twenty years previously for a degree in English literature, or had worked for a dozen years after that for a literary publisher, appeared to make little difference: I felt as breathless and ill-equipped as it was possible to be.

No matter. By chipping away under cover of darkness, I had finally got myself inside the pantry. And the trick then is to believe; to develop some counter-confidence that will temporarily overcome or pull the rug from whatever it is that tells you, you have no right to be there, you are unqualified, unskilled; just to get on and do it.

There is no substitute for doing: no amount of reading the greatest works in literature will turn you into a great writer, no amount of listening to a great violinist will turn you into a violin-player, no amount of looking at great works of art will turn you into a great artist. Only once you have started to experience the weight of the paintbrush, the texture, the colour, the canvas for yourself, can you begin to see better what you are looking for and what you are looking at. Only then can you begin to develop some understanding of what the pitfalls might be and to appreciate the method, the tricks and turns of negotiation. Practice is everything. Like a child learning to walk, you have to discover it for yourself: the balance, the tottering, the leap of faith that puts one foot in front of the other and then again, and again until miraculously you have reached the other side of the room.

Convinced that there must be *some* documentary evidence relating to the writing of my first novel, I spent a morning ransacking old boxes, trying to retrieve irretrievable e-mails, sifting through damp papers typed on both sides and in no particular order. I came up with very little except confirmation of what I knew already – that the construction was chaotic.

I suspect that it is fearfulness and anxiety about form that attracts many first-time novelists to using overtly biographical material. It is easy to imagine that in doing so, the tricky question of structure can be pre-empted or short-circuited. But as I found out, it is not so simple.

I had narrowed the timescale of my novel to the duration of one long summer holiday in the late 1970s, spent by the Tennant family in a remote cottage in Northumberland. The summer is marked by the breakdown of the parents' marriage and its effect on the four children, as related by the eldest of them, 15-year-old Ruth. The dogmatism of biographical fact (the family and situation very closely resembled my own) soon weighed like a millstone round my neck. Having constantly to measure up to the rival narrative of memory – an attempt to be 'true' to the memory – was as inhibiting as a straightjacket and a gag. When I ought to have been testing the writing against itself, I was continually testing it against the stubborn trajectory of actuality.

I can pinpoint exactly the week in which I began to look at my material in a more serious, structured way. It was the summer of 2004 and, despairing of ever getting anywhere, I had booked myself onto a five-day Arvon creative writing course. That course supplied a week out of life, away from a young daughter, away from a demanding, full-time job, away from the telephone and the Internet. The tutors were Joanna Briscoe and Charlotte Mendelson. Being among writers, taking writing seriously, was in itself a great boon. Small suggestions and encouragements at the right time can have a tremendous impact. By this time I had about 20,000 words of biographical material, but was feeling horribly constricted by my choice of narrator and with little sense of direction. That brief course was enough to give me courage – *en*couragement – and momentum. Joanna Briscoe suggested I go off at a tangent and explore a different voice. In the space of a morning, I came up with Alison Burden, the entirely fictional mother of the farming family, hovering at the periphery of Ruth's story. I imagined Alison lying in bed with her husband, her parents-in-law in the bedroom next door, 'him trying to keep movement to a minimum, to just the squeak picked up by the springs, as if deep in the mattress the reeds of a tiny harmonica had been planted'.[3]

It was a leap into the unknown, but having made it and found that it was possible to create a materially concrete world out of a detail just as vividly as from the didactic narrative of memory, I had opened up a way forward and out. The discovery gave me the nerve to venture into unchartered territory, and it freed me from the constant obligation to test the material I was writing for 'truth'. I found that I didn't need the prop of actuality – that in fact it was a great liberation to *make it up*. It showed me too that in terms of resource, biography need not be taken too literally – in one guise or another, it accounts for a great deal, if not all 'fiction'. This was a structural as well as a material discovery. It had the advantage too of paving a future – because I wanted to be able to convince myself that I could make it up, if I had to, *again*.

It was around this time too that I made another rudimentary discovery: how cheap and available words are. Before then, like any beginner, I had guarded jealously anything that arrived on the printed page. Words are worthless in themselves; they are only the raw material – I had to learn to be more cavalier. There is no particular secret to writing the stuff. It is everywhere. And it is as cheap as pins. But it is a common misapprehension to mistake the words themselves for 'form'. Words are protean creatures, they can be as beguiling and beautiful as they can be lumpy and wanton. It is safer to regard them en masse, as a slab of clay or a hunk of granite. The question of form begins here: in developing an alertness to the collective materiality of words, to the ways in which they hug or repulse one another, in pairs, in phrases, in sentences; to the shaping, the honing and the cut, cut, cutting. In this sense, structure and writing are intricately, tortuously related. And the fundamental lesson is that there will be waste – huge amounts of waste.

The cool logic of mathematics can help. 1000 words, I came to see, was not impossible to write, on a good day. Even 1000 words a week would produce 52,000 words in a year – almost a novel. Being mathematical takes the preciousness out of production. The most sensible thing I learned was how to let go of words, the first step to editing. In fact, at one time, my novel was called, *The Art of Losing*, an art that every aspiring writer needs to master.

There are bound to be as many approaches to form as there are people, as there are books to be written. I know there are some writers – and not all of them men – who conceive of a beautifully structured novel and then write it. *Silas Marner* springs to mind, or *Brideshead Revisited*, both of which appeared to flow from their authors' pens, composed in a remarkably short period of time (somewhere between three and six months). I entered the literary world less fully formed and in the process of writing that first novel (and my next) I have gone round in circles, up blind alleys, constantly re-jigging, re-arranging.

There are some writers who are not content to sign off a page until it is right. I know, on the contrary, that I must allow myself to return and return and return. It may have something to do with an ability to sustain chaos, something I appear to be horribly good at. What I write has to be provisional because it sniffs out its structure as it goes along. Like concrete or like water, it finds its level or its place to go.

To write this way is a slow and arduous process, reliant on trial and error, false starts, false trails. There is the constant threat that something unforeseen, further up the line, will snarl up everything in its wake.

In my first novel, having hit upon the liberation of different voices and viewpoints, I became so carried away that there was a time when the narrative chopped and changed so furiously the whole thing collapsed in a dizzy, incoherent heap. Nonetheless, the experiment turned out to be a helpful one: it drove the novel forwards at a point when it had stalled, and it got me to explore territory I might otherwise have left unexplored. I learned along the way that there has to be good reason within the story itself for using any such narrative device. Structure has to relate to content.

In the end, I held off introducing that second voice – Alison's – until Ruth and her family relationships had been firmly established. Alison Burden's narrative begins 80 pages into the novel and connects to her recent encounter with Ruth's family: 'Her eyes prickled in irritation at the timing of it, the way that whole family descended on the valley, more and more children trampling around, just at the point when it was unbearable again.'[4] There needs to be a perceptible rationale behind a shift in narrative perspective, otherwise the reader will flinch at the grinding of the gears. Ruth's family's annual summer holiday is a sharp reminder to Alison of her son's death in August, and it is as she speaks that the two parallel stories of breakdown and loss begin to entwine.

Everyone approaches things differently and I am optimistic enough to think that there is more than one way to skin a rabbit; and more than one way to cook a rabbit; and plenty of ways no doubt to have a stew with no rabbit in it at all. My choice of metaphor is deliberately visceral. It is important to bear in mind, however, that like a diner at a restaurant, all a reader is interested in is the end result when the whole mucky, chaotic process of preparation has been tidied up and put away. As long as the dish tastes good, then few people – barring connoisseurs – are too bothered about how the meal was put together. Ideally, all these things should be rendered irrelevant by the pleasure of eating and tasting.

The chef's experience of eating is different from the diner's: it is heightened by his or her knowledge of cooking. In the same way, a writer must develop their skills – a heightened sensitivity to aesthetics combined with an ability to butcher – that will enable him or her to be a decent critic of their own work in progress.

Eudora Welty in her brilliant memoir, *One Writer's Beginnings*, is clear-sighted on the differences between writer and reader, and writer as reader, or 'listener'[5] as she prefers to put it, and how closely related this delicate relationship is to form. In an earlier piece on 'the plot of the short story', she poses the question 'Where does form come from – how do you "get it"?' And this is her answer:

> My guess is that form is evolved. It is the residue, the thrown-off shape, of the very act of writing... It is the work, its manifestation in addition to the characters, the plot, the sensory impressions – it is the result of these which comes to more than their mathematical total... From the writer's point of view we might say that form is somehow connected with the process of the story's work – that form *is* the work. From the reader's point of view, we might say that form is connected with recognition; it is what makes us know, in a story, what we are looking at...[6]

In a short story, it is entirely possible for the narrative to find its shape organically. Because a novel is by definition a more complicated, large-scale edifice, it takes a keen instinct for structure – or as Eudora Welty puts it, for 'the beauty of organization' – to achieve as convincing a result. Even if you lack that instinct (as I do) and still feel compelled to tackle a longer work, all is not necessarily lost: it may not be the quickest or the surest method, but in flailing around for solutions, structural decisions will inevitably be made or arrived at. I can pinpoint three such occasions in the writing of *According to Ruth*.

Stories and mythologies accrue and proliferate around all families. In mine, among my siblings, we shared a passion for the 1970 film *The Railway Children*. This was before the days of video or DVD, so every time we saw the film, perhaps two or three times over our childhoods, it renewed its impact forcefully. Each of us identified with, or was identified as, one of the three 'railway' children. It helped us to frame our place in our own family and locate us in a wider world in which we too might be heroes. This childhood identification provided me with a model structure. It became a way of characterizing and presenting an unknown family in a recognizable way. The novel plays upon the disjunction between the children's-book story and the painful reality of the situation in hand. The comparison becomes a sort of architectural riff in the novel – there to be exploited and/or subverted:

> If I hadn't been Ruth, I would have been Bobbie. The cottage always reminds me of *The Railway Children*, partly because of the endless games we used to play in the Railway Children dresses Mummy made us years ago that we wore, in the end, over our jeans, and partly

because, in my mind, *The Railway Children* stood for the inevitability of things working out, which is how I used to imagine life did and would. It was the good version of our lives, the version without swearing and rows, the version where, given that everything came right in the end, the father had to go only in order for him to come back.[7]

The reference to the pre-existing narrative opens up a space by setting up an expectation: we know the father will leave. And after that, there are two possible outcomes: either, he will come back, or, defying expectations, he won't. There are countless studies that argue what a limited number of basic stories there are in the world – seven? In every single novel there will be allusions to variations of other stories, each with their own series of expectations that can either be fulfilled or subverted. Very simply, my novel was driven by the question, does he come back?

My second offering is to do with visualization. Writing is such an intangible, unquantifiable activity that it is a great help to have an active, physical metaphor for it – hammering or chipping or polishing; to think of words as having materiality and substance. Although I am the least domestic person I know, the image that I found myself referring to most frequently was an old-fashioned, domestic one: that of quilt-making. I imagined my bits and pieces as scraps of material stitched together painstakingly, adding up inevitably over time to something bigger.

Later on, much later, when the novel had somehow to become a three-dimensional object, it helped to think of it in architectural terms. What you are creating and defining is a space – a space that can be inhabited by the reader without them worrying that the walls, the ceiling, the sky is going to cave in. It might be a palace, a house, a shack or a den. In *According to Ruth*, my structure was a tent, made up of patchwork walls with various supporting poles on which to hang everything.

My poles were those scenes that exerted the strongest hold on me, both visually and, as the novel progressed, metaphorically. The telephone box scene at the beginning provided the tall pole at the front opening of the tent. Visually, this scene establishes the relationship between the mother and father and children: the children as witnesses observing, from a distance, the implosion of their parents' marriage:

She was talking to the door of the booth, holding out her hands to it. Daddy was all black until his head, still attached to the receiver, swivelled round showing the pale skin of his face. She began knocking hesitantly, politely, on the glass, tapping with her knuckles like Little Red Riding Hood. Then, suddenly, a slap with the palm of her hand, and another, and another.[8]

Towards the end of the novel the scene is replayed, this time from Lizzie, the mother's point of view, and things have changed:

> She knew where he was headed and she knew he'd already given himself up, he would be talking, negotiating, reassuring the face on the other end of the line in that coaxing voice she'd long ago forgotten the sound of. Whatever she was going to say, she knew she had lost.[9]

The children have vanished from the picture altogether. The recapitulation of that scene is, to the novel, the twin pole that serves to support the back end of the structure. It is both an echo and a deepening of the emotional ramifications of the earlier description.

The other key scene for me, which was a movable prop on which much of the surrounding material hung, was the drowning of the calf. When Robert, the farm boy, manages to haul the creature out of the mill pond, Ruth sees,

> a shiny, oily mound of black bagpipe dead weight, half out of the water. The rope was around the front legs and had pulled the calf forward onto its knees, throwing its head back. I could see quite clearly the tiny, scratchy beginnings of whiskers on its chin, the purple-blue cushion of its out-turned lips, one solitary fly, parading there. And its eyes, its eyelashes, its legs, tangled in river, the little nutty hooves, the soft drum of him, contained in his own pouch, and snot dribbling out of his mouth and nose like the river being wrung out.[10]

This was the first scene I wrote that made the connection between Ruth and Robert Burden; the first scene, written and framed in a way that wasn't 'reminiscence' and in which I established Ruth's voice as distinct from my own. The calf began to exert a metaphorical hold on the novel too. It became a physical incarnation of the losses experienced elsewhere – directly reminiscent in narrative terms of two previous deaths in the Burden household, and suggestive of the submerged griefs in Ruth's family over the breakdown of her parents' marriage. These few pages were also the ones, which, after that Arvon course, I sent out to an agent, who a week or two later expressed the longed-for desire to 'see more'.

From that point, the scene became my standard, one I knew I had to match elsewhere.

The final structural prompt for me was the title. It may seem a small thing, but it was no coincidence that the title to the novel proved every bit as elusive as the structure. I had various working titles – *Under The Bam Bush*, *The Art of Losing* – and hundreds of others, listed over pages of notebooks, each new one casting the book in a different light.

At the eleventh hour, months after the novel had been accepted for publication, I arrived at *According to Ruth*. The title evolved directly out of the final editing, a process whose prime object was to further knit the two central narratives/families of the book together. With encouragement from my editor, James Gurbutt, I developed an idea that had been only hinted at – the characters as reflections and reminders of one another. This mirroring happens most obviously within a family, but I extended it more consciously beyond. What do the two mothers, Alison and Lizzie, see in each other? How does the Burden's dead son Daniel relate to Ruth's younger brother Jack? Why does Ruth's father Jon remind Alison of her former lover Johnny? This interconnectedness between characters and narratives was a further way of structuring and developing the story. It helped strengthen the world of the novel, providing an illusion of objective containment: 'recognition' could be seen to operate internally between characters on the page.

In the process of tightening everything up around the new title, I made my final breakthrough. What if *all* the voices were in fact Ruth's? There was already a structural logic to this conclusion. Ruth's was the only first person narrative, all the others were expressed in the third person. I realized that in one swoop, all my anxieties about truthfulness might be allayed. By using that word 'according', the novel declared its partiality from the outset. What it promised was not 'the truth', but a *version* of the truth. It was as if the key had been turned: finally, form had become a condition rather than an imposition.

I cannot imagine that writing a first novel is much different from writing a second or a third or a fourth. Unless you are writing to a formula, the only difference is that having achieved it once, you are a tiny bit further on in the belief that you might do so again. All that is required now – trembling in the pantry – is to recapture that sense of daring.

To this end, I suggest you hunt out George Herbert's poem, 'Love'. Among other things, it is a poem about dwellings, about belief and about food.

Look at what happens when the guest in the poem, 'guilty of dust and sin', draws back from entering Love's house. Love, with a straightforward, exonerating imperative, dismisses all self-doubt:

> 'You must sit down', says Love, 'and taste my meat'.
> So I did sit and eat.[11]

Notes

1. S. Townsend Warner (1982) 'Women as Writers' in *Collected Poems* (Manchester: Carcanet), p. 271.
2. H. James (2003) *The Portrait of a Lady* (London: Penguin Classics), pp. 50–1.
3. J. Feaver (2007) *According to Ruth* (London: Vintage), p. 99.
4. Ibid., 81.
5. E. Welty (1984) *One Writer's Beginnings* (London: Faber), p. 12.
6. E. Welty (2006) 'The Plot of the Short Story' in D. Gioia and R. S. Gwynn (eds) *The Art of the Short Story* (New York and London: Longman), p. 830.
7. J. Feaver (2007) *According to Ruth* (London: Vintage), p. 11.
8. Ibid., 1.
9. Ibid., 190.
10. Ibid., 141.
11. G. Herbert (2004) *The Complete English Poems* (London: Penguin), p. 178.

Part V
The Business of Publishing

17

An Agent's Perspective

Hannah Westland

I was having tea at a friend's house recently when her six-year-old daughter came into the room and sidled up to me. 'Is it true you get books published?' she asked, wide-eyed and expectant.

'Well, yes', I said, 'in a way that's exactly what I try to do'.

Encouraged, she went on; 'Because *I've* written a book.'

'*Really*? How clever of you. So what kind of book have you written?'

'It's a *yellow* one', she replied, without missing a beat.

I often think of this exchange when I'm asked by new writers for advice on how to find an agent for their first novel, and also when asked what I, as an agent building a list of new writers, am looking for. Unfortunately, there's no straightforward answer to either of these questions, just as I'm sure you have no answer as straightforward as 'yellow' to explain what your novel is about or why you've written it. But I am going to try, in this chapter, to explain something of the process by which I make the decision to represent a writer. I'll also try to give you some ideas about how to work out who the right agent for you might be.

Our agency is sent dozens of manuscripts every week. I personally receive three or four a day, and I take on only one or two new novelists a year (half of my list is non-fiction, and half fiction, so I do take on a number of writers not writing novels, too). Generally, it takes me between three to six months to respond to submissions. So how do you make your writing stand out amidst this sea of new work? It might be reassuring to know that this isn't actually all that difficult. I can reject out of hand at least 50 per cent of the submissions made to me because they're from writers writing in genres, or about subjects, that aren't my specialization. Before approaching anyone, therefore, it's very important to do your homework. All agents are different, and have their own particular taste and interests. Some online research will give you a good idea as to who might be interested in your work. On a basic level, this simply means if you've written a sci-fi novel don't send it to an agent who doesn't represent sci-fi. On a more useful level, doing this preliminary research is your first step in considering what the right agent will be able to do for you.

Primarily, your literary agent needs to understand and appreciate who you are as a writer. Out of this understanding comes all of the practical things they should be able to do for you: from being a trusted critic able to offer editorial advice when you're developing new work; to knowing which publishers are going to be interested in what you're doing; to striking deals that reflect the financial reward your book deserves, in its likely market; to helping you be proactive in marketing and promoting your work in a landscape where writers can no longer remain in glorious 'ivory tower' isolation.

In order to find the person with whom you're most likely to want to have this both practical *and* creative relationship, you need first to appeal to us as readers. The standard submissions guidelines for most agencies ask for a covering letter, synopsis and the first 50 pages of your manuscript. I personally don't feel that a synopsis is important, but a good covering letter is. Reading a full plot outline of your book won't tell me if I'm going to like your writing. A demonstration of the seriousness of your intentions as a writer, an indication of your motivation for writing the book, the writers who have influenced you, and how you would describe its style – these are the things that will draw me in, and all of these things can be included in a covering letter. A writer I took on sent me a brilliant letter with her submission, and I'll include it in full below as a helpful example:

Dear Hannah

I am writing to your agency on the recommendation of Sir Andrew Motion, who has supervised my fiction writing for the past five years.

I recently completed my novel CONFUSION, and I am keen to secure an agent as soon as possible. Seeing from your website that you welcome debut writers I particularly wanted to approach you. I enclose a synopsis, along with the first 50 pages.

CONFUSION has been written and refined as part of a Creative Writing PhD, for which I have also been writing a thesis about the 'realist gothic' genre, appraising my own work alongside that of Hilary Mantel and Iris Murdoch (as you can imagine, this is extremely unnerving!).

I hope you'll enjoy what I'm told is an unusual and distinctive writing style. As a child, I was brought up to memorise tracts of the 1611 Bible and sing rather elderly Victorian hymns, and if the content of what I memorised hasn't materially influenced my voice, the cadences seem to have done. I never had the slightest interest in developing a style – all I've ever wanted to achieve is making a reader turn the pages until the end – but it's there, and it's mine.

The novel arose from an interest in how people behave when enclosed in a strange, oppressive environment – I wanted to create a building that was as much an agent in the plot as the characters. It also plays with the idea of a main protagonist who has escaped any real involvement in the lives of others, and is therefore ripe for falling in love, in all sorts of unsuitable ways, with the most unexpected people. It is set over six days at the climax of a heat-wave, and intersperses conventional third-person narrative with a diary kept by the increasingly baffled central character.

Looking to the future, I am planning my second novel, which will be set in the Philippines during a time of political unrest. I lived in Manila for some months in my early twenties, and wrote about it soon after (an essay for which I won the Shiva Naipaul Memorial prize). I would like to draw more deeply on my experiences of a country as miserable as it is beautiful.

Many thanks for your time. Needless to say I would be free to talk at any time that suits you, and look forward to hearing from you.

All best,

Sarah Perry

It wasn't Sarah's connection to a high-profile writer (Motion), or even that she was completing a PhD in creative writing, that drew me in. Although both of these things *did* help to demonstrate that she's serious about writing, which is helpful, most of the writers I represent don't have creative writing qualifications. What I found irresistible was how she described her writing and what she was trying to explore in her novel, in both personal and literary terms, as well as demonstrating that she had focused ambitions for future books. I read the 50 pages she submitted right away, and loved them as much as I expected to. We worked together on some final revisions of her novel and the manuscript was submitted to publishers at the end of the summer, 2011.

Writers sometimes ask why we only accept the first 50 pages of their manuscript in the first instance, and worry that these pages won't be the most representative of their novel as a whole. Of course, there are practical reasons: think of the amount of paper, or the weight of our inboxes. But it's also simply that reading 50 pages of your book will give me an idea as to whether I like your writing enough to want to read more. This is an incredibly subjective business, and Sarah's letter illustrates this well, for while it really spoke to me, perhaps it didn't intrigue you in the slightest? I loved the pages of her novel she'd sent, but that doesn't mean they'd appeal as much to other agents. All of us can tell stories about the book we turned down that went on to be a bestseller – but this doesn't mean we were wrong to do so, or can't tell the difference between what's good and what isn't. It just means we really only deserve to represent those writers whose work we feel passionate about.

In this industry our taste is a practical consideration: it is what our relationships with editors at publishing houses are built on. From the moment we become interested in a submission we're reading, we're instinctively thinking about which editors might agree, and what our chances of selling the manuscript are. It's your job – partly with the manner of your approach but mainly with the brilliance of your writing – to convince us that we should represent you. Once you've done this, it's our job to firstly convince editors as to why they should publish you, and then secondly to help ensure that they publish you well.

The publishing industry is going through a period of intense change. The rise of digital technology and e-books, and the decline of high-street retailers and the traditional print-media are all challenging the structure and nature of what we do. At the same time, as the creative writing industry expands and the Internet offers opportunities for self-publishing, more people than ever are trying to become writers. As a result, it can sometimes seem harder than ever for new writers to get a foot in the door. But, as I hope I've managed to explain, most agents are engaged in this writing and reading business for the same reasons you are – because we're passionate about and committed to good writing and books. A good agent will be a consistent ally for you in this challenging terrain, helping to demystify the publishing process and identify new opportunities that arise out of the changes that are taking place.

The truth is, the insight and advice offered by writers in this book will give you far more valuable wisdom than I can on getting your writing published. The most useful thing you can do with your time is to keep working hard at your writing. You know why you're doing it, and I firmly believe that if you're talented and serious about it, then you will find a good agent and publisher who understand why you're doing it too, and they will want to work hard to ensure that you find readers who feel the same.

18

The Role of the Editor

Helen Garnons-Williams

One of the difficulties in trying to offer advice on how to get a first novel published is that writers want there to be rules. They may have spent months, sometimes years writing their novel; they may, or may not, have found a literary agent; and now it can be tempting to believe that if only they gain a place on the right creative writing course, or use the right wording in their submission letters, or work out what the secret password is, then their novel will make it on to the desk of an editor who will immediately see its potential, and make an offer for it the very next day.

But the trouble is that, as the essays in this book testify, there are no hard and fast rules for getting a novel published. In the same way, alas, that there are no hard and fast rules for publishers to follow in order to get a book on to the bestseller lists, or the review pages, or the tables at the front of high-street bookstores. Or at least, if there are, someone has yet to share them with me.

Publishing, and indeed, reading, is such a subjective business. Powered by the twin engines of passion and enthusiasm, it is a business built on taste, and taste is an unpredictable and deeply personal thing. Editors are employed, among other reasons, for their taste. In this essay, while I will endeavour to explain what our role involves, I will, I hope, also reassure first-time writers that the science behind our decision-making process is not entirely an exact one.

I have been lucky enough to be an acquiring editor, and to work with some fantastic authors, for just over ten years. My job, among other things, is to read literary novels that are submitted to our publishing house. The vast majority of these novels come from agents, and there are *vast* numbers of agents, so those manuscripts that are unsolicited, or that reach me by other means tend, unfortunately, to get pushed to the bottom of the pile. This is because I know that books submitted to me by agents have already had something of a filter applied to them. If the agent is any good, the book will have been sent to me because the agent knows me and knows my taste. They will be aware that it is likely to be the kind of novel to which I would respond well.

So, I read the submissions, and then I make a judgement call based on my reaction to them. If I think I have found one that we should pursue, I share it with my colleagues and then we meet to discuss the book at our acquisitions meeting. If they share my enthusiasm (or at least, if enough of them do to convince me that we could publish the novel with the collective passion required to give it its best shot) we will then make an offer for it. And if our offer is accepted, after a process that may involve an auction against other publishers, or just a negotiation over terms with the agent, and most likely a meeting or telephone conversation with the author, we will then schedule the novel and publish it around 12–18 months later. Those months will be taken up with editing and copyediting, putting together the jacket, working out our sales, marketing and publicity strategies for the novel, and selling it in to the trade. The editor is involved in all of these processes to a greater or lesser extent.

But I wanted to pause for a moment on the question of that judgement call. What makes an editor want to buy one novel and not another? I wish I could give a precise and helpful answer to this, but I am not sure there is one. As a publisher on a literary imprint, I am fortunate enough to have a pretty wide brief. I can buy historical novels, contemporary novels, comic novels, poetic novels, novels that skim the edges of fantasy or crime, ones that will hopefully attract the attention of prize judges, and ones that will become word-of-mouth successes and still be read in several years' time. So rather than looking for any specific criteria, I have to follow my gut instinct, and I have to hope (as indeed, do my employers) that my gut is in sync with the guts of a good number of readers and book buyers.

If I find myself unable to put a book down, if I race to the end and then immediately want to go and tell someone else about it, if I find the characters hanging around in my head a couple of days later, or if I read and reread certain paragraphs because I am struck by the author's descriptions or observations, then I begin to suspect that I may have something special in my hands. At that point, I then have to put on my rather more commercial hat and try and think about where (and when) we would put it on our list. Does it compete too closely with another similar title? Will my sales team be able to go out and sell it in the one-minute slot they have to pitch a book to a retailer? By this I mean, can they convey the essence of this particular novel in a way that will make the bookseller choose that book over the hundreds of others competing for the same slot? This is not to say that the novel in question has to boil down easily to a one-line pitch, but it is important that I bear in mind that I can only ask my sales team to use the argument, 'but it's such a beautiful novel; you just have to read it', very sparingly.

It might be helpful also to explore the many reasons why an editor does *not* pursue a book. I should at this point say that I have tremendous respect for anyone who can complete a novel. It requires dedication, self-belief and not inconsiderable courage. And for anyone who has received a rejection letter that, frustratingly, seems not to offer up a concrete 'reason' for the rejection within it – that talks instead about the editor 'just not loving it enough', or the novel 'not working for them' – then this is intended to alleviate some of that irritation, but also to offer up something of a defence. Of course, many novels are rejected because they simply are not good enough: not original enough, not distinctive enough, or not extraordinary enough. But it may also be because a novel happens to be set in South Africa in 1892, and it may happen to arrive on an editor's desk after he or she has just waded through a slew of other historical novels set in South Africa. The editor may, understandably, be feeling a little fatigued with that setting. On the other hand, the editor may have just come out of a meeting with the latest high-street bookseller to be facing bankruptcy, and may be feeling utterly demoralized and unable to take a chance on a novel that is not likely to sell very many copies – even though the writer may obviously be very talented.

The editor may be under pressure to reply to emails from 12 literary agents, all of whom have set deadlines for a response for the next day, in the hope that they will have a deal to announce before the upcoming International Bookfair. To respond in time the editor is only able to look at the first 50 pages of the novel, and it may well be that on page 51 the evidence of an author's true brilliance only really becomes apparent. The editor's list may already be full up for the next two years. Or – and this is the most likely scenario – it may be that the editor just doesn't fall in love with it and is not able to explain the reasons for feeling this way, in the same way that people don't always know why a film or a play, or for that matter a person, can leave them cold regardless of how accomplished they might be. In the many cases when the wonderful alchemy I have described earlier just doesn't take place – no matter how much the author's talent may be in evidence – the editor is likely to turn down the novel because they know that they would be a poor champion for it.

For the role of the editor, in my experience at least, is above all to be a loyal – and vocal – champion for a novel, both inside and outside their publishing house. From the moment of first reading it, up to publication and far beyond, the editor is the person who is constantly pitching the novel, pushing for it to be entered for prizes and promotions (in the face of competition that is both external and internal), and expending tremendous amounts of energy on making sure that the book is noticed and read by as many people as possible.

So, we follow our gut instincts. And our guts can sometimes be wonderfully right and, quite often, dismally wrong. Every editor (or at least every editor I know) has a list of novels that 'got away': books that just didn't strike a chord with them, books that they really didn't like at all, or books that they didn't feel confident enough to take a chance on. And these books have gone on to be fantastically successful for someone else. Most of us have, on occasion, felt a little like the bad fairy at Sleeping Beauty's christening, when we have turned up to award ceremonies for literary prizes to see books that we turned down go on to achieve glory.

But then, most 'first time novelists' that I have worked with also have their own list of novels that have 'got away' in a different sense, which may be gathering dust under their beds. These novels were either sent out to literary agents and publishers and came back with crushing rejection letters, or they simply never quite turned out the way the author intended. But, in the writing of them, those authors learned invaluable skills that went on to help shape the 'debut' novel that did, eventually, get published.

One of the most celebrated editors of recent decades, Robert Gottlieb – who edited, among others, Joseph Heller, John le Carré and Toni Morrison – once said, when interviewed in the Paris Review, 'editing is simply the application of the common sense of any good reader'.[1] If being a 'good reader' is vital to the acquisition process, it is also at the heart of the process of editing itself. This is a process that begins straight after a novel has been acquired. Though, as I will explain below, it can sometimes start before.

The editing process is different with every author. Sometimes it involves writing only a page of brief notes pointing out minor inconsistencies or inaccuracies. At other times it is a process involving several drafts, with my initial notes dealing with the macro level of the book – questions of plot and structure – and then, with each subsequent draft, focusing each time more closely on the lines themselves.

On more than one occasion, however, I have found that it is only after going through a first round of edits and effectively moving around some of the furniture of the novel, that the author and I have discovered the equivalent of a gaping great hole in the floorboards. Those moments can be disheartening for us both, but in the end (and after a little structural repair work!) it has resulted in a finer, more coherent book.

Some authors like to have editorial discussions in person, others prefer to be emailed notes and left to wrestle with them alone, only phoning or emailing every now and then to run queries by me. Some authors – particularly when they are writing the second book in a two-book contract – like to send me the first half of their novel, so that they can get a steer on it in case they have veered off in the wrong direction. When I edit I rarely try and offer solutions to editorial problems; rather, I point out what I see as a problem and then engage in a dialogue with the author about it. The author then, having worked through the problem, nearly always comes up with a far more elegant solution than one that I could have dreamt up.

In all cases, editing is an organic and a collaborative process. And it's usually a very enjoyable one. It is also somewhat akin to working in the diplomatic service. The art of persuasion, therefore, is key. As is knowing which battles to pick.

Being an editor is a strange job because there is no 'training' for it. It helps to have read widely, and indeed obsessively. And one can certainly learn how to put one's point across diplomatically; how to suggest a change, how to know when not to push a point, and how to gently nudge an author out of a rut and into a more productive furrow. But if you were to give five editors the same manuscript, the chances are they would come up with five different sets of editorial notes. There would be some common ground, but they would almost certainly suggest different ways in which the author should – or indeed, should not – change their book.

For a writer, working with an editor is something of a leap of faith. One of my authors once asked, when he was querying one of the changes I was suggesting he make to his novel, 'What if I were to have this same conversation with another editor, and what if they felt the same way that I do about not changing this particular element?' How was he to know I was right? For that matter, how was *I*? It was a good question, and I offered him two answers.

The first was this: those other editors hadn't actually made an offer for his novel. So even if they might have had good editorial suggestions, the fact that they didn't love the book enough to try and publish it in the first place, would suggest that he and they might not have seen eye-to-eye. And secondly, there *was* no way of knowing whether or not I was right. I acquired the novel in the belief that my taste would chime with the taste of a fair few readers in the market, and so I now represented those readers. If I couldn't understand something or was struggling to be convinced by it, then there was a good chance that they would be too.

Diana Athill talks about the benefits of working with an editor on BBC Radio 4's Open Book: 'What one learns when you're working with an editor, is that actually very few people get their books read extremely attentively by anybody. A writer is dying to have his or her work read with complete attention. And here is this editor person, and the one thing they have done is they have paid full attention to your work, which is very gratifying.'[2] An editor edits a book because they care about it hugely, and because they want it to fulfil its potential, to be the best novel it can possibly be. They ideally draw out the best from a writer and encourage them to go the extra mile.

This means something different for every author. Some writers hold the detailed world of a novel in their head, and they live so long with their characters and the backdrop to them, that they sometimes don't realize they haven't taken them out of their heads and put them on to the page. Occasionally, I have asked a question about a particular character and the author has answered it comprehensively, and then been shocked to discover that almost all of the information they have given me wasn't actually in the book.

Conversely – and this is often the case with historical novels, or novels with a strong political agenda – the author has sometimes done so much research and has become so fascinated by the subject, that they can not resist dumping all of that research on to the page (if only to make the hours spent swatting away in the library seem worthwhile). In those cases, the editor's job is to help the author to sift the novel so that the politics and history shake down and the characters and story rise up. In the end, the great majority of their research may not make it into the novel, yet if they have done it well it will colour and shape the narrative itself.

It has become a truism that editors no longer edit: that they only want to read polished, near-perfect novels, and that they have neither the time nor inclination to work with an author to weave the threads of a manuscript into a rich tapestry of a finished novel. I think of this truism from time to time, and find that it doesn't quite chime with my experience as I am going through the fourth draft of a novel, a year into working with the author, and realizing that in the last round of revisions we unwittingly uncovered an enormous plot hole.

What is true is that in a tough retail context, in which the book trade is contracting, it is harder to get debut novels through an acquisition meeting, particularly if they are in a raw state, and where sales, marketing and publicity teams have only the assurance of the editor that the book will *eventually* be wonderful. Thankfully, these teams do tend to trust their editors, but it is hard to get them to read something twice, if only because of logistics. While doing all the things that their jobs in sales, marketing and publicity require them to do, they are also busy reading other new manuscripts and making themselves familiar with books on their existing list. Consequently, there is a risk that if they have already read something once (and not been overly impressed by it), then they will be reluctant to return to it – or will at least struggle to read it with fresh eyes. For this reason, it is in the editor's and author's best interests to get the novel into as good a shape as possible *before* it is circulated to the rest of the publishing house.

So, for me, this has meant that several times I have gone back to the author and the agent when a novel has been submitted, and I have asked – if no other offers are forthcoming – to meet the author to discuss my editorial suggestions, and to see whether they would be amenable to revising the novel. This is done on the understanding that I still can't guarantee to make them an offer, but that they will have a far better chance of receiving one from us if I can show my colleagues a revised draft rather than the original. This represents a different kind of leap of faith for both the author and the editor. The author does not know whether the work they do will result in their getting a publishing deal, and the editor does not know whether the work they do will result in their acquiring the novel. But in the cases where I have done this (and one of them was with the first novel by one of my fellow contributors to this collection) the gamble on both sides has usually paid off. The authors have revised the manuscripts and when I felt they were strong enough to share with my colleagues, I did so, and they fell in love with the books. Their enthusiasm was crucial. It has meant that the novels could be published with conviction by the whole team, and it is this collective passion that can give a book a fighting chance.

Because chance does play a part, both in terms of finding a publisher and of a published book becoming successful out in the world. This is something that can be disheartening, but it should also be consoling. Publishing is full of passionate, committed editors who are longing to read books that set their pulses racing, and to find authors with distinctive, original voices. When we find them we want to work with them (if they need it), to make them even more distinctive and original and to champion them in this overcrowded, difficult and unpredictable market. There may not be any hard and fast rules to becoming a successful novelist (or indeed a successful publisher), but perhaps this simply means that you have the freedom to make up your own.

Notes

1. Interview with Robert Gottlieb by Larissa MacFarquhar, http://www.theparisreview.org/interviews/1760/the-art-of-editing-no-1-robert-gottlieb, date accessed 15 October 2011.
2. Diana Athill, quoted in article by Chris Walters, http://booksprung.com/five-editors-and-authors-discuss-the-role-of-the-editor, date accessed 6 January 2010.

19
Baby, You've Got It Made

Lionel Shriver

You've sold your first novel! After years of scraping by as a sales minion in the Apple Store and making time for your fledgling manuscript when peers were slumped before box sets of 'The Wire', you have finally distinguished yourself from the cesspool of fellow aspirants, so many of whom, unlike you, have no talent.

Your real life has now begun. A long career stretches before you, full of feverish, wee-smalls inspiration at a keyboard and fractious debates about free will with feisty intellectual equals in coffee shops. Before your appearances at the Royal Festival Hall, the organizers will confide that tickets sold out weeks ago. When in the mood for a change of scene, you will occasionally deign to accept creative-writing junkets on Greek islands or Cape Cod. Other notable authors will beg you to blurb their latest. Literary festivals in comely locales will bombard you with requests to make room in your cluttered calendar for readings; when you condescend to say yes, audiences will be hushed, women in packed houses prone to weep. Book supplements will ring up, desperate for your opinion on the declining use of the semicolon.

In due course, weary of switchbacked signing queues and constant imprecations for comment in the world of letters, you will retreat to an isolated windblown coast, where you'll settle in a palatial but quirky five-bedroom house (ivy, you decide; limestone), its front porch open to the lulling of waves, its back lush with a large garden (sweet peas, you envision, fox gloves – somehow wild and disciplined at once, much like your books), all financed with the lavish proceeds of your 20-some novels, film adaptations and hundreds of translation deals. Here you will complete your finest work, while critics marvel how you've maintained such high standards into your eighties. Perhaps once in a decade, a journalist will badger you into granting an interview, subsequently reprinted everywhere from *The International New York Times* to the *China Morning Post*. Once you win the International Booker, you will already have won so many prizes that you'll feel rather beyond them, or at least you'll feel strongly that they should be reserved for less recognized authors who could still benefit from the accolades. Your death at 97 will command double-page spreads... although that is assuming that in 2075 they still have newspapers... Damn. The crystal ball has begun to cloud.

I would never want to piss on the parade of anyone who has finally signed a contract for a first novel. I'll never forget when I got the news that a publisher wanted to buy my own first novel (sequentially my second, but I had already demoted the first one to Practice Novel). I was on a 4000-mile cycling trip of Western Europe, in the small town of Teruel, Spain. Leaving the bike at a B&B, I checked in with my New York agent, stuffing pesetas into a dilapidated roadside phone box while the sound repeatedly cut off. I admit it: when I made out that Random House was bidding the unimaginable sum of $10,000 for *The Female of the Species*, I cried.

Well might I have cried. For I made the mistake of most first novelists in assuming that I had got past the crucial hump, and the hard part was over.

To the contrary, I was letting myself in for nearly two decades of struggle and disappointment, and my education in the vicissitudes of publishing had barely begun. Its reputation notwithstanding, writing for a living is not a romantic business, and though it is not my place to discourage anyone who aspires to an occupation that I must still love or I'd do something else, best go into it with your eyes open.

First off, to backtrack a bit, in the lead-up to my first book contract I lost my best friend. We'd met at Columbia University's Master of Fine Arts programme, where we both studied fiction writing, and continued to see a lot of each other into our latter twenties. More than by a mutual enthusiasm for Elvis Costello ('Every day, I write the book!'), we were united by a common ambition to become professional novelists. Yet after *The Female of the Species* attracted the interest of a senior editor at Harper & Row, my graduate-school buddy grew touchy. She picked a fight – such an extravagant fight that she involved her husband, whom I barely knew. For weeks, they took turns sending me hate mail, each letter more lacerating than the last, weaponizing every confidence I'd ever shared into ammunition. The rift was terminal.

Twenty-six years later, recollection of a then-baffling cascade of character assassination still makes me wince. But from this distance, the explanation for the spectacular falling out is obvious: jealousy. That senior editor had been uncannily complimentary about my potential, delivering the encouragement from on high for which all unpublished writers are so hungry, and I'm still grateful for the elderly woman's timely generosity. Yet, a fraction older than I, my friend had already written several unpublished novels – she dashed off a new one every six months – while Shriver the Sidekick had written only two; justice, in her view, dictated that her picture beam from a dust jacket first. Although in the end Harper & Row (now HarperCollins) declined *The Female of the Species*, my friend's fears of being beaten to the publishing punch were well founded: Harper's interest was a harbinger of acceptance to come. In fact, travelling satisfyingly full circle, I am currently published in English by HarperCollins worldwide.

You may take from that anecdote that I had poor social judgement as a young adult. Probably. But I mention this tale because aspiring writers often cling to one another, sharing drafts of new chapters or short stories, pooling information about agents, signing up for courses. Yet this it's-us-against-the-world camaraderie can quickly dissolve the moment one of you makes the cut. My friend from graduate school essentially flew into an hysterical rage the moment it appeared I was about to get my own book published and she still hadn't published any of hers. Pathetic, if typical, and for all I know if the publisher were on the other foot I'd have picked a fight with her. I can't vouch for the other arts, but something about writing attracts people who are both rivalrous and insecure, a characterization from which I cannot exempt my younger self. Be forewarned, then: publication may cost you a friend or two. Indeed, at every level of achievement I've experienced in this biz, I've made the depressing discovery that it is more comfortable to consort with fellow writers who are enjoying (or failing to enjoy) the same broad stratum of recognition. So disagreeable is this instinctive career apartheid that (with a few wonderful exceptions) I've found the best answer is to avoid chumming with other writers altogether.

More cheerfully, the interim between acceptance and publication of *The Female of the Species* was delightful. I returned from my bike trip to sample my first *editorial lunch*, a languid, protracted affair with appetizers and wine at which I wore my most fetching of frocks. I was touched that when my editor moved from Random House to Farrar, Strauss & Giroux he took me with him.

Yet I look back with horror on the way I contended with attendant technical froufrou. In those days, I placed blind trust in the Big Important Publishing House, whose employees were professionals and thus clearly knew how to do their jobs. I was cooperative with my editor, and revised whatever he suggested. Sent flap copy for approval, I signed off without changing a word. I let the copyeditor correct whatever she liked. I accepted the first cover design (and I was lucky – it was good – which must have been why, to my consternation, another publisher soon hijacked the same design, a doctored version of Henri Rousseau's 'The Dream', for a Gabriel Garcia Marquez novel). When I received my first-pass proofs, I flipped idly through the pages in a spirit of self-congratulation, relishing the typeset manuscript as object.

Now, on the editorial front, my biddability as a fledgling was for the best. Nevertheless, it took me two or three more books to register that editors make *suggestions*, which writers are free to disregard. Your name is on the cover; you take the heat from reviewers; you are the boss. I have learned both to trust my instincts, and to pick my battles with care. I'd never advise first novelists to be arrogant and recalcitrant, and sometimes your editor is spot on. But occasionally you have to fight your corner, and in numerous instances my bloody-mindedness has paid off.

On all other fronts – copyediting, proofreading, fact-checking, back copy, author bios, cover letters to reviewers, publicity materials, and catalogue copy – my unquestioning faith in the professional skills of publishing employees was poorly placed. Over the years, I have repeatedly been sent copy that would attach to my work in some manner that was not only ungrammatical and awkward, but that described a book that no one of sound mind would conceivably want to read. If you're no good at this promo stuff, fine, depend on the pros, who are most likely 23-year-old products of an educational system that has never taught the most basic rules of grammar and punctuation, much less the finer points of prose style. So maybe it isn't their fault, but most lower-order publishing employees could not write their way out of a paper bag. Ever since I got wise to this, I have rigorously rewritten every scrap of text associated with my book. Trust not! And while the cover of my first novel turned out well, I have since been sent all manner of ghastly images, wholesale rejection of which has earned me a reputation for being difficult that doesn't bother me in the slightest.

Yet I fault myself for that casual passivity ('Ha! Look at that! There's my name big as life on the title page!') while flipping through several iterations of my first novel – copyediting; first, second, and third passes – when at each of these junctures I was provided a precious opportunity to polish the text and correct mistakes. It is not true that because the manuscript has been professionally proofread there are therefore no missing commas, no misspellings, and no confusions of 'heroine' with 'heroin'. Because this epiphany arrived late in the day, my first several books contain multiple errors.

American publication of *The Female of the Species* was generally enjoyable. Flattered to be interviewed at all, I wasn't bothered that accounts of my then-short life were often inaccurate. Because most of the reviews were positive, I didn't get upset when their authors misunderstood the gist of the novel, misquoted the text, mischaracterized the plot, or themselves wrote so poorly that by association even admiring notices reflected badly on my book. Given that my protagonist was an anthropologist, both interviews and reviews made far too much of the fact that I was once a student of Margaret Meade's. (In truth, along with 400 other classmates, I'd taken a dreadful course at Columbia that was run by graduate assistants, at which Ms Meade made grand appearances with her famous stick exactly twice.) But I didn't care; at least these distortions were in the paper at all.

From the perspective of contemporary publishing, I was fortunate. When my first novel was published in 1986, newspapers and magazines were commercially healthy, and there was still such a thing as a book section. A profusion of medium-sized-city papers still had literary editors, while many of these papers have since converted to mere web pages or gone to the wall. Consequently, I garnered, what, perhaps 20 reviews? But if that novel were published today, it would be lucky to get one or two. The *New York Times Book Review* is the last remaining independent book supplement in American newspapers. The print media's Incredibly Shrinking Book Page has spread to the UK as well. And take it from me: blog reviews are not the same.

Accordingly, publishing your first novel today can be terribly painful if your expectations are still governed by the old reviewing model. The small space devoted to book reviews in most newspapers and magazines is now almost all consumed by the latest offerings from writers who've already made a name for themselves – probably in the era when review space was more generous. In other words, *I* am stealing your review space. After going to all that work, smoothing your first hardback lovingly in your hands, maybe organizing a book party (don't expect your publisher to throw one – not any more), only to confront stupefying silence, your daily searches on Google turning up a clutter of strangers and maybe a genealogical web page on your surname... Well, it's devastating. Recently a friend of mine published an excellent non-fiction book in the UK that got exactly one mainstream review. Alas, unless you're one of the lucky few whose publisher has decided to pull out all the stops for a debut – and hoopla doesn't always work, either – this indifference to new voices in what remains of the mainstream media is commonplace.

Of course, when you're ignored, you *think* you crave attention. But there's a variety of review to which neglect is far preferable.

The one and only foreign rights deal *The Female of the Species* secured was in the UK. As it happened, when the British edition was published I was living in Belfast, so I got to experience the UK publication up close and personal. Very personal. The book couldn't have generated any in-house 'buzz' at Viking, since they wouldn't even spring for my 50-minute flight to London from Aldergrove Airport. So I paid for a ticket to Heathrow myself, just in case my presence in town could help with publicity. Er, what publicity? My editor spent all of 35 minutes with me, taking me to a café in the building. She bought me a sandwich.

Once I'd returned home to Belfast, Viking posted me a sheaf of photo-copies, with neither a cover letter nor even a commiserating Post-it. The reviews were vicious. An unknown American first-novelist would have been routinely assigned to young, ambitious, and themselves unknown journalists who were not going to make their mark by fawning. Now, I do truly believe they didn't like my book. But there was no mincing of words, no pulling of punches. The language was catty, full of wicked point-scoring at my expense. I have since developed a high regard for the compassion of the current books editor at the *Economist*, Fiammetta Rocco, who will never review a first novel unless she can run a posi-tive notice. The policy is dead sound. One needn't crush an ant with an anvil. I have latterly installed the same policy myself: for years now, I have filed no first-novel reviews unless they were nice. For pouring that envelope from Viking out on my Belfast bed was like opening mail contaminated with anthrax. Right, after ten books, I've grown a thicker skin. But one can't reasonably expect any first novelist to be able to take in stride snide assertions that a book is so badly written that it's 'a bit of a giggle'. Being brutalized at the start of a career isn't good for character or improving of output, either. It is discouraging, full stop. Moreover, don't imagine that you're so sophisticated that you can brush this stuff off. Whether or not you admit it, having strangers pour scorn on your one and only published novel stings, and nettles like 'bit of a giggle' are likely to stick in your memory for life.

Yet now that I've got my mind right, I realize that both my pleasure in the good reviews and my despair at the bad ones were misguided. Nei-ther sort was of profound consequence, and I submit this as someone who has herself written hundreds of reviews of other people's novels. I'm not quite sure why, but reviews do not sell books. Maybe no one reads reviews; maybe no one believes them. Yet while largely having embraced the truism that reviews don't sell books, publishers continue to plan so-called review-driven publicity campaigns. (Translation: no-money publicity campaigns.) Curiously, the publishing industry is still befuddled by what *does* sell books, which is one reason publicists continue to pursue reviews that don't matter: they don't know what else to do.

As a neophyte, my most fundamental misconception was that reaping critical acclaim was the point. I thought the object of releasing a novel was getting my head patted. I wanted an A on my homework. But that's living in a child's world, and out here in the adult one what matters is money. Even literary houses and small presses care first and foremost about sales. This isn't a cynical perspective, merely a realistic one. Publishers are not charities, and if companies do not, on average, run in the black, they perish.

The Female of the Species made what was then regarded as a reputable showing, selling about 8000 copies in hardback. It didn't earn me any royalties beyond my initial advance. Penguin picked up the paperback rights, and so ignorantly oblivious to sales figures was I in the olden days that I've no idea how many copies the paperback sold. In any event, a 'reputable showing' is quite distinct from a blockbuster success. We can always hold out the hope that you will be one of those charmed sorts who come out with a *Goodbye, Columbus* or *Bright Lights, Big City* that catapults you into the big time overnight. But becoming a household name with your first novel is the exception. My experience is more the norm. I did not have it made. I had not necessarily kicked off a lifelong career. And here is the bad news: there is only one thing harder than getting a first novel published. That's getting a second novel published.

Though the years between 1986 and 2005 (when one of my novels finally became a bestseller) sponsored a string of crushing disappointments, triggering periodic descent into what I'd call rational depression, in retrospect I'm inclined to see my occupational history through the soft-focus filter of a glass half-full. Despite dismal sales, I kept getting novels into print somewhere. Depressed, maybe, but I didn't kill myself. Never regarding myself as having decisively arrived probably honed me into a better writer. Hilariously, being an irredeemable nobody spared me harassment to file a fritter of distracting journalism; no one implored me to give interviews, attend festivals or go on author's tours. Thus I was able to concentrate more fully on my books than I've been able to do since my seventh novel took off. Now that I enjoy what little security this career ever offers, my story has a happy ending.

When I exulted at my first book offer, literally dancing away from that Spanish phone box, I'm glad no one warned me how hard a row I had yet to hoe, so perhaps this whole essay is hypocritical. After all, if you are publishing your first novel, you will find out everything I've told you for yourself.

Besides, the publishing scene has become much more complicated since my debut. These days a novice author has to weigh the benefits of going the traditional route versus self-publishing on the Internet or selling a manuscript for e-book distribution directly to Amazon. The publishing industry is both confusing and confused now. Technological innovations that many establishment publishers view as threats are often, for new authors, opportunities. On the downside, broad access to readerships in cyberspace means that none of us is ever firmly distinguished from the 'cesspool of other aspirants', even after securing a contract with a mainstream press. The cesspool (a few of whose denizens are fearfully talented) is always with us. Now anyone can publish a novel. That's wonderful and horrifying in equal measure.

Despite my cautions here, I review my earlier life with no regrets. I'm glad I had a hard time in publishing for nearly two decades. I revile complacency, and accomplishments that had come too easily I'd be apt to take for granted; instead I am actively grateful to have found a readership at last.

My experience of publication may often have been woeful, but writing the novels themselves has consistently been a kick. In fact, I wrote my first novel in a state of playfulness and exhilaration that visits less frequently now, so I would urge you to cherish the excitement of creating something from nothing – bringing non-existent characters to life, making things happen with the tips of your fingers, getting into words ideas you never even knew were lurking in your head – before this process, oft repeated, becomes inevitably more workaday. Lately when writing novels I am more anxious, more self-conscious, better read and thus more aware of how many other books are out there, more worried about whether the world needs one more. Thus I grow nostalgic for the days I was still typing on an IBM Selectric in a rent-stabilized walk-up in Queens, living on raw carrots and cheap beer. I christened Gray Kaiser, Errol McEchern and Raphael Sarasola with no certainty that other people would ever meet these characters between hard covers, and I still had a ball. Why, the sheer dodginess of my ambition, the wild unlikelihood that I would ever succeed in becoming a professional novelist, must have been part of the fun, like taking myself up on a dare.

I may have reservations now about some of the unorthodox structural choices I made in *The Female of the Species*, and my style has improved. But I still fancy its sense of abandon and gleeful willingness to break the rules. There is a kind of book one writes for the very first time, which is why some authors, like Richard Yates or Joseph Heller, never quite exceeded the exceptional quality of their first novels. You should certainly be alert to the fact that if you do get a publisher you've surmounted only one hurdle of many to come. But you're a fiction writer. You like story. How marvellous, that yours is just beginning.

Index

According to Ruth, 155, 159–60, 162
The Accrington Antiphonary, 139
Achebe, C., 129
Adult Children of Alcoholics, 121
adult fiction, 3, 123–4
  categorization of, 123
The Advocates of Darkness,
    138, 145
  final draft, 147
aerial mapping, 113
agrarian life style, 130
airport fiction, 18
alcoholism, 120
  far-reaching consequences, 122
Aldiss, B., 144
Alexandra, 35
Alex y Robert, 76, 80, 83–5
alienation level, 33
American woman represents the
    sophistication, 79
amygdala, 116
Anglo-Irish middle classes, 91
Animal Farm, 134
Arkwright residents, 62
The Art of Losing, 157, 162
The Art of Writing Fiction, 100,
    102, 121
Ashdown, I., 3, 8, 9, 119–25
Ashley, C., 117
Athill, D., 177
Attitude, 59
Atwood, M., 9
Auster, P., 97, 106
author bios, 183
autobiography, 19

The Bacchae, 50, 53–4
back copy, 183
Bad Sex Award, 32
Bakhtin, M., 4
Bank, I., 113
Barry, S., 96

BBC Radio
  Derby, 62
  Four, 83
  Open Book, 177
bedsprings, invention of, 91
Bhattacharya, S., 6, 9, 10, 148–53
biographical fact, dogmatism of, 156
biographical material, 155–6
bipolar disorder, 63
birdwatching, semi-rural, 61
Blackmoor, 58–9, 63–5
  dissolution of, 61
  school project, 61
  subject of, 64
blank empty page, 19
blockbusters, 18
Bloom, H., 5
Bonny, A., 90–3, 95
Book at Bedtime, 83
Book of Knots, 116
book supplements, 180
Bouquet of Barbed Wire, 3
Bovary, E., 28
Brice Heath, S., 4
Brideshead Revisited, 157
Briscoe, J., 156
British naval history and weaponry, 91
Broyard, A., 34
The Buddha of Suburbia, 22–4
Bullfight, 82
bullfighting, 8, 76–85
  book, 84
  in the novel, extended description
    of, 83–4
buoyancy, 111
Burroway, J., 8

Cameron, J., 100
Camus, A., 29
Caribou Island, 44–5
Cartwrights, 61
casting characters, 123
catalogue copy, 183

catastrophic dereliction, 20
Catholic vs. Protestant, 104
cause-and-event thread, 111
certainty of the moment, 7
The Changeling, 89–90, 93–5
  image of strange child, 90
  main character of, 94
  many speaking voices, 95
  multi-voiced quality of, 94
  phrases in, 93
  plot and structure in, 94
Chapman, M., 8, 49–57
Chaudhuri, A., 133
Chekhov, 17–19
child labour, 138
child of an alcoholic parent, 121
China Morning Post, 181
Coetzee, J. M., 135
Complicity, 113
confessional nature of the book, 152
Conrad, J., 144
consumerism, 5
contemporary publishing, 184
continual evolution, 6
copyediting, 173, 183
cosmopolitan tale, 78
Costello, E., 181
council housing, 104
cover design, 183
cover letters to reviewers, 183
Cowan, A., 5, 8, 9, 99–107, 121
Crafting Scenes, 112
creative writing, 29, 37, 119
crime fiction, 73
criminal investigation, 38
The Crossing, 146
cyberspace, 187

Darlingji: The True Love Story of Nargis
  and Sunil Dutt, 67–70
  writing experience, 70
Darwin, E., 113
day-dreaming, 19
Dead Man's Shoes, 65
Death in the Afternoon, 76, 81
de Musset, A., 23
denationalization, 104
denigration, 20
depth and direction, 143

Desai, K., 5, 8, 66–75
Desmond Elliott Prize, 58
  see also Blackmoor
The Devil's Music, 108–9, 117
  Andrew, the adult's voice, 114–17
  Andy, the child's voice, 110–13
  complexity of structure of, 114
  Mother's Voice, 113–14
didacticism, 18
Didion, J., 150
digital technology, 11, 170
disharmonies, 21
dismemberment, 33
displaced persons, 104
divine madness, 50
DNA test, 119
documentary evidence, 155
double vision, 140
dramatic intensity, 4
drugs, 22, 31, 38

Eagleton, T., 6
e-books, 170, 187
Economist, 185
editing
  line-by-line, 10
  organic and collaborative process
    of, 10, 176
  time-consuming, 114
editorial advice, 168
editorial front, 183
editor's role, 11, 172–9
  author bios, 183
  back copy, 183
  catalogue copy, 183
  copyediting, 173, 183
  cover letters to reviewers, 183
  editing process, 175
  fact-checking, 183
  marketing, 173
  meeting or telephone conversation
    with author, 173
  negotiation with agent, 173
  proofreading, 183
  publicity, 173, 183
  solutions to editorial problems, 176
  structural repair, 176
Egri, L., 145
Eliot, G., 3

emotional disarray, 22
epistolary form, 10, 150–3
experience, 17, 21, 119
  love and hate, 17
experimentation, 110, 114
extended members, 119
Eyre, J., 3–4

fact-checking, 183
fantasy, 19, 33, 159, 173
fatherhood, memoir, 153
fear of failure, 99
Feaver, J., 5, 9, 10, 154–63
female foeticide, 68
The Female of the Species, 181–2, 184,
  186, 188
  foreign rights deal, 185
  unorthodox structural choices, 188
fiction, 1, 3–6, 8–9, 12, 19, 34, 39–40,
  49, 52, 63, 67, 69, 73–4, 97, 100,
  103, 120, 123, 142, 146, 150, 153,
  157, 167, 181, 184, 188
  adult, 3, 123–4
  airport, 18
  character, 120
  crime, 73
  make-believe of, 19
  teenage, 123
Finland
  bilingual part, 54
  female character, 52
  socially progressive, 52
  working women, 52
first-person narration, 9, 113, 122,
  124, 141, 162
Flagstaff Lake, 36–8, 40, 42
flap copy, 183
Flaubert, G., 3, 28, 29
food stamps, 28, 31
Ford, M. F., 151
Forna, A., 111
Forster, E. M., 2, 9, 30, 101, 102, 144
fragmentary scenes, 141–2
Frost, R., 96
Fulbright Grant exchange, 54
Fulworth, A., 92, 94–5
functional building design, 49
funereal pronouncements, 5

Gardner, J., 9, 10, 113
Garnons-Williams, H., 10–11, 172
gendercide, 69, 71, 73–4
gender-conditioned perspective, 103
gender identity, notions of, 60
gender justice, 73
genetic similarities, 119
Gilbert, S., 29
Glasshopper, 119, 122, 124–5
  class divisions that are integral
    to, 124
  distinct voices, 124
  location was fundamental, 124
  shifting time zones, 124
  story for adults, 122
Goa, 73
Goldberg, N., 110
Gone With the Wind, 30
The Good Soldier, 151
Gottlieb, R., 175
The Great Divorce, 30
The Great Gatsby, 140
Greek mythology, 120
Greybeard, 144
Gurbutt, J., 162
gut instinct of publishing, 11

Habila, H., 7, 9, 129–36
half-siblings, 119
HarperCollins, 182
Harper & Row, 181–2
Heart of Darkness, 144
Heath, S. B., 4
Heller, J., 175, 188
Hemingway, E., 76, 80, 81, 82
Hemingway critics, 76
Herbert, G., 162
Heyman, K., 114
high-street bookstores, 172
  decline of, 170
Hill, S., 12
Hoban, R., 141
Hogan, E., 5, 8, 58
hotbed of apathy, 27
Houdini, H., 109
Howard's End, 30
How Fiction Works, 132
Huckleberry Finn, 144
Huizinga, J., 141

human discourse, 29
hurrying temptation, 99
hysteria, 27

idioms, 94
If I Could Tell You, 148, 153
imagination, 4, 6–8, 19–20, 22–4,
   26–7, 36, 58, 64, 67, 91, 94,
   108, 115, 120, 143, 149–50
imaginative breed of literary
   event, 1
Imaginative Writing, 8
The Immortals, 133
index cards, 62, 112
India
   accounts of women in jail, 73
   cinema, 68
   female foeticide, 68
   gendercide, 69
   ill-treatment of women by a
      patriarchal society, 71
   infanticide, 68
   Mumbai riots, 68
   partition of, 68
industrial revolution, 138, 140, 146
industrial sabotage, 138
infanticide, 68
inner signature, 8, 96
inspiration and finished form, balance
   between, 41
*Inspiration, Research, Voice and
   Form*, 6–7
intellectual disarray, 22
International New York Times, 181
introductory session on writing
   the novel, 1
Irish rural lore, 91

James, H., 29, 132, 154
journalist
   ambivalence, 64
   personality of, 18

Kafka, F., 135
kaleidoscope-like research, 91
Karenina, A., 4
Keats, J., 91
Kennedy, J., 144
Kipling, R., 110

Kundera, M., 2, 91
Kureishi, H., 2, 7, 17

labour of novel-writing, 89
Land of Lost Content, 141
landscape, 44–5, 49–50, 58, 91,
   144, 168
Langhorne, K., 145
Laurel, S., 138–40
Lawrence, D. H., 145
le Carré, J., 175
Leisureland, 105
linear step-by-step form, 2
line-by-line editing, 10
literary agent, 153, 168, 172, 174–5
literary classics, 3
literary festivals, 1, 180
literary question, 29
logistics, 178

MacLeod, A., 2, 8, 9, 89–97
Madame Bovary, 27
maiden voyage of the novelist, 33–5
*The Mail on Sunday Novel
   Competition*, 124
   see also Glasshopper
Man Booker Prize, 3
Manchester City Library, 142–3
Mantel, H., 3, 9, 94, 169
market forces, fetishization of, 104
Marr, A., 5
Martin, V., 7, 11, 12, 26–35
Marvin, G., 82
masochism, fantastic acts of, 27
McCarthy, C., 146
McDowell, M., 123
medieval torture contraption, 136
memoir, 148–50, 153, 158
micro festivals, emergence of, 1
military souvenirs, 38
miners' strike, nuances of, 62
miners welfare teams, 59
miracles, 27
misogyny or prejudice, 60
modicum of authority, 30
monetarism, 104
Moore, L., 7
Morrison, T., 94, 175
Mortimer, Sir John, 124

Mrs Dalloway, 130
Mumbai riots, 68
My Beautiful Laundrette, 22
mystery and magic of the imaginative
　process, 117
mystical moments in researching, 8
mythologies, 159
My Treasure, 109

Nabokov, V., 29
Napoleon, 38–40, 141
　retreat from Moscow, 141
narration
　first-person, 9, 113, 122, 124,
　　141, 162
　second-person, 7, 113–14
narrator, 27, 30, 33, 37–41, 53, 73, 94,
　　102–6, 110, 123, 150–3, 156
National Book Foundation, 5
National Coalmining Museum, 64
nature personification, 27
negative capability state, 91
Negotiating with the Dead, 9
New York Times, 34, 184
night-dreaming, 19
non-fiction, research for, 67
Northern stereotypes, passion for, 59
novel-writing
　challenge of, 41
　introductory session, 1
　joy of, 41
　labour of, 89
Nueva España, 81
nuns, 26–9, 56
　pragmatism of, 28
　romance of, 26

Observer, 5
Observer Sport Monthly, 148
obsessions, 7, 31
Obstfeld, R., 112, 113
O'Connor, F., 138
Odyssey, 133
Okri, B., 96
One Writer's Beginnings, 158
online research, 168
optimism, 121, 143, 146–7
oral rhythms, 94
Orange Prize, 12

Origins of Love, 72
Orwell, G., 96
Osborne, J., 82
Our Wife, 138

Penal Colony, 135
Penguin, 186
personal history, 7
Pig, 99–106
　anxious prevarication, 101
　autobiographical aspect of, 103
　fairly assessment, 103
　preliminary research, 102
Pilgrim's Progress, 134
pirate sub-culture, 91
plot-direction, 143
Poon, W., 8, 76–86
pornography, 38
Portrait of a Lady, 154
post-industrial landscape, 105
post-modernism, fantastical, 104
postmodern novel, 153
postmodern subversiveness, 152
post-partum psychosis (PPP), 62–4
posttraumatic stress disorder, 116
Powells.com, 45
prescriptive or didactic, 2
professional writers, 1–2
proofreading, 183
Property, 30
Proulx, A., 11
public-facing documents, 63
publicity campaigns,
　review-driven, 186
publicity materials, 183
public readings, 1
Pullman, P., 146
Punjab, 8, 70–2

Quang Tri incident, 38–9
quotidian normalcy, 53

The Railway Children, 159–60
ranch, 85
　see also bullfight
Random House, 181–2
realism, 27
Reality Hunger: A Manifesto, 4
The Real Oliver Twist, 140

reassurance of research, 8
Red Book, 57
Reid, R., 141
religious vocation, 29
research
   mystical moments in, 8
   for non-fiction, 67
   reassurance of, 8
resembled writing, 101
Riddley Walker, 141, 143, 146
   elliptical tradition of, 146
Rocco, F., 185
rocky islands, archipelago of, 51
Rogers, J., 62
   see also BBC Radio, Derby
Roman Catholic, 26
romanticism, 27
rope-making, 109
Roth, P., 152
Royal Society of Arts, 154
Rusbridge, J., 7, 8, 9, 108–17
Rushdie vs. mullahs, 21
Ruskin, J., 84

saintly, 27
scepticism, 18, 21
sci-fi novel, 168
Sebald, W. G., 99
second-person narration, 7, 113–14
The Secret Scripture, 96
Skibsrud, J., 7, 10, 36–43
self-delusion, 32
self-expression, 115
self-imposed deadlines, 67
self-publishing, 170, 187
self-sabotaging impulse, 99
Seligman, C., 5
sensuality, 33
The Sentimentalists, 37, 39–40, 42
   conceiving idea, 42
   moment of inspiration, 40
Set in Motion, 29–31, 34–5
Shields, D., 4
short fiction, 138, 142, 144
short story, 22, 100, 119–20, 135,
   138, 159
   plot of, 159
Shukman, H., 144
Siegel, L., 4

Silas Marner, 157
Sinclair, I., 141
Sister Tutor, 56
Skywalking, 144
slang, 122
slave rebellions, 91
slave-trade practices, 91
Slim pamphlets, 63
   see also post-partum psychosis (PPP)
Smoke, 84
   see also Alex y Robert
social advancement, 105
social networking, language of, 80
Solaratoff, T., 115
Sontag, S., 5
Spanish Civil War, 77
speaking voice, immediacy of, 151
spiritual solutions, 18
Squiggle Game, 108
   see also Winnicott, D. W.
staying still, temptation of, 99
Steegmuller translation, 28
step-children, 119
step-siblings, 119
Stewarts & Lloyds, 103
storytelling, power of, 94–5, 109
The Stranger, 29–30
String: A Technique of
   Communication, 108
structuring problems, 150
subject to death, 78
submissions
   respond time, 167
   standard guidelines, 168
   synopsis, 168
subversiveness, postmodern, 152
The Sun Also Rises, 81
superstition and mythology,
   elements, 50
surgery, innovations in, 49
Suvanto, fictional institution, 49
Swann, D., 3, 9, 138
Swift, G., 120
synchronicity, unexpected moments
   of, 3, 125

Tanizaki, J., 29
teenage fiction, categorization of, 123
Thatcherism, 104

tightening everything, process of, 162
timescale, 156
Tolstoy, 18
Townsend Warner, S., 154
trades union law, reform of, 104
Trespass, 30
truism, 177, 186
Twain, M., 144
typeset manuscript, 183

unarticulated intentions of young
    woman, 30
Under The Bam Bush, 162
unexpected gifts, 6
unsavoury articles, 38

vague, reinstatement of, 91
Vietnam War, 38
Viking, 185
visualization, 10, 160
vividness, 33

Waiting for an Angel, 129, 131–2
    beginning, 132
    chain of events, 133
    empathy, 131
    instinct, 131
    postcolonial or postmodern, 130
    self-contained chapter, 129
    sense of achievement, 129
    structuring, 132
    talent, 131
Waiting for the Barbarians, 135

Waller, J., 140
Warner, S. T., 154
Watts, N., 2
The Way We Write, 120
Weldon, F., 124
Welty, E., 124, 158, 159
Western maleness, 86
Wharton, E., 29, 130
Why I Write, 96
Williams, R., 102
Winnicott, D. W., 108, 109, 110, 117
Witness the Night, 68–9, 74
    gripping page turner, 74
    research for, 69
    story of Bengali girl, 69–70
Woititz, J., 121
women
    oppression of, 73
    privacy of, 54
Wonderworld, 104
Wood, J., 133
Woodward, G., 95
Woolf, V., 94, 105, 130
word-of-mouth successes, 173
Writing a Novel, 2
The Writing of Fiction, succinct
    style, 130

Yates, R., 188
You Must Like Cricket? 148
Your Presence Is Requested at Suvanto, 49
YouTube, 78

Printed by Printforce, United Kingdom